W9-AAT-265

FOUNDATION

Building
Sentence
Skills

Third Edition

THOMAS R. NEUBURGER

Moorpark College

HOUGHTON MIFFLIN COMPANY / BOSTON

DALLAS   GENEVA, ILLINOIS   PALO ALTO   PRINCETON, NEW JERSEY

Cover photograph by Edward F. Wheeler

Copyright © 1989 by Houghton Mifflin Company. All rights
reserved.

No part of this work may be reproduced or transmitted in any
form or by any means, electronic or mechanical, including
photocopying and recording, or by any information storage or
retrieval system without the prior written permission of Houghton
Mifflin Company unless such copying is expressly permitted by
federal copyright law. Address inquiries to College Permissions,
Houghton Mifflin Company, One Beacon Street, Boston,
Massachusetts 02108.

Library of Congress Catalog Card Number: 88-81352

ISBN: 0-395-35028-X

FGHIJ-CS-998765

CONTENTS

UNIT   II   Beyond simple sentences

UNIT   IV   Verbs

UNIT V   Nouns and pronouns

UNIT VI   Punctuation and spelling

UNIT　　VII　　Writing paragraphs and essays

xi Contents

PREFACE
To the Third Edition

During my 13 years as an instructor of developmental English at City Colleges in Chicago, I found that many of my students had trouble recognizing and correcting sentence-level errors in their own writing. I concluded that most developmental-writing students were able to improve their writing significantly if they (1) understood basic sentence structure and then (2) frequently practiced applying this understanding to their own work. A number of basic writing texts emphasize either sentence structure or practice activities; *Foundation* combines *both* strategies in a single text.

Foundation begins by introducing students to core sentence elements and moves on to teach relationships between and among elements; it then shows students how to make correct judgments about sentence structure and word usage in the context of those elements. To apply and test their knowledge of sentence structure, students are taught a sentence marking system in easy-to-understand steps.

What's New In The Third Edition?

Organization   *Foundation*, Third Edition, has been carefully organized so that the material it presents is both carefully paced and flexible to use:

■ Instructors can choose between two basic paths through the text. Units 1 through 3, (Chapters 1 through 10), provide a step-by-step sequence through the elements of basic sentence structure. Units 4 through 7, (Chapters 11 through 20), offer a wealth of material to supplement and reinforce that sequence. Instructors thus can teach the chapters in the book sequentially, with Units 4 through 7 working primarily to reinforce Units 1 through 3, or they can interleave material in Units 4 through 7 with Units 1 through 3 as needed.

■ Students work through each chapter in the Third Edition in carefully paced segments of instruction. Each stage provides abundant explanatory text, displayed examples, and exercise material. An end-of-chapter writing assignment provides a final opportunity for practice with that chapter's material.

Chapter Previews and Reviews   Each chapter opens with a list of material to be covered and closes with a review of that information, providing students both with advance organizers and handy summaries.

Related Skill Sections   Fifteen of the 20 chapters in this edition include a Related Skill section, in which the student is asked to apply a related aspect of punctuation, grammar, or usage to that chapter's material. These sections reinforce the student's understanding of the interrelationship among sentence elements.

Review Exercises   Review exercises now include both sentence- and paragraph-level work. Each chapter now has at least two review exercises, and many review exercises include work in editing, sentence-combining, and controlled composition.

Chapter Writing Assignments   End-of-chapter writing assignments have been expanded to include helpful advice on pre-writing, drafting, and revising techniques. In addition, each assignment covers one of the eight rhetorical modes, preparing the student for the next composition course he or she is likely to take.

Answer Key   This edition has been revised so that the in-text Answer Key contains half of the answers from every exercise set in the book, thus allowing for student self-testing over all the material taught.

Ancillary Material

Instructor's Support Package   The Instructor's Support Package contains handouts of rules on grammar, usage, spelling, and punctuation as well as one half of the answers to the text questions. In addition, it contains two forms of a Diagnostic and Mastery test, which can be administered to classes or to individual students. Three forms of a supplemental chapter test and at least one quiz per chapter are also included.

Computerized Tests   Software versions of the Diagnostic and Mastery Tests and two forms of the chapter tests are available on Apple and IBM diskettes.

Acknowledgments

I would like to express my appreciation to all who helped in the preparation of this book. Special thanks go to my colleagues Professors James Russell and Sterling Washington of Malcolm X College for their assistance in building the program from which *Foundation* grew. I am also grateful to the following reviewers for their helpful comments and suggestions:

Steve Arnold   *Eldorado College, California*
Carley Rees Bogarad   *State University of New York at New Paltz, New York*

Michael L. Burke	*Eastfield College, Texas*
Catherine A. Carlson	*North Hennepin Community College, Minnesota*
Sigrun Coffman	*Truckee Meadows Community College, Nevada*
John M. Corley	*Merced College, California*
Joyce L. Crawford	*Miami-Dade Community College, Florida*
Joseph W. Daniels	*Valdosta State College, Georgia*
Robert Dees	*Orange Coast Community College, California*
Francine L. DeFrance	*Cerritos College, California*
Lulie E. Felder	*Sumter Area Technical College, South Carolina*
Carolyn E. Gordon	*Cuyahoga Community College, Ohio*
Roslyn J. Harper	*Trident Technical College, South Carolina*
Gloria Hooper	*Honolulu Community College, Hawaii*
Jenine E. Kemp	*Highland Park Community College, Michigan*
Terry D. Manning	*Tulsa Junior College, Oklahoma*
Diane Martin	*Eastfield College, Texas*
Timothy A. Miank	*Lansing Community College, Michigan*
Joanne Pinkston	*Daytona Beach Community College, Florida*
Barbara A. Reyman	*Arapahoe Community College, Colorado*
William Ronald Runyan	*Salem College, West Virginia*
Jan Zlotnick Schmidt	*State University of New York at New Paltz, New York*
George H. Steele	*Community College of Baltimore, Maryland*

This book is dedicated to D. and H. with love.

T.R.N.

xiv

U N I T
I

The structure
of simple
sentences

Writing is one of the miracles of our culture. It is an excellent way of recording and communicating ideas, a useful tool for getting things done, and a satisfying means of expressing yourself. As a result, being able to write well is a valuable skill, one well worth having. The rewards of good writing can benefit your personal life, your school life, and your work life.

Good writing has many qualities. Its sentences are complete, correctly written, and readable, and its paragraphs contain logical and well-presented ideas. In this book, we will focus mainly on correct sentence writing. Other English books and courses deal with sentence clarity and paragraph logic.

1

Finding the main parts of a sentence

Chapter Preview

This chapter will show you

1. How to find **action verbs** and **linking verbs** in simple sentences.

2. How to use the **subject question** to find the **subject** of a verb.

3. How to use the **object question** to find
   a. the **object** of an action verb.
   b. the **complement** following a linking verb.

In addition, a RELATED SKILL section will show you how to use **commas to punctuate lists** of subjects or verbs.

Let's start our study by looking at the main parts of a complete simple sentence.

THE SIMPLE SENTENCE

The backbone of every paragraph is the sentence. What is a sentence?

The simplest sentence has at least two parts — a **subject** and a **verb**. Many sentences have other words in them, but no sentence can be complete if it doesn't have at least a subject and a verb.

Complete sentence

Angelica cried.

Why is this sentence complete? It has a subject and a verb, and because there are no words like *if* or *when* connecting it to something else, *Angelica cried* is a complete sentence.

Some sentences may seem complete because they are long. But without at least a subject and verb, they are not *grammatically* complete. The following, for example, is not a complete sentence:

Not a complete sentence

An old gardener named Cornelius working hard to pull the weeds out of our future rose bed

This example is not complete because it does not have a subject and a verb. When you learn to recognize the parts of a sentence, you will see easily why this sentence is not complete.

The chapters in this unit will help you find the main parts of **simple sentences** — those that contain only one subject and verb pair and no connecting word like *if*. Chapter 6 will teach you how to recognize incomplete sentences. Incomplete sentences, called **fragments**, do not belong in college and professional writing.

Learn to recognize complete sentences by first learning to find subjects and verbs. Let's start with the verb.

FINDING THE VERB

Every complete sentence has a **verb** — a word or group of words that states

An **action** that something is doing, or

that something **exists**, or

that something **equals** or is related to something else

Verbs that show action (the first group) are called **action verbs**.

Verbs that show existence or "equals" (the second and third groups) are called **verbs of being** or **linking verbs**.

Action Verbs

Most verbs are **action verbs**. Action verbs show that something is happening, has happened, or will happen.

> **Action verb**
>
> Brunhilda **speaks** fifth-century Latin with a fourth-century accent.

One way to find the action verb in a sentence is to ask yourself, "What's happening in the sentence?" In the example above, someone *speaks* something. Because *speaks* is an action and the other words of the sentence are not, the verb in the sentence is *speaks*.

Marking the Verb

In this book, we will always mark verbs by circling them.

> Brunhilda (speaks) fifth-century Latin with a fourth-century accent.

Here are a few more examples of verbs that show actions. Each of these sentences contains a one-word action verb.

> Pablo (bought) a pickleburger and fries.

> My brother (runs) his own business.

> Every complete sentence (has) a subject and a verb.

The following exercise contains sentences with one-word action verbs. Practice finding the verbs in these sentences. If you run into trouble, ask yourself, "What's happening in this sentence?"

The answers to the odd-numbered sentences in this exercise and others are found in the back of the book. Use them after you do each of the exercises to check your work.

Exercise 1

Finding Action Verbs

Circle the **verb** in the following sentences.

1. Wanda laughs at all of his jokes.

2. Bruno found his way to the bank at last.

3. The *Titanic* sank in 1912.

4. Mario bought pizza for all of us.

5. Many of her students succeeded because of her help.

6. The news of last night's fire shocked the entire community.

7. This restaurant serves fresh fish daily.

8. Bob found the correct answer on page 243.

9. The best essay in this group received a grade of B +.

10. The roofing tar splashed into the pool.

Verbs That Show Existence or "Equals"

Not all verbs show actions. Some verbs show that something

> Exists, or
>
> "Equals" something else

When a verb shows existence, it is technically called a **verb of being**. When a verb shows that something "equals" something else, it is called a **linking verb**. Learning the names, however, is less important than finding them in sentences.

Verbs Like *Is*

One of the most important groups of non-action verbs includes verbs like *is* and *are*. Sometimes verbs like *is* show that something exists.

> *Is* showing existence
>
> The book (is) under the table.

This sentence tells us that the book exists (and also *where* it exists).

6 The structure of simple sentences

Sometimes verbs like *is* show that something "equals" something else by connecting (or linking) two words or ideas in an "equals" relationship.

***Is* showing "equals"**

His brother (**is**) a dance instructor.

brother = instructor

This sentence tells us that *brother* "equals" *instructor*. Linking verbs like *is* can also connect a word to a description of that word.

The test (**was**) difficult.

test = difficult

In this sentence, *difficult* describes the test.
One-word verbs in this group include

am

are

was

were

and phrases like *will be* and *might have been*. (Verb phrases — groups of words that act like one-word verbs — will be discussed in greater detail in Chapter 2.)

Verbs Like *Appears*

Other verbs can also be used as linking verbs. These verbs include words like

seems

appears

becomes

and sense words like

feels

smells

looks

sounds

tastes

When these words are used as linking verbs, they mean almost the same as *is*. Compare the following sentences.

Linking verbs

The meal (tastes) good.

The meal is good.

Most of these verbs can be used as either action verbs or linking verbs, depending on their meaning. Compare the following sentences.

Linking verb

Mr. Enriquez (looks) handsome in that suit.

Action verb

Mr. Enriquez (looks) at his watch frequently.

In the first sentence, the verb *looks* means "equals" — Mr. Enriquez "equals" handsome. In the second, Mr. Enriquez is doing the action of "looking." He doesn't equal anything.

The following exercise contains sentences with verbs that show existence or "equals."

Exercise 2

Finding Linking Verbs and Verbs of Being

Circle the **verb** in the following sentences.

example

Hilda (seemed) tired all afternoon.

1. This book is on the required reading list.

2. The photograph looked better in black and white.

3. Most of Gayle's answers were correct.

4. The group's last two songs sounded alike.

5. Brad Palmer is the youngest pledge at Eta Eta Pi.

6. All of her courses this semester were tough.

7. These comparisons seem inaccurate.

8. The best rebounder was Larry Darwin.

9. On first sight, the old man appeared stronger than before.

10. The problems became more difficult later in the semester.

The next exercise contains sentences with both types of verbs, action and linking. Keep in mind that words like *appeared* and *looked* can be either action or linking verbs, depending on how they are used.

Exercise 3	**Finding Verbs**

Circle the **verb** in the following sentences. Then tell what kind of verb you have circled by writing

a. Action if the verb is an action verb.

b. Linking if the verb is a linking verb or verb of being.

example	_action_ Bradley's hat (fell) into the open well.

_____A_____ 1. Byron showed great courage during his father's

recent illness.

_____L_____ 2. Kurt was with him every evening after work.

_____A_____ 3. I saw James yesterday on his way to the beach.

_____A_____ 4. Earvin's suitcase weighed 47 pounds.

_____A_____ 5. He returned the calculator to Abdul the

next morning.

_____A_____ 6. The Lakers played their best game last night.

_____L_____ 7. Pollock looked unusually tired this morning.

_____A_____ 8. We looked everywhere in the theater for his watch.

_____A_____ 9. The ghost appears every morning around

breakfast time.

_____L_____ 10. The example appears on page 425.

_____A_____ 11. The cavalry charged the enemy position three times.

_____A_____ 12. Her magic tricks always delighted the

younger children.

_____L_____ 13. The locket was in the drawer all the time.

_____L_____ 14. This earthquake felt stronger than the last one.

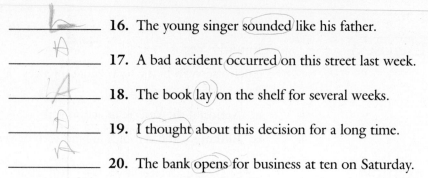

___A___ 15. Alice (wanted) more mayonnaise on her

chicken sandwich.

___L___ 16. The young singer (sounded) like his father.

___A___ 17. A bad accident (occurred) on this street last week.

___A___ 18. The book (lay) on the shelf for several weeks.

___A___ 19. I (thought) about this decision for a long time.

___A___ 20. The bank (opens) for business at ten on Saturday.

Being able to find verbs is an important skill. You will need it to continue in this text. See your instructor now if you are having trouble with these exercises.

FINDING THE SUBJECT

The other main part of a complete sentence is the **subject**. Together, the subject and the verb form the core idea — the backbone — of the sentence. All of the other ideas in the sentence are built on that core idea.

The Subject Question

Once you have found the verb of a sentence, it is usually easy to find its **subject**. Just ask the subject question.

	Subject Question
Ask	*who?* or *what?*
then say	the verb
Example:	**Jacob** runs the store.
	Who runs?
	What runs?

The answer to the subject question — usually one word — is the subject of that verb.

Most subjects appear before the verbs they are connected to. This is their **normal position**.

For example, let's find the subject of the following sentence.

Abdul brought the money with him.

To find the subject of the sentence, we first look for the verb. In this case, the action of the sentence is *brought*.

Abdul (brought) the money with him.

Now use the subject question to find the subject. Ask "who?" or "what?" and then say the verb, *brought*.

**Subject
question**   *Who* brought?

**Answer
(one word)**   *Abdul*

Abdul is the subject. *Abdul brought* is the core idea — the backbone — of the sentence.

Marking the Subject

In this book, we will mark subjects with a double underline.

Abdul (brought) the money with him.

Nouns and Pronouns as Subjects

The subject is usually either a

noun   a word that names a person, place, thing, or idea (like *Buick* or *love*), or

pronoun   a word that takes the place of a noun (like *she* or *someone*)

Both nouns and pronouns are common in sentences. Each of these kinds of words has many uses, as you will see. Therefore, try to avoid marking the first noun or pronoun you find as the subject of the sentence. Use the subject question to confirm that your choice is correct.

You will find more information about nouns in Chapter 14. You will find more information about pronouns in some of the Related Skill sections, such as the one later in this chapter. In addition, all pronoun information is summed up in Chapter 15.

Let's use the subject question to find the subjects of these sentences. The verbs have already been marked.

Valinda (won) fourteen million in the lottery.

Subject question	*Who* won?

Answer (one word)	*Valinda*

Valinda is the subject. *Valinda won* is the core of the sentence (subject + verb).

Valinda (won) fourteen million in the lottery.

The next one is a little harder.

Mr. Penwicker's father (built) this college by himself.

Subject question	*Who* built?

Answer (one word)	*Father*

Father is the subject, not *Mr. Penwicker*. Note that the sentence says that the father built the college. We have no idea what Mr. Penwicker did.
   Watch out for this kind of sentence when looking for subjects.

Mr. Penwicker's **father** (built) this college by himself.

   Now for one more:

The history lesson (was) a long one.

Subject question	*What* was (a long one)?

Answer (one word)	*Lesson*

Lesson is the subject of the sentence. Note that the subject is *lesson*, not *history lesson*.

The history **lesson** (was) a long one.

   Almost all subjects are one word long. When you mark subjects, choose one word unless you know for sure that the subject is a phrase.

Names as Subjects

All of the subjects you have seen so far have been one word long. Capitalized names are an important exception to this rule.

Capitalized names are often **phrases** — groups of words that act like one word. In this case, the phrase acts like a one-word subject.

Find the subject in the following sentence.

Dr. Mary Park (gave) her final exams last week.

**Subject
question**   *Who* gave?

**Answer
(name)**   *Dr. Mary Park*

The subject of this sentence is *Dr. Mary Park* — a capitalized name and title. When a name is the subject of a sentence, mark the whole name as the subject.

Dr. Mary Park (gave) her final exams last week.

A SIMPLE SENTENCE PICTURE

We can now begin to make a picture of a simple complete sentence, leaving room for the parts of the sentence we will study later.

SUBJECT   —   VERB

The subject and the verb are capitalized in the diagram above because they are required in every complete sentence. All other parts of the sentence are optional.

Exercise 4

Finding Subjects

The verb of each of these sentences is already marked. Find the **subject** by asking the subject question. Then underline it twice.

Unless the subject is a capitalized name or title, *do not mark more than one word*.

example

The season (ended) with a victory.

1. The pass (landed) in the end zone.

2. The chair in the corner (needs) a new coat of varnish.

3. Mike's little brother already (has) his own bank account.

4. The science class (meets) in the planetarium today.

5. Last year's American history final examination (was) not

very difficult.

6. Dr. Banning (answered) all of the questions from the audience.

7. 1985 (was) an excellent one for the college.

8. *Noises Off* (plays) all year at the Morris Civic Auditorium.

9. A good concert pianist (practices) almost every day.

10. Ruth Hemingway (spoke) to the class about nutrition.

Exercise 5

Finding Subjects and Verbs

In this exercise, the verbs are not marked. Mark each sentence by working in the following order.

a. Circle the **verb**.

b. Ask the **subject question**.

c. Underline the **subject** twice.

example

The medicine cabinet (was) empty.

1. We agreed with all of her arguments.

2. The best comedian in the show was eleven years old.

3. The manager spoke highly of the team's talent.

4. Unlike the last president, Dr. Aaron places a high priority

on research.

5. Schoenbaum attended two years at Penwicker Law School.

6. She was the best student in his class.

7. Commuters from the northern suburbs waited three hours for a train

into town this morning.

8. The carburetor needed replacement badly.

9. Charlie's dancing instructor called in sick this week.

10. The puppy spent last night in a box in the basement.

11. The oldest student in the class looks like a bank president.

12. He is actually a prominent local sculptor.

13. KKRP's local weatherman guessed wrong this morning.

14. It rained all day.

15. The victims reported the burglary themselves.

16. Wrecking Crew won the race by four lengths.

17. Almost Late came in second.

18. A painful limp slowed his walk.

19. Vice President Uhara addressed the graduating seniors.

20. The Consequential Insurance Company issued the policy last year.

FINDING THE OBJECT OR COMPLEMENT

The last of the sentence parts that contain the core idea is either the **object** or the **complement**.

Not every sentence has an object or complement, and no sentence will have both. But if either the object or complement is present, it is an important extension of the idea contained in the subject and verb.

SUBJECT — VERB — **Object or Complement**

Let's look at objects and complements more closely.

Objects of Action Verbs

The **object of the verb** (also called the **direct object**) receives the action of the verb. Only action verbs can have objects, since linking verbs do not show actions.

The Object Question

If you can find the verb, you can find the object. Just ask the object question.

Object Question

Say   the verb

then ask   *whom?* or *what?*

Example: Carlos saw the **movie**.

                    Saw **whom**?

                    Saw **what**?

If the verb is an action verb, the answer to the object question — usually one word — is the object. Objects, like subjects, can be either nouns or pronouns.

   The **normal position** for objects is, as you might have guessed, after the verb. Let's look at some examples.

   The construction <u>company</u> (built) the library in

   eighteen months.

Object question   Built *what?*

Answer (one word)   *Library*

Library is the object of the verb *built*. *Company built library* (subject – verb – object) is the core idea of this sentence.

          company   —   built   —   library

Here's another sentence with an action verb and an object.

   <u>Vernetta</u> (answered) Sarah's letter immediately.

Object question   Answered *what?*

Answer (one word)   *Letter*

Notice that the object is *letter*, not *Sarah's*. *Sarah's* may look like an object, but the core of the sentence is *Vernetta answered letter*.

          Vernetta   —   answered   —   letter

Marking Objects

Mark the object of an action verb by underlining it once.

The construction <u>company</u> (built) the **library** in eighteen months.

<u>Vernetta</u> (answered) Sarah's **letter** immediately.

Sentences Without Objects

Many sentences do not have objects. These sentences won't give you a sensible answer to the object question. In this case, simply leave the sentence without a marked object. You will probably be right.

The campus <u>bookstore</u> (opens) at noon today.

Object question   Opens *what?*

Answer (one word)   (no answer in sentence)

From what the sentence tells us, there is no answer to the object question. Therefore, the sentence has no object.

Notice that *at noon today* answers the question "opens when?", not "opens what?" The question "opens what?" would need an answer like "envelopes." No "whom" or "what" answer makes sense in this sentence. Therefore, the sentence has no object.

The campus <u>bookstore</u> (opens) at noon today.
                    (NO OBJECT)

Names as Objects

Capitalized names are used as objects in the same way they are used as subjects.

My <u>mother</u> (saw) *Gone With the Wind* seventeen times.

Object question   Saw *what?*

Answer
(name)   *Gone With the Wind*

Since *Gone With the Wind* is a capitalized name, we underline the whole name as the object.

My <u>mother</u> (saw) *Gone With the Wind* seven-

teen times.

Exercise 6

Finding Objects

Each of the verbs in this exercise is an action verb, and the verbs and subjects are already marked.

Find the **object** by asking the **object question**. Then underline it once. If a sentence has no object, write **NO OBJECT** in the margin.

Unless the object is a capitalized name or title, *do not mark more than one word*.

examples   <u>Alice</u> (opened) the <u>newspaper</u> to the sports section.

NO OBJECT   <u>She</u> (looked) for the college basketball report.

1. <u>Jimmy</u> (watched) the old <u>man</u> across the street.

2. <u>Antonio</u> (wrote) a <u>book</u> about life in the Army.

3. <u>Marie</u> (saw) an <u>advertisement</u> for a licensed nurse.

4. Her <u>students</u> (noticed) a <u>change</u> in her teaching.

No object 5. <u>Mr. Valdez</u> (ran) for the city council.

No object 6. The <u>phone</u> (rang) several times.

No object 7. <u>Mr. White</u> (answered) immediately.

8. Wanda's high <u>school</u> (produced) *South Pacific* last spring.

No object 9. <u>Wanda</u> (sang) in *South Pacific*.

10. <u>Ms. Stockwood</u> never (understood) the problem.

Complements Following Linking Verbs

Since verbs like *am, is,* and *seems* are not actions, they cannot have objects. But they are often followed by words that answer the object question. These words are called **complements**.

SUBJECT — LINKING VERB — **Complement**

Since the meaning of a linking verb is "equals," complements equal or describe the subject. (The word *complement* comes from the verb *to complete.* Complements "complete" the subject.)

Though complements are different from objects, the object question can be used to find them. Let's look at some examples.

The <u>instructor</u> (is) Ms. Black.

**Object
question**   Is *who?*

**Answer
(name)**   *Ms. Black*

Even though *Ms. Black* looks like an object in this sentence, it is a complement because of the linking verb *is.*

The instructor (is) **Ms. Black.**
instructor   =   Ms. Black

Let's try another one.

The <u>winner</u> (was) she.

**Object
question**   Was *who?*

**Answer
(one word)**   *She*

She is a complement because it follows a linking verb (*was*) and it answers the object question.

Remember, if a sentence has an answer for the object question, you must check the *verb* to see if the answer is an object or a complement.

If the verb is   an **action** verb

**the answer to
the object
question is**   an **object**

If the verb is	a **linking** verb
the answer to the object question is	a **complement**

Marking Complements

Mark complements by underlining them once and writing COMP above them.

COMP
The <u>instructor</u> (is) <u>Ms. Black</u>.

Descriptive Words (Adjectives) as Complements

Most complements are nouns (words like *student* and *car*) or pronouns (words like *she* and *that*).

Noun complement

COMP
Our new <u>neighbor</u> (is) a <u>student</u> at Penwicker

College.

Pronoun complement

COMP
Our new <u>neighbor</u> (is) <u>she</u>.

In these sentences, both *student* and *she* are complements. Both answer the object question, and both follow a linking verb.

Some complements, however, are **adjectives** — words that describe nouns and pronouns. The following sentence shows an adjective used as a complement.

Adjective complement

COMP
Our new <u>neighbor</u> (is) <u>young</u>.

Young describes neighbor ("young neighbor"). Because it answers the object question

Object question	Is *what*?

Answer
(one word)   *Young*

and follows a linking verb, *young* is a complement and should be marked as one. (Adjectives will be discussed in greater detail in Chapter 3.)

Names as Complements

Names are used as complements in the same way they are used as subjects and objects. When a capitalized name is the complement, mark the whole name as the complement.

Name as complement

COMP
The best <u>novel</u> in the store (was) *The Tin Drum.*

Exercise 7

Finding Complements

Each of the verbs in this exercise is a linking verb or verb of being, and the verbs and subjects are already marked.

Find the **complement** by asking the **object question**. Then underline it once and write **COMP** above it. If a sentence has no complement, write **NO COMP** in the margin.

Unless the complement is a capitalized name or title, *do not mark more than one word.*

examples

COMP
<u>Mr. Valdano</u> (was) a <u>man</u> of his word.

NO COMP <u>Your jacket</u> (is) under the cushion on the couch.

1. <u>I</u> (am) a <u>student</u> in this class.   *COMP*

2. The second <u>boxer</u> (looked) <u>tired.</u>   *COMP*

3. Linda's <u>brother</u> (is) an <u>accountant</u> for a law firm.   *Comp*

4. The <u>ghost</u> (was) a <u>member</u> of the football team.   *COMP*

5. <u>He</u> (seems) <u>unhappy</u> with the score of today's game.   *CoMP*

6. <u>This</u> (seems) like a good day for skiing.   NO COMP

7. <u>Ben</u> (is) <u>one</u> of the actors.   *COMP*

8. <u>They</u> (looked) <u>eager</u> for a part in the play.   *COMP*

9. The <u>answer</u> to question seven (is) *The Maltese Falcon*. [COMP]

10. Several <u>stores</u> in our neighborhood (are) members of [COMP]

Neighborhood Watch.

The following exercises will help you practice finding objects and complements.

Exercise 8

Finding Objects and Complements

The verbs and subjects of the following sentences have already been marked for you.

Find the **object** or **complement** in the following sentences by asking the **object question.** If the sentence has an object or complement, underline it once. Write COMP above any complement.

Remember that objects follow action verbs and complements follow linking verbs.

examples

Francine (moved) the <u>television</u> into the living room.

                  COMP

Our <u>television</u> (is) a German <u>brand</u>.

1. The insurance <u>examiner</u> (arrived) this morning.

2. <u>Kelly's Bar</u> (offers) a special every Monday night.

3. <u>Mark Williams</u> (is) this year's starting <u>quarterback</u>. [COMP]

4. The <u>report</u> (named) the Democratic candidate as one of

   the stockholders.

5. The <u>Timson County Library</u> (collapsed) shortly after

   its construction.

6. Fortunately no <u>injuries</u> (occurred).

7. The final <u>speaker</u> of the evening (offered) several solutions to the

   budget problem.

8. <u>Sherlock Holmes</u> (is) popular. [COMP]

9. <u>Sherlock Holmes</u> (is) a popular fictional <u>detective</u>. *COMP*

10. The <u>novel</u> (told) yet another story of forbidden passion.

MARKING SENTENCES

As you have discovered, many of the exercises in this book ask you to mark sentences to show that you understand their structure. Doing these exercises helps you in three ways.

1. Knowing sentence structure will help you punctuate correctly.

   Readers need to have certain sentence structures pointed out to them. This makes reading easier. You will soon see, for example, that it is easier to read a list of three subjects if commas are used between them.

   If you're having trouble punctuating the sentences you write, it may be because you're having trouble seeing the structures within those sentences. Learning to mark sentences accurately will help you learn those structures.

   Then, when you study the rules of correct punctuation in Units 2 and 3, you will always know how and where to apply those rules. Sentence marking will improve your punctuation greatly.

2. Knowing sentence structure will help you choose verb, pronoun, and noun forms correctly.

   Many words have more than one form. *Is* and *are,* for example, are both present tense forms of the verb *to be. Who* and *whom* are both forms of the same pronoun. In order to use these words correctly, you need to understand the structure of the sentences they are in.

   You cannot choose between *is* and *are* if you cannot find the subject, since the verb form must match the form of the subject. This can be difficult to do, however, since many sentences are complicated. Without a knowledge of sentence structure, their subjects are not at all obvious.

   In the same way, you cannot choose between *who* and *whom* if you do not know whether the word is used as a subject, object, or complement. It is even easier to choose between singular and plural forms of some nouns if you know the structure of the sentence they are in.

   You will study *how* to use verb, noun, and pronoun forms in Units 4 and 5. Accurate sentence marking will teach you *where* to use them.

3. Finally, knowing sentence structure will gradually improve your writing style.

   There are always many ways to express the same idea. However, many student writers express an idea in only one way — as though they were speaking it.

   A knowledge of sentence structure will make you aware that ideas can be expressed in several ways. As a result, your writing will slowly, but steadily, move toward clearer and more readable sentences.

For all of these reasons, you should do the marking exercises in FOUNDATION carefully. Eventually, you will know the structure of a sentence on sight, and your writing will improve as a result.

In the following exercise you can apply your knowledge of each of the marks you've learned in this chapter.

Exercise 9

Finding Verbs, Subjects, Objects, and Complements

In each of the following sentences, mark the

a. **verb**

b. **subject**

c. **object** or **complement**, if any.

examples

The store manager (is) unhappy [COMP] with last week's sales report.

Julio (answered) the phone on the first ring.

1. The suspect showed no evidence of guilt.

2. Demonstrators swarmed through the European city.

3. The fire started in a stairwell.

4. The store manager later installed an expensive sprinkler system.

5. The instructions seem complicated. [COMP]

6. Barry's father sent a coffee maker.

7. It arrived yesterday.

8. This is the best college in the state. [COMP]

9. The Coho Club gives charitable meals each year at this time.

10. Few governments are ready for tax reform. [COMP]

11. Our local team won easily.

12. The new camera operator's work was excellent. [COMP]

13. Odell appeared sleepy all through Dr. Week's morning lecture. [COMP]

14. But Julio's question woke him up.

24 The structure of simple sentences

15. Most books in this store are historical novels.

16. The film at the Nuart Theater was boring.

17. Once more, alien beings from a dying planet invaded an

    unsuspecting Earth.

18. In a field miles from any town, two strange craft landed quietly.

19. Dr. Willard eventually understood the meaning of this event.

20. But by then the theater was empty.

RELATED SKILL   USING COMMAS WITH MORE THAN ONE SUBJECT OR VERB

Now let's put some of this information to use. In Related Skill sections, we will show you ways to apply what you have learned to your writing.

Some Related Skills, like this one, will introduce a related aspect of punctuation. (All of the punctuation you will learn in this book is summarized in Chapter 17.) Other Related Skills may show you how pronouns should be used in the sentence element you have just studied.

In this section, we will look at sentences in which the subject or the verb has been "multiplied."

As you probably know, many sentences have more than one subject or verb. These multiple subjects and verbs form a list, or "series."

Two Subjects

The **President** and **Congress** finally (reached) an

agreement.

Technically, more than one subject is called a **compound subject**. This simply means that the two (or three, or four) subjects act as one subject. Each is a subject of the verb, and each answers the subject question.

Subject question   *Who* reached?

25 Finding the main parts of a sentence

When a sentence has more than one subject or verb, mark each subject or verb.

The **President** and **Congress** finally (reached) an

agreement.

Punctuating sentences that contain lists is sometimes a problem. The solution lies in knowing how many items are in the list.

Punctuating Items in a List or Series

Do not use commas to separate items in a list of two items.

Use commas to separate items in a list or series of three or more items.

If you know how many items are being joined in the list, you will have no problem punctuating it. A list of two items in a sentence is not punctuated.

Two Subjects

┌─NO COMMA

The **President** and **Congress** finally (reached) an

agreement.

A list of three items in a sentence is punctuated with commas.

Three Subjects

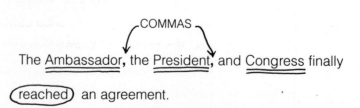

The Ambassador, the President, and Congress finally

(reached) an agreement.

Note that commas are used to separate *each* item in the list. It would be incorrect to punctuate the sentence above as follows:

Incorrect

COMMA NEEDED HERE

The <u>Ambassador</u>, the <u>President</u> ↓ ,and <u>Congress</u> finally

(reached) an agreement.

Be careful with sentences that contain two verbs that are widely separated by other words. Do not use a comma to punctuate a list of two items.

Two Verbs

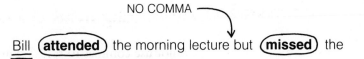

NO COMMA ——

<u>Bill</u> (**attended**) the morning lecture but (**missed**) the

afternoon session.

Three Verbs

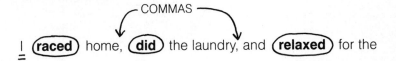

— COMMAS —

<u>I</u> (**raced**) home, (**did**) the laundry, and (**relaxed**) for the

rest of the evening.

The words most often used to join subjects, verbs, and other compounded sentence parts are *and, or, but, nor.*

Skill Exercise

Punctuating Items in a List

Do the following for each sentence in this exercise.

a. Mark each **verb** and **subject**.

b. **Punctuate** the sentence correctly.

c. If a sentence is already punctuated correctly, write **OK** in the margin.

example

The sales <u>manager</u> , the tech support <u>manager</u> , and their <u>staff</u>

(met) at Bullwinkle's last Friday for lunch.

27 Finding the main parts of a sentence

1. The president and her secretary received copies of the report.

2. "Crunch" McCord "Big Ben" Butterfield and "Mad Dog" Magruder tackled the halfback with a fine defensive play.

3. Our engineering staff designed the computer built it and wrote the manual within three months.

4. The engineering staff designed the computer and built it themselves.

5. Each of his first three mystery novels has an unusual one-word title.

6. *Rimshot Hindsight* and *Bulldog* were three best-selling novels.

7. Gold silver platinum and rare coins lay in heaps near the burial site.

8. Loyola and Notre Dame did well on Thursday.

9. Chapters seven nine and thirteen are Mr. Mealy's responsibility.

10. The light dims fades and drifts from sight again.

11. The Search Committee met in the afternoon discussed the candi-dates and reached no conclusions.

12. Marcie Steve and Lara won radios in the bookstore contest.

13. Steve brought the camera and placed the lighting equipment.

14. Neither the diplomat nor his assistant knew the contents of the letter.

15. The Chicago Bears the Anaheim Rams and the Irwindale Raiders made the playoffs this year.

16. The networks promoted the boxing event and sold most of their advertising time.

17. Walter played hard but lost in the last few minutes.

18. Red blue green and ocher are Susette's favorite colors.

19. LaWanda dances at the Roxie sings at the Rosemont and per-

    forms in plays at the Westjoy Palace Showroom.

20. Marx and Lenin preached and wrote to millions.

Chapter Review

In this chapter you learned that

1. The **required parts of a sentence** are the subject
   and verb.

2. **Action verbs** show the action of a sentence.

3. **Linking verbs** and **verbs of being** show that something
   exists or "equals" something.

4. The **subject question** (like *Who runs?*) can help you find
   the subject of a verb.

5. The **object question** (like *Runs what?*) can help you find
   both objects and complements.

6. Only **action verbs have objects.**

7. Only **linking verbs have complements.**

A RELATED SKILL section showed you how to **punctuate lists**.

1. Do not use commas to separate items in a list
   of two items.

2. Use commas to separate items in a list of three
   or more items.

Review Exercise 1

Mark the **verb, subject,** and **object** or **complement** of each of the following sentences.

1. Mr. Riley purchased the brown house on the corner.

2. Earvin was unhappy with his score on the quiz.

3. Last evening Byron spoke to his grandmother.

4. James wants another car for his son.

5. Mrs. Green committed the murder in the library with the wrench.

6. Kareem read several history books for his research paper.

7. The food inspector is my cousin.

8. Several military policemen asked questions of the landlord.

9. These apartments are too expensive for my family.

10. She looked happy this morning.

11. The grocery store on the corner lost business steadily.

12. Our dry cleaning is ready.

13. Mike White was the high school spelling champion.

14. Your father is at the game.

15. Sheila appeared sleepy after the hike.

16. Wendell went to his brother's house for dinner.

17. My husband works for the electric company.

18. That was his last chance.

19. The magazine promised delivery in seven days.

20. *Murder Without a Motive* was my favorite novel last year.

Review Exercise 2

Mark the **verb**, **subject**, and **object** or **complement** of each sentence in the following paragraph.

The twentieth century saw the birth of a new form of storytelling.

A combination of metal, celluloid, glass, and wire produced a technical miracle. The result had a tremendous effect on the minds of millions. Of course, this art form is the motion picture. For many people the motion picture is the most important art form of the century.

Chapter 1 Writing Assignment

Write a brief **physical description** of an interesting scene in your neighborhood using short, simple sentences.

When you have made a final copy of your description, mark each **verb**, **subject**, **object**, or **complement**. (Remember — keep your sentences short.)

Hints for Writing Descriptions

Good descriptions are not just lists of details about a subject; they are details that *prove* something about the subject — some emotional response or impression that the writer wants to share with the reader.

In a good description, the writer is not telling only about a person or a lake, but about a *kind* person or a *peaceful* lake.

Your description can succeed nicely if you follow the advice below.

Before the rough draft:

1. Choose a scene that will be interesting for you to write about.

2. Look at the scene in person and decide on a feeling about it — an emotional response — that you want your readers to feel.

3. Make notes about the scene before you write. Include the emotional impression you want to create and the physical details that will support that feeling.

4. Edit your notes, leaving out the details that aren't needed or that don't support the emotional impression.

5. Recopy the details that remain in the order you wish to use them. Remember that the reader has to "see" this scene through your eyes. Make sure the details are listed in an order that you consider effective.

Writing the rough draft:

1. Start your rough draft by writing an opening sentence or two that mentions
   a. The scene you are going to describe, and
   b. The feeling you have about that scene.

2. Then, using your edited list, describe the scene so that your reader is convinced that your feeling is accurate.

3. As you describe the scene, use your best, most colorful language.

4. Write a closing sentence that either

   a. Restates your feeling about the scene, or
   b. Completes your description with a detail that seems to be an appropriate ending.

After the rough draft:

1. Do your best to correct any errors on this first copy.

2. Make any other changes you think will make your paragraph more interesting and readable.

3. Recopy your corrected paragraph on a clean sheet of paper, and turn in all of your work.

2
More about simple sentences

Chapter Preview

This chapter will show you

1. How to find **verb phrases** in simple sentences.

2. How to find **adverbs** that interrupt verb phrases.

3. How to find the subject and verb in sentences with **reversed word order**.

In addition, a special RELATED SKILL section will show you how to recognize **active** and **passive voice verbs**.

VERB PHRASES

In Chapter 1 you worked with one-word verbs. These verbs showed action and linking ideas that occurred in either the present time or the past time.

One-word verbs that show present time actions are called **present tense verbs**.

> **Present tense verbs**
>
> Mr. Mack (sees) another exit from the building.
>
> Lucia (is) this year's class president.

One-word verbs that show past time actions are called **past tense verbs**.

> **Past tense verbs**
>
> Mr. Mack (saw) another exit from the building.
>
> Lucia (was) last year's class president.

Every verb has a one-word present and past tense form.

Many sentences, however, contain not one-word verbs, but **verb phrases**, groups of words that act like one-word verbs. For these sentences, finding the verb means finding the verb phrase.

FINDING VERB PHRASES

Every one-word verb can be changed into a verb phrase. Compare the following sentences.

> Mr. Mack **sees** another exit from the building.
> Mr. Mack **will see** another exit from the building.

> Lucia **is** this year's class president.
> Lucia **could have been** this year's class president.

Though verb phrases come in different lengths, they all look the same and have the same structure. Each ends with an **action** or **linking word**, and each is preceded by one or more **helping verbs**:

HELPING VERB(S) + ACTION or LINKING WORD

In the sentences above, for example, the verb phrases are *will see* and *could have been*. *Will, could,* and *have* are helping verbs. *See* is an action word, and *been* is a linking word.

The action or linking word — the last word in the verb phrase — always contains its meaning. For example:

Helping verb(s) + action or linking word

will	**see**
may	**run**
could	**be**
have been	**running**
should be	**seen**
could have	**been**

The action or linking word can be

A present tense verb form like *run, see,* or *own*

A word made from a verb, like *running, seen,* or *owned*

In Chapter 8 you will study words made from verbs, called **verbals**, in more detail. Here, simply notice that two kinds of verbals can be used in verb phrases — the *-ing* word (like *running*) and a form called the **past participle** (like *seen* and *owned*).

Marking Verb Phrases

Mark verb phrases just like other verbs, with a circle.

Mr. Mack (will see) another exit from the building.

Lucia (could have been) this year's class president.

Finding Helping Verbs

What are helping verbs and how can you learn to recognize them? The easiest and quickest way is to learn the helping verb list.

It is short, and if you refer to it often in this chapter, you will find that you have learned it rather quickly.

35 More about simple sentences

Helping Verbs

1	2	3	4	5
shall	should	do	have	am
will	would	does	has	is
can	could	did	had	are
may	might			was
must				were
				be
				been
				being

Note that some of the words in columns 3, 4, and 5 can also be one-word verbs. To tell how one of these words is used, look at its position.

If it is the last word in a verb phrase, it is the action or linking word and carries the meaning of the verb phrase. If it is NOT the last word in a verb phrase, it is used as a helping verb.

As helping verb

I (**did** see) the answer.

We (**have** found) one of your earrings near the crime.

They (**are** looking) for your assistant.

As one-word verb

I (**did**) the job yesterday.

We (**have**) the earring in the evidence locker.

They (**are**) assistants in the learning laboratory.

Action and Linking Verb Phrases

When verb phrases contain action ideas, most students have little trouble recognizing them. But verb phrases that contain linking-verb ideas sometimes cause difficulty.

Compare the following sentences.

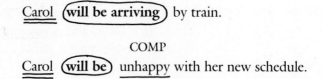

Carol (**will be arriving**) by train.

COMP
Carol (**will be**) unhappy with her new schedule.

The first sentence contains the three-word verb phrase *will be arriving*. *Arriving* is the main action of the sentence. Both *will* and *be* are used as helping verbs.

The second sentence, on the other hand, contains the two-word phrase *will be*. Notice that *will be* contains a linking idea and that *unhappy* is a complement, not an action.

In sentences like these, don't be tempted to mark words like *unhappy* as part of the verb phrase.

Most of the linking verb phrases that cause this confusion end in the following words

be	(*will be*)
been	(*has been*)
being	(*is being*)

Look carefully at verb phrases containing these words to see if the meaning is an action or a linking idea. Mark the verb phrase accordingly.

The following exercises will help you find verb phrases in simple sentences. As usual, the more difficult sentences are toward the end of this group.

Try to get at least 80% of the answers correct. If after doing your best you cannot get a score of 80% or better, talk to your instructor. Finding verb phrases is an important part of your work in this book.

Exercise 1

Finding Action Verb Phrases

Circle the **verb** or **verb phrase** in each of the following sentences. Use the helping verb list on page 36 to help you.

All of the verbs in this exercise are action verbs.

example

The class (has been moved) to the Science Hall.

Shorter verb phrases:

1. *The Great Train Robbery* (was made) in 1903.

2. The Barkleys (will go) to the Catskills this summer.

3. This morning I (will eat) a small breakfast.

4. Wilma (has done) the best job possible.

5. Tonight's dinner (was prepared) by my daughter.

6. The roses in the garden (are growing) in sandy soil.

7. Kiley's girlfriend (should bring) extra plates.

8. The game has lasted over two hours.

9. We have read those novels in our last literature class.

10. Mr. Wilkes was registering earlier this evening.

Longer verb phrases:

11. The books should have arrived by now.

12. The food will have been delivered by five o'clock.

13. Tremaine, a transfer student from Maine, will be joining us in March.

14. The actors have been practicing for the opening.

15. The girls in the hall could have been listening.

16. Bennett could have wanted a larger share in the project.

17. That song should have been sung earlier in the evening.

18. Sammie has been working nights for several semesters.

19. She will be looking for a new job.

20. The box has been sent by courier mail.

Exercise 2	Finding Linking Verb Phrases

Circle the **verb** or **verb phrase** in each of the following sentences. Use the helping verb list on page 36 to help you.

All of the verbs in this exercise are linking verbs.

example
This sign (should have been) easier to see.

1. The garden will be ready for planting tomorrow.

2. The situation will look better in the morning.

3. Margaret has been class president the last three years.

4. Their assignments could have been ready last Monday.

5. This roast should taste better than the last one.

6. Walter is being difficult about lending the car.

7. The study guides should have been available earlier.

8. In this class the students are responsible for photographic developing fees.

9. This is a common complaint.

10. These classes have been larger in past semesters.

The next exercise includes both action and linking verbs. In addition, it asks you to find and mark certain important helping verbs — the *have* and *be* helping verbs in columns 4 and 5 of the helping verb list.

Exercise 3

Finding Action and Linking Verb Phrases

For each sentence in this exercise

a. Mark the **verb** or **verb phrase** in each of the following sentences. Use the helping verb list on page 36 to help you.

b. Place an **X** above all *have*- and *be*-group helping verbs.

c. Write **action** on the line if the verb is an action verb, and **linking** if the verb is a linking verb.

examples

action ____ The fraternity (has been asking) for contributions to its scholarship fund.

linking ____ My parents (have been) in Idaho since May 21.

Action ____ 1. The clock had rung several times already.

Action ____ 2. We should have ordered pizza.

LINK ____ 3. Marcy's new job could be a wonderful opportunity.

Action ____ 4. The pie should have been left in the oven longer.

LINK ____ 5. The dog had become irritated by all the fire alarms.

LINK ____ 6. The computer system has been installed by a consultant from Lanfil Technologies.

Action ____ 7. She has flown more than ten thousand miles in the last few years.

Action **8.** Dr. Shea has been trying for years to win the councilman's seat.

Action **9.** The boss will arrive in a few weeks.

LINK **10.** Marv Murphy has been a broadcaster in this area for more than fifteen years.

Action **11.** Jim might have gone to the Coho Club.

Action **12.** She practiced the flute for years before performing in public.

Action **13.** The gladiolas have been attacked by the neighborhood cats.

Action **14.** The books will be sent by first-class mail.

LINK **15.** Mr. Lacy has been a resident since June.

Action **16.** The buses were running on a special schedule during the snowstorm.

LINK **17.** Terry's essay should have been finished by now.

LINK **18.** Law enforcement can be a challenging career.

Action **19.** The sauce should have tasted more like pepper.

Action **20.** The world has been made safe for democracy.

Words That Interrupt Verb Phrases

Sometimes a word that is not part of the verb phrase appears between words of the phrase. For example

I have always enjoyed apricots.

Have enjoyed is the verb of this sentence. It follows the rules about verb phrases.

1. _Enjoyed_ is an action word.

2. _Have_ is on the helping verb list.

The word *always* cannot be part of the verb phrase. Words like *always* are called **adverbs**. Adverbs describe verbs. *Always* describes the verb of the sentence by telling *when* the action occurred.

Here are some more examples of adverbs in verb phrases.

Morten (had) **never** (been selected) for a committee.

The salad (was) **frequently** (served) with a creamy

dill dressing.

Adverbs will be discussed in detail in Chapter 3. For now, be careful of the helping verbs you mark. Remember — if a word does not appear on the helping verb list that you've been using in this chapter, it is NOT a helping verb.

Helping Verbs

1	2	3	4	5
shall	should	do	have	am
will	would	does	has	is
can	could	did	had	are
may	might			was
must				were
				be
				been
				being

The Adverb NOT

The adverb *not* is often found in the middle of a verb phrase.

Hester (could) **not** (believe) the charges against her.

Not is often contracted in verb phrases.

Hester (could) **n't** (believe) the charges against her.

Even though *not* is printed as part of the verb (as *couldn't*), it is still an adverb and not a helping verb. When you circle verbs like this, leave *not* or *n't* out of the circle.

The following exercise contains examples of verb phrases with interrupting words.

Exercise 4

Verb Phrases with Adverbs

Mark the **verb** or **verb phrase** in each of the following sentences. Then place an **X** above all *have-* and *be-*group helping verbs.

Make sure that all of the helping verbs you circle appear on the helping verb list on page 41.

example

The battle (was) not (won) by the infantry.

1. They (could) not (have married) at a better time.

2. Myron (has) always (wanted) a career in the arts.

3. The deal (has) already (been negotiated) by our lawyers.

4. Problems like that (are) seldom (solved) through anger.

5. The Roman eighth legion (has) successfully (penetrated) the enemy

    rear guard.

6. This (could) possibly (have been) her greatest year.

7. Power never (remained) with his branch of the family.

8. Myron (had) never before (been elected) to a class office.

9. These storms (do) not usually (last) more than three days.

10. Her sister's husband (could) possibly (continue) in the job for

    another year.

11. We (could) never (have bought) the bonds by ourselves.

12. The leading actress (is) usually late.

13. The players (have been practicing) by themselves.

14. She (was) never happy with her major.

15. *La Vita Nuova*, Dante's first major work, (is) seldom (read) today.

16. It (is) also one of his greatest.

17. The news (has been brought) to you by Lanfil, makers of today's tech-

    nology today.

18. Treatments for alcoholism (are) often (advertised) in this area.

19. Brian was not interested in the offer.

20. Her choice of residence should never have become an issue.

FINDING VERB PHRASES IN PARAGRAPHS

By now you are probably pretty good at finding verb phrases in exercise sentences. The ultimate goal, however, is to find them (and correct them, if necessary) in your own paragraphs. This is not as easy to do.

As a step toward that goal, the next exercise asks you to find verb phrases in a printed paragraph that contains writing similar to what you will encounter in college. This short paragraph is about why musical plays (like *Oklahoma* and *Cats*) are popular.

Your job (if you choose to accept it) is to find each verb phrase and mark it accurately. Be careful — many of these sentences are long and have more than one verb.

However, if you work carefully, use your common sense about what is being said, and mark only verb phrases that follow the rules, you should do very well.

Exercise 5

Finding Verb Phrases in Paragraphs

For each sentence in this exercise

a. Mark the **verb** or **verb phrase** in each of the following sentences. Use the helping verb list on page 41 to help you.

b. Place an **X** over all *have-* and *be-*group helping verbs.

Be careful. Some of these sentences have more than one verb.

His advice, though sound, has seldom been taken , but his success has never been doubted

Good Broadway musicals have often had longer stage lives than good straight plays. This does not surprise me. Good musical plays, like *Oklahoma* and *Cats,* are enjoyed by more people. They are usually considered a "brighter" form of entertainment. Their subjects are often happier than those of serious plays. Musical theater promises an evening of fun. It should not be a mystery, therefore, that older musicals are frequently revived. Audiences never tire of good music, and few serious plays can successfully compete with the good fun of a great musical.

Verb phrases allow us to tell more about an action than one-word verbs do. Verb phrases allow us to tell

1. The **time** of a future action

> Mr. Hamilton **will bring** extra money for our trips.

2. The **mode** of an action (for example, that an action is not a fact, but a possibility)

   Statement of Fact

   Viola **plays** first base on her weekend softball team.

   Statement of Possibility

   Viola **might play** first base on her weekend softball team.

3. The **completion** of an action

   Action Completed

   Judge Otto **served** time for selling false drivers' licenses.

   Action Completed in the Recent Past

   Judge Otto **has served** time for selling false drivers' licenses.

   Action Completed in the Distant Past

   Judge Otto **had served** time for selling false drivers' licenses.

   Action Still Going On

   Judge Otto **is serving** time for selling false drivers' licenses.

4. The **direction** of an action (for example, that the subject is the receiver of the action instead of the doer)

Whenever possible

Subject as Doer of Action

The referee **postponed** the game because of snow.

Subject as Receiver of Action

The game **was postponed** because of snow.

This last group of verb phrases is especially important. Good writers make the subject the doer of the action wherever possible.

Verbs that make the subject the doer of the action (like *postponed*) are called **active voice** verbs. Sentences with active voice verbs are stronger and more readable.

Verbs that say the subject is the receiver of the action (like *was postponed*) are called **passive voice** verbs. Sentences with passive voice verbs are weaker and less interesting to read. You should use the passive voice only when there is no better way to communicate your idea.

To see the difference between active and passive voice verbs clearly, let's look at the example sentences above.

In the first sentence, the subject (*referee*) did the postponing. You can imagine the action going from the subject, through the active voice verb (*postponed*), toward the object (*game*).

Active Voice Verb

referee **postponed** game

X ——————→

In the second sentence, the action goes back toward the subject. *Game* is the receiver of the action.

Passive Voice Verb

game **was postponed**

←——————

Notice that sentences with passive voice verbs don't always tell the doer of the action. (In the second sentence, did the referee postpone the game? We don't know.)

45 More about simple sentences

To recognize active and passive voice, remember —

If the subject is   the **doer** of the action

the verb is   **active** voice

If the subject is   the **receiver** of the action

the verb is   **passive** voice

Practice finding active and passive verbs by doing the following exercise.

Skill Exercise

Finding Active and Passive Voice Verbs

Mark each **verb** and its **subject** in each of the following sentences. Then write **active** or **passive** on the line to show whether the subject is the doer or the receiver of the action.

| example |

active   Passionella (wrote) an excellent biology final.

A   **1.** The briefcase lay against the desk.

P   **2.** That deodorant manufacturer is being sued.

A   **3.** She has found an important archaeological site.

A   **4.** The sky had been turning gray all afternoon.

P   **5.** The game was seen by thousands of football fans.

P   **6.** Each airplane was inspected before takeoff.

A   **7.** Mr. Carola has been answering all questions.

P   **8.** All questions have been answered except one.

A   **9.** What happened to Manuel's history book?

P   **10.** The room was rented to a young Pakistani couple.

SENTENCES WITH REVERSED WORD ORDER

In some sentences the natural order of the main words — subject, verb, object or complement — is changed. These changes occur most often in the following situations:

Asking questions

Giving orders

"Here is/There is . . ." sentences

Changing emphasis

Recognizing these situations will help you mark and punctuate sentences correctly. It will also help you in choosing the correct verb form.

Asking Questions

To ask a question in writing, we often change the order of the words in the sentence. The new sentence often has part or all of the verb in front of the subject.

Statement (normal word order)

Alma (**has been elected**) treasurer this year.

Question (reversed word order)

(Has) Alma (**been elected**) treasurer this year?

Verb phrases are often used in questions. Notice that the question ends with a question mark, not a period.

Questions That Add *Do, Does,* and *Did*

Sometimes statements with one-word verbs are turned into questions by using the helping verbs *do, does,* or *did.*

Statement (normal word order)

Our customers (**want**) better service.

Question (reversed word order)

(**Do**) our customers (**want**) better service?

Questions That Start with *Who, Whom, Which,* and *What*

Some sentences use the pronouns *who, whom, which,* and *what* to show that they are questions, not statements. When this is so, the question words appear at the beginning of the sentence.

47 More about simple sentences

In the following example, the pronoun *what* is the object of the verb phrase *did ask*. Notice that the answer to the question supplies the meaning of the question word *what*.

What (did) you (ask) me?

Only when the question word is also the subject of the sentence will the sentence be printed in normal word order.

Who (spoke) at the reception?

Notice that in the above sentence, the subject form *who* is used.

Other commonly used question words are *when, where, why,* and *how*. Though these words are usually not the subject or object of the sentence, most questions that contain them also show reversed word order.

Why (are) you (looking) at me like that?

Exercise 6

Marking Questions

Mark the **verb**, **subject**, and **object** or **complement**, if any, of each of the following sentences.

| example |

(Is) the answer (found) on the worksheet?

1. Why was your lab report late?

2. Has Imad been seeing Billy's sister?

3. Who has discovered the answer to problem 17?

4. Has she appeared in other plays?

5. When will the next train leave?

6. Was corn harvested in this area?

7. Did you notice Pablo's new car?

8. Why was the curtain hung upside down?

9. Did Jennifer ever find her lab notebook?

10. Does this answer your question?

Giving Orders

Sentences that contain requests, commands, or directions also show a kind of reversed word order. In these sentences, though, words are not moved around, but *removed*.

The word taken out is the subject *you*. The absence of *you* gives the verb of the request or command more force, since it starts the sentence.

Command

(Stand) next to the door.

Even though *you* is not written in the sentence, it is still understood to be there.

Command

<<u>You</u>> (Stand) next to the door.

Mark the missing subject of a request or command as a **hidden word** by adding it above the sentence and underlining it twice.

Command

You (Stand) next to the door.

Exercise 7

Marking Commands

Mark the **verb**, **subject**, and **object** or **complement** of each of the following sentences. If the subject is the hidden word *you*, add it above the sentence and mark it correctly.

example

You (Return) your <u>books</u> to the library soon.

1. Please (answer) all questions on the examination.

2. <u>You</u> (know) the <u>reason</u> for our visit.

3. (Stand) quietly.

4. (Give) the <u>book</u> to Ms. Abraham after class.

5. The <u>computer</u> (needs) a larger power <u>supply</u>.

6. (Begin) with the information printed in the back of the report.

7. (Read) <u>this</u>.

8. (Stop.)

9. <u>He</u> (saw) <u>everything</u>.

10. (Look) at the picture carefully.

"Here is/There is . . ." Sentences

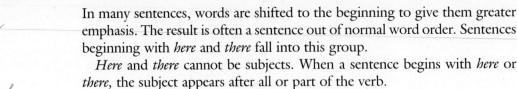

In many sentences, words are shifted to the beginning to give them greater emphasis. The result is often a sentence out of normal word order. Sentences beginning with *here* and *there* fall into this group.

Here and *there* cannot be subjects. When a sentence begins with *here* or *there,* the subject appears after all or part of the verb.

Study the following sentences. In both of them, the subject is *books.*

Reversed word order

Here ⟨are⟩ your <u>books</u>.

Normal word order

Your <u>books</u> ⟨are⟩ here.

Even where *there* does not refer to a specific place, it still cannot be the subject.

Reversed word order

There ⟨are⟩ three <u>men</u> ⟨waiting⟩ in your office.

Test this marking by putting the sentence into normal word order without the word *there.*

Normal word order

Three <u>men</u> ⟨are waiting⟩ in your office.

| Exercise 8 | Marking "Here Is / There Is . . ." Sentences |

Mark the **verb, subject,** and **object** or **complement** of each of the following sentences.

| example | Here ⟨are⟩ the <u>answers</u> to the first ten questions. |

1. There ⟨are⟩ the other <u>copies</u> of my class notes.

2. Here ⟨comes⟩ the first <u>customer</u>.

3. There ⟨is⟩ an <u>example</u> of good lab technique.

4. *<u>Claire</u>* ⟨is⟩ the <u>title</u> of one of her best novels.

5. There ⟨were⟩ <u>visitors</u> ⟨staying⟩ at Appleby House this weekend.

6. It was a surprise to us.

7. Here are the extra diskettes for your computer.

8. There is only one word processor in this office.

9. Here stood the Old West Church.

10. There was also an Indian mission here once.

Changing Emphasis with Reversed Word Order

Many sentences are not written in normal word order so that a word or phrase can be emphasized. Usually, phrases to be emphasized are brought to the beginning of the sentence.

For example, in each of the following sentences, emphasized words appear at the beginning.

Reversed word order

A fine doctor you are !

Into the meadow walked a young deer.

The first sentence emphasizes *doctor,* the object of the verb. The second emphasizes *into the meadow.*

Here is how these sentences would appear in normal word order.

Normal word order

You are a fine doctor!

A young deer walked into the meadow.

Exercise 9

Other Sentences with Reversed Word Order

Many of the sentences in this exercise contain reversed word order. Mark the **verb**, **subject**, and **object** or **complement** of each of the following sentences. If the sentence is in reversed word order, rewrite it in normal word order. If the sentence is not in reversed word order, write "normal" on the line.

example

On the blackboard is tomorrow's homework assignment.

Tomorrow's homework assignment

is on the blackboard.

51 More about simple sentences

1. Into the room walked three players from the soccer team.

Three players walked into the room.

2. A blank page is the writer's worst enemy.

3. To Mr. Hogan came the last of the transceivers.

The last of the transceivers came to Mr. Hogan.

4. A fine student he became!

He became a fine student.

5. On the shelf sat the stack of newspapers.

The stack of newspapers sat on the shelf.

The following exercise includes all of the kinds of sentences you have been studying.

Exercise 10

Reversed Word Order

Mark the **verb**, **subject**, and **object** or **complement** of each of the following sentences.

1. Is this the way to Beauville?

2. Here is a recent map of this region.

3. Who lives in the house now?

4. Look at the article on the back page.

5. The corner needs repainting.

6. One book has disappeared each week for the last month.

Know **7.** There are no more copies of the essay.

8. Was she the first lawyer on the case?

9. Stop at the first apartment on the left.

10. There were ants in the kitchen this morning.

Chapter Review

In this chapter you learned that

1. A **verb phrase** acts like a one-word verb.

2. A verb phrase = **helping verb(s) + action or linking word**.

3. The **action** or **linking word** contains the meaning of the verb phrase.

4. A **helping verb** is a word from the helping verb list.

5. Words that describe verbs (**adverbs**) sometimes interrupt verb phrases.

6. Sentences that have **reversed word order** include

   a. Questions
   b. Commands
   c. "Here is/there is . . ." sentences
   d. Sentences with changing emphasis

A special RELATED SKILL section showed you about **active** and **passive voice verbs**.

1. Active voice — the subject is the doer of the action.

2. Passive voice — the subject is the receiver of the action.

Review Exercise 1

Mark the **verb**, **subject**, and **object** or **complement** in each of the following sentences. Watch for sentences with reversed word order.

example

 Are you waiting for the train?

1. Rain has been falling steadily for weeks.

2. This is next month's rent. *COMP*

3. Here is next month's rent.

4. We have seldom seen a dance performance as good as Damon's.

5. Martha has been saving her money for a new car.

6. Martha has been careful with her money. *COMP*

7. Please send another order form. *YOU*

8. An order form was already sent by first-class mail.

9. This accident could have been avoided.

10. This accident could easily have been avoided.

11. Don't stop the car yet. *YOU*

12. I couldn't find a replacement for the light bulb.

13. Was this man waiting for Dr. Valdez?

14. What is the name of your cousin from New York? *COMP*

15. Where did you leave the checkbook?

16. I left the checkbook in the back of the car.

17. Susan must have liked her psychology class.

18. She has been practicing on everyone in her dorm.

19. Irma might never have reached home safely without your help.

20. Is Bernie having another beach party?

Review Exercise 2 ———————————

Mark the **verb**, **subject**, and **object** or **complement** of each sentence in the following paragraph. Watch for sentences with reversed word order.

Do you need a printed copy of one of the reports on your computer?

There are several ways to do this. The simplest way, however, is this. Press *COMP* *YOU* the F1 key on the keyboard. The screen will list all of the reports that are yours. Then move the flashing cursor with the arrow keys. In this way a report can be chosen for copying. Finally, press the ENTER key. The computer will automatically print the report for you.

Review Exercise 3

Each of the sentences in this exercise is written in the passive voice. **Recopy** each sentence, **changing all passive voice verbs** to the active voice. Note that you may have to supply a "doer" when rewriting some passive voice sentences.

The biggest basketball game of the season was played last night by the Penwicker Quills. The score was kept close by the opposing team until the last minute of the fourth quarter. Then, with the score even, the ball was stolen by Penwicker guard Brad Palmer. The ball was dribbled to the basket through three opponents. The shot was made. The game was won by that shot. For the rest of the week, Palmer was greeted as a hero everywhere on campus.

The Penwicker Quills played the biggest
basketball game of the season
last night. The opposing team
kept the score close until the
last minute of the fourth quarter.

Chapter 2 Writing Assignment

Write a brief **physical description** of an interesting person. Use at least one **question** and one **"here is/there is" sentence** in your paragraph.

When you have made a final copy of your description, **mark each verb**, **subject**, and **object** or **complement**. Watch carefully for sentences with more than one subject and verb.

Hints for Writing Descriptions

This description will be successful if you follow the same principles you applied in the last Chapter Writing Assignment.

In your first sentence, name your subject and *tell what you are trying to prove* about that person — Mr. Jones is excessively neat; Brianna is tall and attractive; Juan is a colorful dresser. If your description seems to make a point about its subject, your readers will be much more interested in your writing.

Before the rough draft:

1. Choose a person that will be interesting for you to describe.

2. Study the person and, if possible, make notes about his or her appearance.

3. Decide on a main impression or feeling that you want to convey about that person's appearance in your description.

4. Organize and rewrite your notes to include

   a. The impression you want to create about the person's appearance and

   b. The supporting details you want to include in your description

   Make sure that supporting details are listed in an order that the reader can follow easily. You might start with the head, for example, and work your way down, or start with the clothes and end with the face. In any case, make sure your reader doesn't get confused.

Writing the rough draft:

1. Start your rough draft by writing an opening sentence or two that mentions

   a. The person you are going to describe
   b. The point you are going to make about that person's appearance

2. Then, using your edited list, describe the person so that the reader is convinced that the point you are making is correct.

3. As you describe the person, use your best, most colorful language.

4. Write a closing sentence that either

    a. Restates the point you made in your first sentence, or

    b. Completes your description with a detail that feels like an ending.

After the rough draft:

1. Do your best to correct any errors on this first copy.

2. Make any other changes you think will make your paragraph more interesting and readable.

3. Recopy your corrected paragraph on a clean sheet of paper and turn in all of your work.

3
Adjectives and adverbs

Chapter Preview

This chapter will show you

1. How to use the four **adjective questions** to find **adjectives** that describe subjects and objects.

2. How to use the five **adverb questions** to find **adverbs** that describe verbs.

3. How to find **adverbs** that describe adjectives and other adverbs.

In addition, a special RELATED SKILL section will show you how to use the **apostrophe to spell possessive adjectives**.

DESCRIPTIVE WORDS IN SIMPLE SENTENCES

You have seen that the subject, verb, and object or complement are the basic parts of every sentence. But most sentences have other words in them. What do these words do?

Some of these words describe subjects and objects. Words and phrases that describe nouns or pronouns (subjects and objects) are called **adjectives**.

SUBJECT — VERB — **Object**
| |
Adjectives **Adjectives**

Other words describe verbs. Words and phrases that describe verbs are called **adverbs**. Adverbs can also describe adjectives and other adverbs.

SUBJECT — **VERB** — Object
| | |
Adjectives **Adverbs** Adjectives

Complements can be described either by adjectives, if the complement is a noun or pronoun, or by adverbs, if the complement is an adjective.

SUBJECT — VERB — **Complement**
|
Adjectives or **Adverbs**

You've seen adjectives and adverbs in previous chapters. This section will show you how to find adjectives and adverbs in sentences. When you are finished, you will know all of the basic parts of a simple sentence.

Of course, a sentence still needs only a subject and a verb to be complete.

Objects and complements, when they are present, are part of the core idea of the sentence, but not all sentences have them. And even though most sentences would be dry and uninformative without adjectives and adverbs, these words are always optional.

ADJECTIVES

Adjectives are words that describe nouns and pronouns. This means that adjectives describe subjects and objects. In the following sentence, for example, the adjectives *this* and *old* describe the subject *car*.

This old car is mine.

This chapter will show you how to find one-word adjectives like *this* and *old* in simple sentences.

This is a more useful skill than you may realize. If you can find simple adjectives, you can find and punctuate the longer and more complicated adjectives you will study in coming chapters. A great many writers have trouble writing and punctuating these adjectives.

The Adjective Questions

Find adjectives by using the four **adjective questions**. Every adjective answers one of them.

Adjective Questions

First ask   Which
                       What kind
                       How many (or how much)
                       Whose

Then say   the noun or pronoun

Example: **This old** car is mine.

                      Which car?
                      What kind of car?

The Adjective Question "Which?"

Adjectives that tell "which?" either point out a specific person or thing (such as **the** *car* or **that** *salesman*), or they refer to any person or thing (**a** *car* or **any** *salesman*).

Some of the adjectives that answer the question "which?" are:

this	the	a
that		an
these		any
those		

Let's look at an example.

The bookstore has purchased those calendars.

The core idea of this sentence is *bookstore – has purchased – calendars* (subject – verb – object).

The <u>bookstore</u> (has purchased) those <u>calendars</u>.

By asking the adjective question "which?" we discover that the sentence contains two adjectives — *the* and *those*. The adjective *the* describes the subject, and *those* describes the object.

**Adjective
question:** *Which* bookstore?
Answer: *The* bookstore.

**Adjective
question:** *Which* calendars?
Answer: *Those* calendars.

The <u>bookstore</u> (has purchased) those <u>calendars</u>.

If we insert this example into our sentence diagram, the result would look like this.

SUBJECT — VERB — Object
    | |

Adjectives   **Adjectives**

bookstore — has purchased — calendars
   | |

The   **those**

The is a common adjective telling "which." *The* tells us that not just any bookstore, but a specific bookstore, is intended. *A* and *an* also tell "which." (The adjectives *a, an,* and *the* are also called **articles**.)
Consider the following sentence.

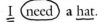

<u>I</u> (need) **a** <u>hat</u>.

I – need – hat is the core of this sentence (subject – verb – object).

**Adjective
question:** *Which* hat?
Answer: *A* hat

The adjective *a* tells "which hat" by showing that no particular hat is being considered at the moment. Any hat will apparently do.

Marking Adjectives

Mark adjectives in sentences by drawing an arrow from the adjective to the word it describes.

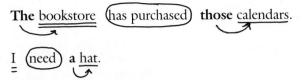

The <u>bookstore</u> (has purchased) **those** <u>calendars</u>.

<u>I</u> (need) **a** <u>hat</u>.

Mark all adjectives, except those used as complements, in this way.

Position of Adjectives

In English, most one-word adjectives appear *before* the words they describe. (In many other languages, this is not the case.)

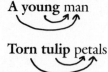

A young man

Torn tulip petals

The chief exceptions to this rule are in sentences like the following.

Her friends (call) her **lucky.**

The Adjective Question "What Kind?"

Adjectives that tell "what kind" are a large group. They include all of the descriptive words like *happy, lucky, red,* and *indescribable,* and many more besides.

The following sentence contains an adjective that tells "what kind."

A **brass** key struck the railing.

By finding the verb and using the subject and object questions, we discover the core of this sentence — *key – struck – railing.*

A **brass** key (struck) the railing.

But the sentence tells us more. It tells us what kind of key.

Adjective
question: *What kind* of key?
Answer: *Brass* key

Brass is an adjective describing *key.*

A **brass** key (struck) the railing.

The Adjective Question "How Many?" or "How Much?"

A third group of adjectives tells "how many" or "how much." Study the following sentence.

Four students received scholarships.

The core of this sentence is *students – received – scholarships* (subject – verb – object).

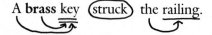

Four students (received) scholarships.

Now let's look for adjectives.

**Adjective
question:**   *How many* students?
Answer: *Four* students

Four is an adjective answering the question "how many?"

Four <u>students</u> (received) <u>scholarships</u>.

Adjectives that tell "how much" are similar to those telling "how many." For example:

<u>Alberta</u> (would like) **more** <u>sugar</u>.

**Adjective
question:**   *How much* sugar?
Answer: *More* sugar

More is an adjective telling "how much." Here it tells "how much sugar."

<u>Alberta</u> (would like) **more** <u>sugar</u>.

Adjectives that tell "how many" or "how much" include numbers (like *one, two,* and so on) and words like *some, many, much, more, all,* and *few.*

Notice, though, that many of these words can also be used by themselves. Compare the following sentences.

Six bottles were broken.

Six were broken.

In the first sentence, *six* is an adjective describing *bottles.*

Six **as adjective**

Six <u>bottles</u> (were broken) .

In the second, *six* is a pronoun acting as the subject.

Six **as pronoun (subject)**

<u>Six</u> (were broken) .

Be careful in marking sentences that contain these words.

The Adjective Question "Whose"

The last group of adjectives are those that tell "whose." Adjectives in this group are called **possessive adjectives** because they show possession, ownership, belonging, or relatedness.

Possessive adjectives are common words. They are made from nouns and pronouns that name owners.

Possessive Adjectives from Nouns

Adjectives that answer the question "whose?" are made by adding an **apostrophe (')** and often an *s* to the ends of nouns. **The part of the word before the apostrophe always names the owner.**

The following sentence contains a possessive adjective.

Benjamin's friends are happy about his promotion.

The core of the sentence is *friends – are – happy* (subject – verb – complement). Notice that the verb is a linking verb.

COMP
Benjamin's <u>friends</u> (are) <u>happy</u> about his promotion.

Now let's look for possessive adjectives.

Adjective question: *Whose* friends?
Answer: *Benjamin's* friends.

Benjamin's is an adjective that tells "whose friends."

COMP
Benjamin's <u>friends</u> (are) <u>happy</u> about his promotion.

Even though the word *Benjamin's* is made from a noun (*Benjamin*), it is an adjective. The part of the word before the apostrophe tells who the "owner" of the friends is — Benjamin.

OWNER
↓

Things as "Owners"

Possessive adjectives are not made just from the names of people. They can be made from the names of things as well.

The **film's** ending was too long.

Naturally the film doesn't own the ending. But the ending does belong to the film. So we speak of a *film's ending* just as we speak of a *book's pages,* a *skirt's hem,* or a *television set's reception.*

Another common use of possessive adjectives is shown in the following sentence.

The company donated a **week's** profits to the Unified

Fund.

Here again, the possessive does not imply real ownership. The company is the true owner of the profits.

Nonetheless, we speak of a "week's profits" to show the relationship between time spent ("week") and the rewards of that time ("profits"). Similar phrases include an *hour's entertainment,* a *moment's pleasure,* and a *month's vacation.*

Possessive Adjectives from Pronouns

Pronouns like *someone* and *anyone* form possessives in the same way as nouns — with an apostrophe and maybe an added *s.*

The possessive adjective form of *someone,* for example, is *someone's.* (Here again, the part of the word before the apostrophe names the owner.)

The personal pronouns and the pronoun *who,* however, have special possessive forms. The following chart shows the possessive adjective forms of these common pronouns.

Possessive Adjectives from Pronouns

Pronoun	Adjective
I	my
you	your
he	his
she	her
it	its
we	our
they	their
who	whose

Note that these words do NOT contain apostrophes. For example, *its* and *it's* are NOT the same word. See Chapter 18 for more information on commonly confused words like these.

Confusing Adjectives and Nouns

It can be tempting to mark some adjectives as subjects and objects. Many adjectives, for example, are spelled the same as nouns. In addition, possessive adjectives, which are often made from nouns, contain capitalized names.

For example, consider the following sentences.

The **letter** opener is kept in this drawer.

Pasadena's air is often smoggy.

The subject of the first sentence is *opener,* not *letter.*

The **letter** opener (is kept) in this drawer.

The opener, not the letter, is kept in the drawer. Even though *letter* might be used as a noun in other sentences, it is an adjective here.

The subject of the second sentence is *air,* not *Pasadena.*

COMP
Pasadena's air (is) often smoggy.

It's the *air* that's smoggy, not the city.

Exercise 1

Marking Sentences with Adjectives

The verb, subject, and object or complement, if any, have been marked for you in the following sentences. Mark each **adjective** by drawing an arrow from it to the word it describes.

Be prepared to say which **adjective question** each adjective answers.

| **example** | Adolph (saw) the new show. |

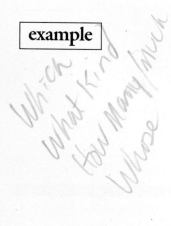

1. The key chain (saved) my life.

COMP
2. She (is) a model student.

3. The old boxes (were inhabited) .

4. These librarians (like) their work.

COMP
5. The largest set (was) available.

66 The structure of simple sentences

6. Barry's broken <u>statues</u> (can be fixed) .

7. His <u>inventory</u> (includes) several new microprocessor <u>chips</u>.

8. Our <u>vans</u> (are) an excellent <u>bargain</u>.
   <small>COMP</small>

9. The Croton daily <u>newspaper</u> (declared) <u>bankruptcy</u>.

10. Several recent <u>videos</u> (have featured) famous film <u>actors</u>.

Exercise 2

Finding One-Word Adjectives

Mark the **verb**, **subject**, and **object** or **complement** in the following sentences. Then draw an arrow from each **adjective** to the word it describes. Be prepared to say which **adjective question** each adjective answers.

example

COMP
The new <u>computer</u> (will be) <u>available</u>.

1. The grocery <u>store</u> reduced its meat <u>prices</u>.

2. Her <u>secretary</u> (left).

3. The downtown <u>theaters</u> (have closed.)

4. This <u>company</u> (has) a few good <u>salespeople</u>.

5. The <u>mailbox</u> (contained) these three utility <u>bills</u>.

6. Fran's <u>cousin</u> (remembered) the <u>evening</u>.

7. <u>Septima</u> (answered) the <u>door</u>.

8. The dark <u>cemetery</u> (frightened) the two <u>children</u>.

9. The Yugoslavian <u>team</u> (played) good <u>basketball</u>.

10. Brady's <u>answers</u> (were) <u>clever</u>. <small>COMP</small>

11. The Andersons' <u>order</u> (is) <u>ready</u>. <small>COMP</small>

12. Mr. Delany's <u>children</u> (bought) Grandpa's <u>car</u>.

13. The karate <u>instructor</u> (offered) several free <u>lessons</u>.

14. Robin's <u>aunt</u> (leads) an all-girl <u>orchestra</u>.

15. <u>We</u> (had) few real <u>differences</u>.

16. Those <u>bananas</u> (are) <u>ripe</u>. <small>COMP</small>

17. The old road is rough.

18. Marnie has found her cousins.

19. The news saddened Michael's two brothers.

20. Each new announcement increased our surprise.

RELATED SKILL   USING THE APOSTROPHE WITH POSSESSIVE ADJECTIVES

All nouns and many pronouns form possessive adjectives by using the **apostrophe (').**

Possessive adjectives answer the question "whose?" They show that someone or something "owns" something. For example:

	Possessive
Noun	**adjective**
man	man's
elbow	elbow's
churches	churches'
ovens	ovens'
John	John's

	Possessive
Pronoun	**adjective**
somebody	somebody's
everyone	everyone's

Spelling possessive adjectives is sometimes a problem. The following rule will help you spell these words correctly.

Using Apostrophes with Possessive Adjectives

To spell possessive adjectives correctly:

1. write the name of the owner or owners

2. add an apostrophe at the end of the word

3. Add an **s** after the apostrophe if the word is either

    a. singular, or
    b. plural not ending in **s.**

Singular means "one" in number. *Plural* means more than "one."

The chief problem in spelling possessive adjectives is the temptation to add the apostrophe *inside* the name of the owner, not after it.

The above rule helps you avoid that temptation. Just be sure to write the word that names the owner or owners first. Then add the apostrophe and **s**, if needed.

Let's look at an example.

Jerline owns a book. It is _____ book.

First, write the name of the owner.

Jerline

Next, add an apostrophe to the end of the word.

Jerline'

Finally, add an *s* after the apostrophe if the word is *singular* or *plural not ending in s*. *Jerline* is singular.

Jerline's

Jerline's is the correct possessive adjective form of *Jerline*.

Jerline owns a book. It is **Jerline's** book.

Notice again that in the completed word, the name of the owner is behind the apostrophe.

OWNER
↓

Jerline 's

Here are some other common possessives.

	Noun or pronoun	Possessive adjective
Singular:	boy	**boy**'s
	boss	**boss**'s
	week	**week**'s
	child	**child**'s
	someone	**someone**'s
	another	**another**'s
	Mr. Jones	**Mr. Jones**'s

Plural ending in **s:**		
	boys	**boys**'
	bosses	**bosses**'
	weeks	**weeks**'
	the Joneses	the **Joneses**'

Plural not ending in **s:**		
	children	**children**'s
	men	**men**'s

Notice that in all cases, the name of the owner is before the apostrophe.

man 's ◄——— OWNERS ———► men 's

church 's ◄——— OWNERS ———► churches '

Skill Exercise 1

Using the Apostrophe with Possessive Adjectives

Tell whether each of the following is singular or plural by writing **S** or **P** on the line to the left. Then write the **correct possessive** form of the word on the line to the right.

example | _____S_____ book ___book 's___

1. _____S_____ woman _____
2. _____S_____ women _____
3. _____S_____ game _____
4. _____P_____ games _____
5. _____S_____ Cleveland _____
6. _____S_____ desk _____
7. _____P_____ desks _____
8. _____P_____ speedboats _____
9. _____S_____ goose _____
10. _____S_____ geese _____
11. _____P_____ sweepstakes _____
12. _____S_____ accountant _____

13. _____ s _____ brother _____

14. _____ s _____ businessmen _____

15. _____ s _____ picture _____

16. _____ s _____ Ms. Nicholson _____

17. _____ s _____ porch _____

18. _____ s _____ box _____

19. _____ p _____ boxes _____

20. _____ s _____ frog _____

Skill Exercise 2

Possessive Adjectives in Sentences

Complete each of the following with the **correct possessive adjective** form of the word in parentheses.

| example |

The _gun's_ accuracy was never questioned.
    (gun)

1. Sharon wants to spend a week at her _friend's_ apartment.
    (friend)

2. The _rifle's_ price is not too high.
    (rifle)

3. I followed the _satellite's_ orbit across the night sky.
    (satellite)

4. It took him _hours'_ work to solve that equation.
    (four hours)

5. _Jesse's_ cat has escaped.
    (Jesse)

6. A _urchin's_ sting can be painful.
    (sea urchin)

7. The _boss's_ wife just called.
    (boss)

8. The whole family will go to _Carlos's_ graduation.
    (Carlos)

9. She checked the _water's_ acidity first.
    (water)

10. A _boys'_ club is being formed in the neighborhood.
    (boys)

11. Researchers studied the _compound's_ properties carefully.
    (compound)

12. At the root of the tentacles sits the _octopus's_ mouth.
    (octopus)

13. We were told to follow the _stewardess's_ instructions.
    (stewardess)

14. You are entitled to ___weeks'___ vacation.
(two weeks)

15. The ___band's___ popularity has risen rapidly.
(band)

16. They contributed to the ___players'___ pension fund.
(players)

17. The ___Ladies'___ Aid Society will hold its first fall meeting on
(Ladies)
September 10.

18. Afterward we went to the ___writers'___ workshop.
(writers)

19. ___Men's___ suits are located in the rear.
(Men)

20. ___Willis's___ grades have improved greatly.
(Willis)

ADVERBS

Adverbs are words that describe verbs, adjectives, and other adverbs. In the following sentence, for example, the adverbs *away* and *rapidly* describe the verb, *drove*.

She drove away rapidly.

This section will show you how to find one-word adverbs like *away* and *rapidly* that describe the verb in simple sentences.

SUBJECT — VERB — Object
| | |
Adjectives   Adverbs   Adjectives

Like the ability to find adjectives, the ability to find adverbs will be more useful than you may realize. If you can find simple adverbs easily, you will be much closer to finding and punctuating the longer and more complicated adverbs you will study in coming chapters.

The Adverb Questions

Adverbs that describe verbs can be identified by using the five **adverb questions**. Every adverb that describes a verb answers one of them.

Adverb Questions

First say   the verb

Then ask   When?
        Where?
        Why?
        How?
        Under what condition? (*or* For sure?)

Example:	She drove **away rapidly**.
	Drove *where?*
	Drove **how?**

These are all of the ways that actions can be described. Let's look at them one at a time.

The Adverb Question "When?"

The first group of adverbs tells *when* the action takes place. It includes such words as *today, never, now, often, seldom,* and *yesterday.*

Any word or phrase that tells when an action happens is an adverb. For example:

<u>Slim</u> (met) <u>Wilma</u> **yesterday**.

Adverb question:	Met **when?**
Answer:	**Yesterday**

Note that if we inserted this example into our sentence diagram, the result would look like this.

$$
\begin{array}{ccccc}
\text{SUBJECT} & - & \textbf{VERB} & - & \text{Object} \\
| & & | & & | \\
& & \textbf{Adverbs} & & \\
\textbf{Slim} & - & \textbf{met} & - & \text{Wilma} \\
& & | & & \\
& & \text{yesterday} & &
\end{array}
$$

Another way to answer the question "when?" is to tell "how often" something occurs. *Twice, seldom, never,* and *frequently* are a few of the many words in this group.

<u>Carlos</u> **seldom** (watches) horror <u>movies</u>.

Adverb question:	Watches *when?*
Answer:	*Seldom*

Marking Adverbs

To mark adverbs, draw an arrow from the adverb to the word it describes.

<u>Slim</u> (met) <u>Wilma</u> **yesterday**.

Carlos **seldom** (watches) horror movies.

Both adjectives and adverbs are marked with arrows because they both describe other words. But notice:

If the arrow points to a   noun or pronoun
the descriptive word is an   adjective

If the arrow points to a(n)   verb, adjective, or adverb
the descriptive word is an   adverb

Position of Adverbs

Like all other English words, adverbs have a normal position — after the verb they describe. However, adverbs can be easily placed elsewhere.

For instance, in the first of the above examples, *yesterday* is in the normal position for adverbs.

Slim (met) Wilma **yesterday**.

In the second, however, *seldom* is out of normal position.

Carlos **seldom** (watches) horror movies.

Look carefully for adverbs when doing the exercises in this chapter. They could be anywhere in the sentence.

The Adverb Question "Where?"

Another large group of adverbs tells *where* an action takes place. *Here* and *there*, two common adverbs, are members of this group. Other adverbs that tell "where" include *nearby, somewhere,* and *nowhere.*

Mr. Gould will play **here**.

Adverb
question: Will play *where?*
Answer: *Here*

In this sentence, *here* describes the verb *will play.*

Mr. Gould (will play) **here**.

Another way to tell "where" is to say in what direction an action occurred. Adverbs that tell "in what direction" include *north, south, up, in, out, away,* and many others.

Infinitessima looked **away**.

**Adverb
question:**   Looked *where?*
Answer: *Away*

Here, the adverb *away* describes the verb *looked.*

Infinitessima (looked) **away.**

The Adverb Question "Why?"

Most adverbs that tell *why* an action occurs are groups of words beginning with words like *because, since, so that,* and the like. These adverbs will be considered in the chapters that follow.

Don't forget, though, that "why?" is one of the adverb questions.

The Adverb Question "How?"

The largest group of adverbs tells *how* an action occurs. Most adverbs that end in -*ly* are members of this group.

My sister wins **easily.**

**Adverb
question:**   Wins *how?*
Answer: *Easily*

In this sentence, *easily* is an adverb telling how she wins. Notice that "how" in this case means "in what way."

My sister (wins) **easily.**

Let's look at another one.

The books fell **noisily.**

**Adverb
question:**   Fell *how?*
Answer: *Noisily*

Noisily is an adverb that describes the verb *fell* by telling how the action happened.

The books (fell) **noisily.**

Most adjectives can be made into adverbs by adding the ending -*ly*. For example:

Adjective	Adverb
awkward	awkwardly
easy	easily
generous	generously
high	highly
short	shortly

In fact, only a few adjectives have adverb forms that do not add -*ly*. The most common of these is *good*.

Adjective	Adverb
good	well

The Adverb Question "Under What Condition?"

A small group of important adverbs shows that a statement is true only if some condition is true.

Sometimes these conditions are stated in adverb phrases and other longer adverbs that begin with words like *if*. Most one-word adverbs, on the other hand, say merely that a condition exists, without specifying what the condition is.

When the condition is not stated, adverbs in this group can be found by asking the question "for sure?" Adverbs like *maybe, certainly,* and *not* are among the most common "under what condition?" adverbs. For example:

> **Maybe** she could borrow your notes.

Adverb question: Will lend *for sure?*
Answer: *Maybe*

Here the adverb *maybe* says that the action *could borrow* is true under some condition that hasn't been stated.

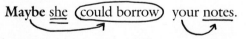

> **Maybe** she could borrow your notes.

Here is another example.

> Dr. Said is **certainly** a demanding instructor.

Adverb question: Is *for sure?*
Answer: *Certainly*

In this sentence, *certainly* is an adverb that describes the verb *is* by saying it is true "for sure."

Dr. Said (is) **certainly** a demanding instructor.

The following list of common adverbs will help you do the exercises in this section. Keep in mind, though, that this list is not complete — a complete list of adverbs would probably fill this chapter!

Some Common Adverbs

When?

yesterday	always	early
today	never	late
tomorrow	often	earlier
now	seldom	later
once	frequently	
usually		

Where?

here	in	north
there	out	south
somewhere	up	
nowhere	down	
everywhere	upstairs	

Why?
This group contains groups of words starting with words like *since* and *because*.

How?

quickly	fast	commonly
slowly	well	noisily
easily		
carefully		

Under what condition? (For sure?)

not	maybe	certainly
also	possibly	perhaps
too		

Note that some adverbs in the "when" and "how" lists, like *early, late, earlier, later, fast,* and *slow* can also be used as adjectives.

Early **as adverb**

Sandra (awakens) early.

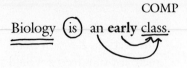

COMP

Biology (is) an **early** <u>class</u>.

Exercise 3

Marking Sentences with Adverbs

Each of the following simple sentences contains only one adverb. **Mark each sentence completely.** Then **tell which adverb question** the adverb answers. (The verb has already been marked for you.)

example

Vote when? Many <u>citizens</u> never (vote) .

_____ 1. Herb seldom (opens) his junk mail.

_____ 2. Coach Phillips (threw) his bat down.

_____ 3. She easily (answered) his questions.

_____ 4. The Blue River Band (played) earlier.

_____ 5. Perhaps she (wants) a different birthday gift.

_____ 6. Bradley (met) her once.

_____ 7. The dog (raced) downstairs.

_____ 8. I never (expected) this promotion.

_____ 9. Everywhere the situation (is) the same.

_____ 10. Jerry (wore) the new shirt daily.

_____ 11. Yesterday Mr. Black (retired) .

_____ 12. Professor Brandt (speaks) well.

_____ 13. Cautiously the children (entered) the dark house.

_____ 14. Now Evelyn (likes) him.

_____ 15. The iron gate (opened) slowly.

_____ 16. The doctor (spoke) carelessly.

_____ 17. They (have) not (filled) the prescription.

_____ **18.** Both secretaries (arrived) late.

_____ **19.** We never (found) the bottle of bleach.

_____ **20.** Your trash (was taken) already.

Adverbs That Describe Adjectives and Adverbs

Words that describe adjectives and adverbs are also called adverbs. These fall into two groups.

The first contains words, like _very_ and _too,_ which are always adverbs. These adverbs also tell "how," but in the sense of "to what degree" rather than "in what way."

Let's look at a few examples. In the following sentence, _very_ is used in this way.

Art is a **very** slow driver.

Here, _very_ describes the adjective _slow._

Adverb
question: _How_ slow?
Answer: _Very_ slow

Art (is) a **very** slow driver.

The next sentence contains the adverb _too._

He speaks **too** quickly.

In this sentence, _too_ describes the adverb _quickly._

Adverb
question: _How_ quickly?
Answer: _Too_ quickly

He (speaks) **too** quickly.

Note that when adjectives are used as complements, adverbs that tell "how" sometimes describe them.

COMP
The children (were) **unusually** quiet.

Other adverbs that describe adjectives and adverbs are harder to spot. These adverbs look like nouns and adjectives.

For example, _hardware_ is often used as a noun. And in the phrase _hardware store, hardware_ is clearly an adjective.

ADJECTIVE
↓
A **hardware** store

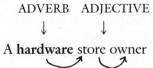

But if *store* becomes an adjective, describing *owner,* for example, *hardware* becomes an adverb.

ADVERB   ADJECTIVE
↓   ↓
A **hardware** store owner

In the example above, *hardware* is technically an adverb because it describes an adjective.

In cases like these, it is not important that you call *hardware* an adverb, as long as you can tell which word it describes.

Confusing Adverbs and Verbs

Students sometimes mark adverbs as verbs. This is especially true of adverbs that appear next to verbs. Be careful to avoid marking these adverbs as parts of verbs or verb phrases.

Theo's parties are **well** attended .

Exercise 4

Finding One-Word Adverbs

The following sentences contain all of the kinds of adverbs that you have studied. **Mark each sentence completely.**

example

I never met a better real estate agent.

1. A very tired little girl climbed upstairs.

2. We answered the disk jockey's questions carefully.

3. The house is too quiet.

4. Too many delegates disliked the minister's proposal.

5. The pictures were remarkably clear.

6. The dean's revised estimates caused even more discussion.

7. Canada possesses very large oil reserves.

80 The structure of simple sentences

8. Perhaps a few moments' rest will calm you.

9. Mike is tired also.

10. The new cover design has just arrived.

Chapter Review

In this chapter you learned that

1. **Adjectives** describe subjects and objects.

2. **Adverbs** describe verbs, adjectives, and other adverbs.

3. The four **adjective questions** (like *Which book?*, *What kind of book?*, *How many books?*, and *Whose book?*) can help you find **adjectives.**

4. The five **adverb questions** (like *Runs when?*, *Runs where?*, *Runs how?*, *Runs why?*, and *Runs under what condition?* or *Runs for sure?*) can help you find **adverbs** that describe verbs.

A RELATED SKILL section showed you about **forming possessive adjectives with apostrophes**.

1. Write the name of the owner or owners in the sentence.

2. Add an apostrophe to the end of the word.

3. Add an **s** after the apostrophe if the word is either singular or plural not ending in **s**.

Review Exercise 1

This exercise contains everything you have learned so far about simple sentences. Mark each **verb**, **subject**, **object** or **complement**, **adjective**, and **adverb** in the following sentences.

If you wish, do the BONUS sentence at the end. Be careful, though. It is more difficult than it appears.

1. Tigers roamed freely.

2. Why isn't Bennie here?

3. You deserve another break today.

4. Her strong fingers tore the wicked manuscript.

5. Yesterday my sister's husband took his first college exam.

6. The books are closed.

7. A young sea lion barked loudly.

8. Stop here.

9. Canada's national anthem is a beautiful song.

10. We sang it proudly.

11. The new shawl draped Maria's shoulders gracefully.

12. We soon found a very tired young boy.

13. Coleman purchased the grocery store yesterday.

14. Mikey's report card showed very good grades.

15. Fortunately the motorcycle still works.

16. Far fewer sunglasses were sold recently.

17. Perhaps you would ask your question again.

18. Angelo didn't rent the Rosewood's new apartment.

19. It was too bright and cheery.

20. Why did you mention Sandra's new Buick?

BONUS: Her investment has finally paid off.

Review Exercise 2

Mark each **verb**, **subject**, **object** or **complement**, **adjective**, and **adverb** in the following paragraph.

The duke slowly entered the dark room. A distant clock loudly struck the midnight hour. The moon appeared momentarily bright. Then heavy clouds killed again all light. Quiet covered his footsteps. The old duke heard no sound. Suddenly, a light breeze crossed his cheek. This startled him. Was he not alone? Which door was open? He turned around too late. Three tall young men and one woman surrounded him. The silence was broken only once.

Review Exercise 3

Recopy each of the following sentences, **changing the underlined words to a one-word adverb** describing the verb.

Marcus worked <u>without making a sound</u>. The light bulb burned <u>in a bright way</u> above his head. Sweat gleamed on his forehead and the upper surfaces of his arms. The room was empty. Through the window he heard <u>with clearness</u> the low roar of the gathering crowd. Marcus shrugged. <u>In quick motions</u> he removed the cover from the ticking device. Holding the wire clippers <u>with loose fingers</u>, he found and snipped the blue wire. <u>All of a sudden</u>, the ticking stopped. Marcus looked up, smiled, and felt for the first time the cold chill of the room. The window he had broken <u>some time ago</u> was still broken. A fine layer of snow fell <u>in peace</u> to the floor.

_____

_____

_____

_____

_____

_____

_____

_____

_____

_____

_____

_____

_____

_____

_____

_____

_____

_____

Chapter 3 Writing Assignment

Write a brief **humorous story** about something one of your friends did.

Make your story short (five to ten sentences) and keep your sentences simple. (Don't use quotations in telling this story; they will make your sentences complicated in structure.)

When you have made a final copy, **mark each adjective** and **adverb**.

Hints for Writing Stories

Every good story has a focus. The focus of this story is its humor. To make this story as successful as possible, be sure to tell your reader to expect a funny story and weed out any details that aren't funny or necessary to the plot.

Before the rough draft:

1. Choose a story that will be interesting to write about.

2. Decide on a feeling that the story will communicate to the reader. (In this case, your story will be _humorous_.)

3. Make a list of all of the events in the story. Then mark on the list the best place to begin.

4. Reread the list of events in your story and cross out any event that doesn't either

    a. Add to the humor, or
    b. Help the story make sense.

Writing the rough draft

1. Write an opening sentence or two that prepares us to listen to your story. Make sure we know that it will be humorous.

2. Tell us where and when the story takes place.

3. Using your list of events, tell your story in a direct, straightforward manner.

4. Use strong action words in telling your story.

After the rough draft

1. Do your best to correct any errors on this first copy.

2. Make any other changes you think will make your story more interesting and readable.

3. Recopy your corrected paragraph on a clean sheet of paper and turn in all of your work.

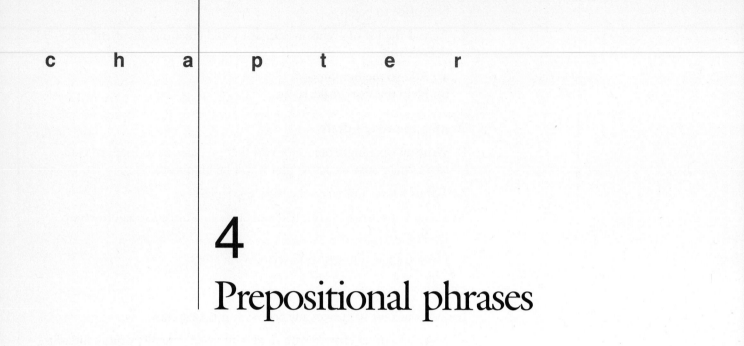

c h a p t e r

4
Prepositional phrases

Chapter Preview

This chapter will show you how to find

1. **Prepositional phrases** in sentences.

2. Two common **phrases with "hidden" prepositions**.
   a. Short "when" phrases
   b. "Indirect objects"

In addition, a special RELATED SKILL section will show you how to find **subjects in difficult sentences** — sentences with prepositional phrases between the subject and the verb.

DESCRIPTIVE PHRASES IN SENTENCES

In earlier chapters you learned about **phrases**, groups of words that act like one word in a sentence. In Chapter 1, you saw how a name acts like a one-word subject, object, or complement. In Chapter 2, you saw how verb phrases act like one-word verbs.

English makes use of other phrases as well. In this chapter you will study **prepositional phrases**, special phrases that act like adjectives and adverbs.

SUBJECT	—	VERB	—	Object
Adjectives		**Adverbs**		**Adjectives**
(words or phrases)		(words or phrases)		(words or phrases)

PREPOSITIONAL PHRASES

Prepositional phrases are short descriptive phrases that begin with a **preposition** — a word like *of* or *from* — and end with an **object of the preposition**, usually a noun or pronoun. Many prepositional phrases also contain adjectives that describe the object.

All of the following are prepositional phrases.

Preposition +	(Adjectives) +	**Object**
to		Fran
for		me
in	the	car
on	his new	desk
over	the	rainbow

Notice that like the object of a verb, the object of a preposition can be found by asking the **object question**.

Object Question

Say	the preposition
then ask	**whom?** or **what?**
Example:	With my younger brother
	With *whom?*
	With *what?*

Using the object question, for example, we find that *brother* is the object of the preposition in the following phrase.

Prepositional phrase

with my younger brother

**Object
question:**   With *whom?*
Answer: *Brother*

Brother is the object of the preposition *with*. Notice that *my* and *younger* are adjectives describing *brother*.

A Short List of Common Prepositions

To help you find prepositional phrases in the exercises that follow, a list of common prepositions is printed below. Notice especially the two- and three-word prepositions, like *because of* and *in spite of*.

Some Common Prepositions

about	beneath	inside	throughout
above	beside	into	to
across	between	like	toward
after	beyond	near	under
against	by	of	underneath
along	despite	off	until
among	down	on	up
around	during	out	upon
at	except	outside	with
before	for	over	within
behind	from	through	without
below	in		

Two- and three-word prepositions

along with	in spite of
because of	next to
except for	out of

Exercise 1

Prepositional Phrases

Tell which of the following are prepositional phrases by writing **YES** or **NO** on the line.

For each prepositional phrase you find, place an **X** above the preposition and **underline** its object.

_____Yes_____ X In the <u>store</u>

_____ **1.** to Joseph

_____ **2.** my bank book

_____ **3.** in my bank book

_____ **4.** because of an unforeseen accident

_____ **5.** an unforeseen accident

_____ **6.** with Marilyn and me

_____ **7.** my youngest daughter's kindergarten class

_____ **8.** for the coming symposium

_____ **9.** in chains

_____ **10.** above the village walls

_____ **11.** several short prepositions

_____ **12.** behind her back

_____ **13.** describing the magazine cover

_____ **14.** Doug's latest record

_____ **15.** outside of this room

_____ **16.** except for General Waller's support

_____ **17.** their many injuries

_____ **18.** minding the store

_____ **19.** despite their anxiety

_____ **20.** running for Congress

Prepositional Phrases Used as Adjectives

It's easy to find how prepositional phrases are used in sentences. *All prepositional phrases are used as either adjectives or adverbs,* and the adjective and adverb questions will identify them for you.

Let's first look at prepositional phrases used as adjectives.

When prepositional phrases act as adjectives, they answer one of the four adjective questions.

> Which?
> What kind?
> How many?
> Whose?

However, most adjective prepositional phrases answer the question "which?"

Consider the following sentence:

> The horse **in the third stall** is mine.

In this sentence, the prepositional phrase *in the third stall* (preposition — *in*; object — *stall*) answers the adjective question "which horse?"

**Adjective
question:** *Which* horse?
Answer: The horse *in the third stall*

Therefore, *in the third stall* is an adjective describing *horse*.

Marking Prepositional Phrases

Like other phrases you will study, prepositional phrases act like one word. In this case, they act like one-word adjectives. To show this, we need two marks — a **grouping** mark and an **adjective** mark.

Therefore, we will mark prepositional phrases by

1. **Grouping** the words of the phrase with **parentheses** (   ).

2. **Drawing an arrow** to the word it describes.

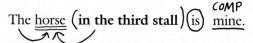

Of course, we could mark the words inside the prepositional phrase as well.

Prepositional phrase

in the third stall

But except in those few places where we need to show the relationship of words in a complex phrase, we will not mark the words within prepositional phrases.

Once you recognize a prepositional phrase, it is usually more important to see how it acts than to see what the words inside the phrase are doing.

By seeing prepositional phrases as just longer adjectives or adverbs, you will see that most sentences are usually rather simple in structure. The sentence we marked above, for example, is really the equivalent of a five-word sentence — a subject, two adjectives, a verb, and a complement.

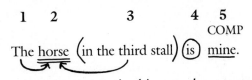

When you look at sentence structure in this way, those sentences that seem complicated become much simpler to analyze.

Prepositional Phrases in a Series

Many sentences have two prepositional phrases in a row, one after the other. When you see this, look at the second phrase carefully. Sometimes it describes the object in the phrase before it, and sometimes not.

Compare the following sentences.

>The gentleman **on the left with the money** is making a deposit.
>
>The gentleman **with the money in his hand** is making a deposit.

In the first sentence, both prepositional phrases describe the subject *gentleman* by answering the question "which?"

Adjective question: *Which gentleman?*
Answer: *On the left*

Adjective question: *Which gentleman?*
Answer: *With the money*

The gentleman (**on the left**)(**with the money**) is making a deposit.

Now look at the second sentence. As before, *with the money* is an adjective describing the subject *gentleman*.

The gentleman (**with the money**) in his hand is making a deposit.

But the second phrase, *in his hand,* describes *money.*

Adjective question: *Which* money?
Answer: The money *in his hand*

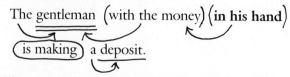

The gentleman (with the money) (**in his hand**)
(is making) a deposit.

Mark sentences with more than one prepositional phrase carefully.

Exercise 2

Prepositional Phrases Used as Adjectives

In the sentences below, the verb, subject, and object or complement, if any, have been marked for you. Mark each **adjective prepositional phrase** with parentheses and an arrow.

example

The sign (on the lawn) (is) new. [COMP]

1. The men from his department (will arrive) soon.

2. A bracelet with emeralds (was shown) Saturday.

3. The answers to these questions (will be discussed) tomorrow.

4. Mr. Burton just (changed) the schedule of deliveries.

5. The lamp by the couch in the living room (needs) a new bulb.

6. One of the graduate students (will help) you.

7. The paper (has printed) most of her letters.

8. The man with the tickets (has) already (left) .

9. Two of these new tennis rackets from Grossen's (are) defective. [COMP]

10. One of us (should answer) the letter from Dr. Black.

Marking Sentences Completely

Many marking exercises in *Foundation* ask you to **mark a sentence completely**. This means "mark what each *word or major phrase* in the sentence is doing." You do not need to show what words inside phrases do. Just show what the phrase itself is doing.

The following sentence, for example, is marked completely.

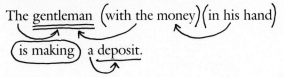

When marking sentences completely, it is best to work in the following order. (These instructions will be expanded as we learn to find other structures.)

Sentence Marking Order (1)

1. **Group prepositional phrases** with parentheses.

2. Mark the **verb**, **subject**, and **object** or **complement**.

3. Starting at the beginning of the sentence, draw **arrows** to show what each **adjective** and **adverb word** or **phrase** describes.

Exercise 3

example

Marking Sentences Completely

Mark each of the following sentences completely.

The sign (on the lawn) is new.

1. The focus of this discussion has shifted.

2. She suggested the film at the NuArt.

3. Several of these envelopes have been opened.

4. We played the team from Argentina.

5. The manager of the store on the corner suggested several of these.

6. Brandon has received two of the tickets.

7. The game of the week is being televised.

8. The men in the front office have spent millions of dollars.

9. Her friend in Alabama wrote another of her long letters.

10. We need a new committee chairman.

Prepositional Phrases Used as Adverbs

Prepositional phrases can also act as adverbs describing verbs.

<pre>
SUBJECT   —   VERB   —   Object
   | | |
Adjectives   Adverbs   Adjectives
(word or phrase) (word or phrase) (word or phrase)
</pre>

When they do act as adverbs, they answer one of the five adverb questions.

> When?
> Where?
> Why?
> How?
> Under what condition? (*or* For sure?)

Let's look at a few examples.

> We stood **in the rain for hours**.

This sentence contains two prepositional phrases used as adverbs. *In the rain* tells where we stood, and *for hours* tells when we stood.

Adverb question: Stood *where?*
Answer: *In the rain*

Adverb question: Stood *when?*
Answer: *For hours*

Adverb prepositional phrases are marked like other prepositional phrases — with **parentheses** (to show that they act like one word) and an **arrow** to the word or phrase they describe.

> We (stood)(**in the rain**)(**for hours**) .

Here is one more example.

> Congress passed the Mining Act **for the wrong reasons**.

In this sentence the prepositional phrase *for the wrong reasons* tells why the act was passed.

Adverb question: Passed *why?*
Answer: *For the wrong reasons*

Congress (passed) the Mining Act (for the wrong reasons) .

"Prepositions" Used as Adverbs

When doing the exercises in this section, keep in mind that many of the prepositions on the list on page 88 can be used by themselves as adverbs.

The following sentence, for example, does NOT contain a prepositional phrase.

Turn off the light.

Off is an adverb that describes the verb *turn*, and *light* is the object of the verb (not the preposition). *Light* answers the question "turn what?", not the question "off what?"

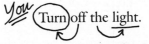

By the way, this sentence is a good example of an adverb with an "extended" meaning. *Off* answers the adverb question "where?" The expression *turn off* goes back to the days when switches were knobs that were literally turned. Off was one of the positions (places) on the switch. *Off* answers the adverb question "where?"

Now, of course, "turn off" has yet another extended meaning — to offend someone. Nevertheless, *off* is still an adverb, and it still tells "where," if only symbolically.

Short "When" Phrases

You have seen how commands are written without the subject *you*. In the same way, some prepositional phrases that tell "when" are written without the preposition. For example:

> **Every Christmas Eve** Mr. Ryan celebrates with his sister.
>
> **Last weekend** Heather worked on her taxes.

We read these sentences as though the preposition were present but "hidden." Prepositional phrases can be shortened in this way because the hidden word is understood to be there.

> (On) **Every Christmas Eve** Mr. Ryan celebrates with his sister.
>
> (During) **Last weekend** Heather worked on her taxes.

If you have trouble recognizing these phrases as adverbs, look for groups of words that tell "when."

Adverb	
question:	Celebrates *when?*
Answer:	*Every Christmas Eve*

Adverb	
question:	Worked *when?*
Answer:	*Last weekend*

Short "when" phrases are marked like other prepositional phrases — with **parentheses** (to show they act as one word) and an **arrow** to the word or phrase they describe.

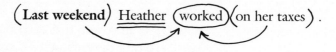

(**Last weekend**) Heather (worked)(on her taxes).

Exercise 4

Prepositional Phrases Used as Adverbs

Mark each sentence completely. Be prepared to tell which question each prepositional phrase answers.

Read these sentences carefully. Some of them may not contain an adverb prepositional phrase.

example

The laundry room (is located)(in the back)(of the house).

1. The mail is usually delivered in the morning on Saturdays.

2. These papers fell off your desk.

3. This week our new teacher canceled all of her classes.

4. In a few minutes the candle will burn out completely.

5. She looked at the baby for hours.

6. The Geology Club is sponsoring the camping trip.

7. Alma spoke to us about her roommate problem.

8. Bill's pipe tobacco smells like old shoe leather.

9. Harold admitted his error with a sly grin.

10. Sunday they rested.

11. Gary reached out for the light pen.

12. Next weekend we will be visiting Newkirk.

13. In the morning this room will look very messy.

14. Tonight the darkness keeps the secret well.

15. Did you go to the bookstore?

16. The blouse was on sale at Batterby's.

17. Send the package by Federated Express.

18. Mickey sent a rose to her room with a short note of apology.

19. She accepted it with some suspicion.

20. It died in her hand.

BONUS: They passed in the final copies of their essays.

Indirect Objects

Another phrase with a hidden preposition has the unusual name of "indirect object." An **indirect object** looks like an object of the verb.

Mr. Potter showed **Ms. Calendar** a better way.

But an indirect object is really an object of the "hidden" preposition *to*, *for*, or *of*. You can find indirect objects with (you guessed it) the **indirect object question**.

Indirect Object Question

Say	the verb
then ask	to whom? for whom? of whom?
Example:	showed to Ms. Calendar
	to whom? for whom? of whom?

Using the indirect object question, we find that Ms. Calendar is the indirect object of the preposition *to*.

Indirect object question:	Showed **to whom?**
Answer:	To *Ms. Calendar*

Mr. Potter showed (to) **Ms. Calendar** a better way.

Mark indirect objects like other adverb phrases, with **parentheses** and an **arrow**. Then write the hidden preposition above its object. (This will make you more aware of indirect objects in other sentences.)

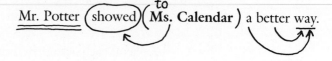

Mr. Potter (showed)(Ms. Calendar) a better way.

Exercise 5

Indirect Objects

Mark each sentence completely. Use the indirect object question to avoid marking indirect objects as objects of the verb.

example

They (gave)(him) their complete attention.

1. He asked us several unusual questions.

2. His superiors offered Colonel Jackson several options.

3. Maureen is giving her vacation in Ireland a lot of thought.

4. Our math instructor awarded each of his students high grades.

5. The officer handed Mr. Furman a ticket for speeding.

6. We wrote the district manager a strong letter of protest.

7. A bonus was offered the production company for an early completion.

8. She offered them a fair settlement.

9. Mr. Bird gave us our papers.

10. Fred told the men in his crew several entertaining lies.

RELATED SKILL FINDING SUBJECTS IN DIFFICULT SENTENCES

As you have noticed, many sentences contain a prepositional phrase between the subject and the verb. Consider this sentence:

The color of my brother's tennis shoes is brown.

The verb is the linking verb *is*.

The color of my brother's tennis shoes (is) brown.

But what is the subject? Because *shoes* is a noun close to the verb, you may be tempted to pick *shoes* as the subject. *Shoes,* however, is the object of the preposition *of.*

Prepositional Phrase

of my brother's tennis shoes

Object question: Of *what*?
Answer: *Shoes*

The subject of a verb is never the object of a preposition. We can avoid mismarking the subject by finding and marking the prepositional phrase *of my brother's tennis shoes* first. Then we can find the correct subject — *color* — more easily.

Correctly marked, the sentence looks like this:

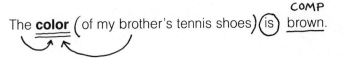

(Notice that if *shoes* were the subject, the verb would be *are,* not *is. Shoes is* is an incorrect subject-verb combination. Chapter 11 discusses matching verbs and subjects in detail.)

Finding the correct subject can be especially difficult when the subject is a pronoun like *one.*

One of the students has brought the tickets.

In this sentence, the subject is *one,* not *students.*

One (of the students) (**has brought**) the tickets.

(Notice again that if the subject was *students,* the correct verb would be *have brought,* not *has brought.*)

You can find subjects more accurately by marking prepositional phrases with parentheses first. Then look for subjects, objects, and complements outside the parentheses.

Skill Exercise

Marking Sentences with Difficult Subjects

Mark each of these sentences completely.

example One (of the cheerleaders) is not here.

1. Each of our new spider plants has mites.

2. The girl in the blue running jacket has finished the quiz early.

3. The reasons for gang warfare are many.

4. My talks with Carlos were interesting.

5. The eyes of the law see far.

6. Suzy's goals for this semester have not been met.

7. The great medicine men of the Wilusi clan are its true leaders.

8. Computers from this manufacturing plant break down easily.

9. Our return to Black Rock was uneventful.

10. Women from this voting district could have predicted

    Dr. Belamo's defeat.

11. Luis, with his superior running ability, quickly passed his

    opponents.

12. The messengers from Sparta are waiting outside.

13. Each of Bilbo's cousins asked another question.

14. All of your answers were correct.

15. The eastern part of the country is experiencing rain.

16. Warm oil from the pan was used.

17. Two of Mr. Park's students have won awards.

18. A heated debate among several members of the track

    team followed.

19. One of the athletes knew Coach Brown already.

20. Some of these exercise sentences are difficult.

Chapter Review

In this chapter you learned that

1. **Prepositional phrase** = preposition (+ adjectives) + object.

2. The **object question** will help you find objects of prepositions.

3. Prepositional phrases always act as **adjectives or adverbs**.

4. Some short "when" phrases have **hidden prepositions**.

5. **"Indirect objects"** are really prepositional phrases with hidden prepositions (usually *for*, *to*, or *of*).

6. **Indirect object question**: Say the verb, then ask "for whom?", "to whom?", or "of whom?"

The RELATED SKILL section showed you how to **find subjects in difficult sentences**.

1. Some sentences have prepositional phrases between the subject and the verb.

2. The object of a preposition is never the subject of the verb.

Review Exercise 1

Mark each of the following sentences completely.

1. The foreman is a good friend of Mr. Garetski.

2. Sister Alicia gave us a letter for Mrs. Walker.

3. Each of us went on the trip.

4. To whom did you give copies of the contract?

5. For whom was this gift purchased?

6. The tickets were sent to her last month by the road manager.

7. At the reception several new albums were previewed.

8. Mr. Alvarado bought his books from the Campus Exchange.

9. Last week the cabinet's decision was overturned by the president.

10. Was the note written to her sister?

11. The letters for Jack have arrived.

12. The guardians of the castle sent him a request for reinforcements.

13. She bought her sister a new briefcase for her birthday.

14. Calistoga County sends you its greetings.

15. Next Friday the monsignor will have made his decision.

16. Wanda's last class meets in the gymnasium during suppertime.

17. One of these sandwiches will do nicely.

18. She saddled the horse with speed.

19. Hamlet asked the king a direct question.

20. None of her counselors would have recommended a break in her schooling.

Review Exercise 2

Mark each sentence of the following paragraphs completely.

Later that night Marian walked onto the old pier. In the past this simple act would have frightened her. The long shadows of the boat in the moonlit waves would have seemed ominous. The rhythmic slap of the water against their hulls would have reminded her of the old days in Virginia before the war. Life had given her rough treatment in those days. She had lost her mother and both of her brothers. The family house by the ocean had been the scene of a dozen tragedies. And always the silence of a little girl's tears had been punctuated by the sound of the endless water.

Marian breathed in slowly and exhaled. Those days were gone. She had made her own way and was stronger because of it. The troubled waters of her past had become the healing waters of her new life. This time Marian listened to the endless motion of the waves with a glad heart.

Chapter 4 Writing Assignment

Write a brief paragraph that uses **examples** to discuss a **bad habit of one of your friends**.

Then mark each **prepositional phrase** in the paragraph.

Hints for Writing Paragraphs with Examples

Using examples is an excellent way to make a point. But to be most effective, they should be well chosen and well written.

Examples are usually either stories or descriptions. In this paragraph, your examples will be stories. To make this paragraph as effective as possible, choose your stories carefully and tell them well by following the hints below.

(If you wish, review the Hints for Writing Paragraphs with Stories in the Chapter 3 Writing Assignment.)

Before the rough draft:

1. Choose a friend with an interesting bad habit, a habit that you dislike. Your paragraph will be more interesting if you have strong feelings about your subject.

2. Make a list of interesting stories that could be used as examples of this habit. (Make this list as long as you can. Your final essay will be better if you have a good list of stories to choose from.)

3. Select two stories from your list and mark the order in which to tell them.

4. For each story, make a short list of the events that make up that story.

5. Reread these lists, and make any changes in them that you think will make your stories more effective.

Writing the rough draft:

1. Start your rough draft by writing an interesting opening sentence or two that mentions your friend and the bad habit.

2. Then tell your first story, beginning with a sentence that starts, "For example." Use your list of events to tell this story.

3. Now tell your second story, beginning with a sentence that starts with a phrase like, "On another occasion." Use your list of events to tell this story also.

4. Write a closing sentence that tells why this person is still your friend in spite of this habit.

After the rough draft:

1. Do your best to correct any errors on this first copy.

2. Make any other changes you think will make your paragraph more interesting and readable.

3. Recopy your corrected paragraph on a clean sheet of paper and turn in all of your work.

UNIT II

Beyond simple sentences

In this unit you will build on what you have already learned about sentences.

Chapter 5 will show you how to combine simple sentences so that the original ideas are equal in importance. Chapter 6 will help you avoid several punctuation errors related to combining equal sentences — including the **run-on sentence**, the **comma splice**, and the **fragment**.

Finally, Chapter 7 will show you how to combine simple sentences so that the original ideas are unequal in importance. When you are finished, you will know quite a bit about writing and punctuating sentences with more than one subject and verb.

5
Joining main clauses into sentences

**Chapter
Preview**

This chapter will show you

1. How **complete sentences** are made from clauses.

2. How to **separate sentences** with periods, question marks, and capital letters.

3. How to **join main clauses** into sentences with semi-colons and comma + conjunctions.

In addition, a RELATED SKILL section will show you how to use **who** and **whom in questions**.

CLAUSES AND SENTENCES

Let's start by looking at one of the basic units of sentence structure — the clause.

What is a Clause?

A **clause** is a group of words which contains a subject and a verb. The following simple sentence is a clause, for example, because it contains a subject and a verb — *revolution – began*.

The <u>revolution</u> (began) in 1849.

Independent and Dependent Clauses

There are two kinds of clauses — independent clauses and dependent clauses.

An **independent clause** is a clause that can stand alone as a sentence.

Notice that all of the simple sentences you have studied have been independent clauses. Each has contained a subject and a verb, and each has stood alone as a sentence.

Independent clauses (main clauses)

<u>We</u> (found) his latest novel in the bookstore.

His early <u>songs</u> (sound) like Bruce Springsteen's.

The <u>revolution</u> (began) in 1849.

An independent clause is often called a **main clause**. We will refer to independent clauses as "main clauses" in this book.

A **dependent clause** is a clause that cannot stand alone as a sentence.

Instead, dependent clauses act like parts of a sentence. As a result, dependent clauses always contain words that connect them to other ideas, words like *after*, *because*, and *for which*.

The following are all dependent clauses. (Notice that they are not followed by periods, since they are not complete sentences.)

Dependent clauses

After the <u>rain</u> (had stopped)

Because her <u>answers</u> (are) usually correct

For which <u>he</u> (was saving) his money

108 Beyond simple sentences

Even though dependent clauses "sound" different from main clauses, dependent clauses contain a subject and a verb, just as main clauses do.

This chapter and the next will be concerned with main clauses — how to punctuate them and how to join more than one into a single sentence. Dependent clauses will be discussed in Chapter 7.

Exercise 1

Recognizing Clauses

None of the following items contains punctuation. Some are clauses, and some are not. Do the following for each one.

a. Mark each **verb** and **subject**.

b. Tell whether the item is a clause or not by writing **CLAUSE** or **NO CLAUSE** on the line.

Remember that if any item has both a subject and verb, it is a clause.

examples

NO CLAUSE The banking assistant from Maryland

CLAUSE That she (was studying) for an important test

_____ 1. Because these events occur frequently

_____ 2. As we already told you

_____ 3. The town was abandoned in 1847

_____ 4. As good as Johnson's essays

_____ 5. The dance was popular in the 1930s

_____ 6. One of the deans will be in touch

_____ 7. If we discover the lost city soon

_____ 8. Which you are replacing

_____ 9. The bandages in the kitchen drawer

_____ 10. That Jerry studied last night

_____ 11. What Jerry did last night

_____ 12. Which my sister recommended

_____ 13. My sister recommended the film

_____ 14. His college application for the fall semester

_____ **15.** A remarkable improvement in writing

_____ **16.** Mr. Larkin was recently promoted to

royalties manager

_____ **17.** Who was recently promoted to royalties manager

_____ **18.** Promoted to royalties manager

_____ **19.** The price is certainly low enough

_____ **20.** To whom the book was lent

Complete Sentences and Fragments

We can now define a sentence. In Chapter 1 we said a sentence must contain a subject and verb. This, of course, is true.

But to define a sentence we need to say more. A **complete sentence** is any group of words that contains at least one main clause. In other words, a sentence is any group of words which

1. Contains a subject and a verb

2. Can stand alone

The opposite of a sentence is a **fragment**. A fragment is any group of words that does not contain at least one main clause.

Fragments

A book of mine

Running in the direction of the main library

A dependent clause, because it cannot stand alone, is always a fragment.

Sentence fragments, whether deliberately or accidentally written, should be avoided in college, professional, and business writing. Fragments will be discussed in detail in Chapter 6, and dependent clauses as fragments will be discussed in Chapter 7.

PUNCTUATING AND CAPITALIZING COMPLETE SENTENCES

Let's look at how sentences are punctuated. We will start with the most basic punctuation first — the punctuation that separates complete sentences from each other. Then we will study the punctuation that joins main clauses into a single sentence.

Complete sentences must be separated from each other. If they aren't, they run together in a very confusing way.

We use punctuation and capital letters to separate sentences from each other.

Separating Sentences

Every complete sentence begins with a capital letter and ends with one of the following punctuation marks.

1. Period   (.)
2. Question mark   (?)
3. Exclamation point   (!)

Periods, question marks, and exclamation points are called **end punctuation** because they are used to end sentences.

Using the Period

The **period** is the punctuation used most often between sentences. It is also the most important.

Here are two sentences that should have a period between them, but don't:

Sentences run together (Incorrect)

The apartment has been empty for two months the last tenants moved to Georgia.

This sentence is really two main clauses run together. Below, we have marked the core of each — the subject, verb, and object or complement.

Notice that there is no punctuation at the **breaking point** between them — the place where one main clause stops and the other one begins.

Main clauses run together (Incorrect)

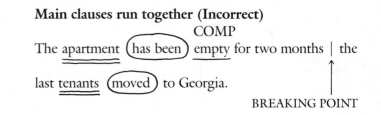

Unless main clauses are correctly joined by punctuation, they must be punctuated as separate sentences — with a period and a capital letter.

Sentences separated with a period (Correct)

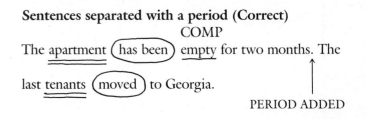

It is an error (called a **run-on sentence**) to write main clauses with no punctuation between them. Using a period to separate the clauses is one way to correct this error.

Capitalizing Complete Sentences

Every complete sentence must start with a **capital letter**. Every sentence in the book you are reading, for example, starts with a capital letter. All of your sentences must begin the same way.

Be especially careful to use capital letters when you correct run-on sentences. Notice how the capital letter is used with the period in the example you just studied.

Main clauses run together (Incorrect)

The apartment has been empty for two months the last tenants moved to Georgia.

Main clauses separated with a period (Correct)

The apartment has been empty for two months. ~~t~~he last tenants moved to Georgia.

Make sure that you use capital letters at the start of all your sentences.

Exercise 2

Using the Period

Some of the following items contain two or more main clauses, and some do not.

a. Mark each **verb**, **subject**, **object**, and **complement**.

b. Place a **period** after each main clause.

c. **Capitalize** the first letter of each sentence.

example

W
~~w~~e (need) more pictures in our dorm room. ~~i~~t (looks) empty without them.

1. the Gatling gun was invented in the 1800s many people thought it would change the West

2. their new album sold several million copies this includes sales in Europe as well

3. the store opened early today maybe Christmas is near

4. the contract clearly restricts the number of units available to discount buyers

5. the technical manual contained several solutions to the problem choose one of them

6. we told Mrs. Gallagher about the snails in the garden she showed us a book on the subject

7. the season ended last week no one noticed

8. the bears discovered the garbage pile in the night this morning the entire area was a mess

9. books with Dr. Hemming's signature on the title page are now worth over $1000 each

10. in the box on the stairs is a small yellow envelope get it for me please

Using the Question Mark and Exclamation Point

In some cases a question mark or exclamation point is used instead of a period to end a sentence.

A **question mark** (?) is used if the writer is asking a question instead of making a statement.

Incorrect

Did you see the Raiders game on TV.

Correct

Did you see the Raiders game on TV?

Review Chapter 2, pages 47–48, for more information on questions and how they are written.

The **exclamation point** (!) is used instead of a period if a writer wants to give special emphasis to a sentence. The following sentence, for example, receives special emphasis because of the exclamation point.

It is important to work in an organized manner!

Exclamation points are most common in dialogue.

"Stop!" she screamed.

Exclamation points are usually considered too dramatic for college and professional writing, and most instructors recommend that you avoid them.

Using Question Marks

Some of the following items contain two or more main clauses, and some do not.

a. Mark each **verb**, **subject**, **object**, and **complement**.

b. Place a **period** or **question mark** after each main clause.

c. **Capitalize** the first letter of each sentence.

example

We (need) more pictures in our dorm room. (Would) you (bring) some back from home with you ?

1. can you hear the speaker would you like to sit closer to the stage

2. those jackets are expensive they are made of the finest leather

3. we need a film projector for today's class would someone get one from the AV closet in the main hall

4. most of the trainees in the forest service are dedicated to ecology

5. why is the car on the lawn did something happen while I was gone

6. place the test tube in the rack then add three drops of acetic acid

7. she wants to bet on one of the horses which do you think has a good chance of winning

8. is this the way to solve problem four I have trouble with anything involving trigonometry

9. the pistol fired accidentally no one was hurt

10. for him the war ended in a cold trench in Belgium he returned to England with the wounded two days later

RELATED SKILL USING *WHO* AND *WHOM* IN QUESTIONS

In Chapter 2 you learned that many questions use question words like *who*, *what*, *which*, and *where*. Most of these words have only one form. *What*, for example, is spelled the same whether used as a subject or an object.

The pronoun *who*, however, is different. When used as a subject, the correct form is *who*. When used as an object, the correct form is *whom*.

Forms of pronouns

Subject Form	Object Form
who	whom

If the *who*-form is needed, *whom* is not correct. It is therefore important to recognize how *who* is used. The following sentence uses *who* as the subject of a question.

***Who* as subject**

Who asked you to the dance?

Who (asked) you (to the dance) ?

The following sentences, on the other hand, use *whom* as an object.

***Whom* as object of verb**

Whom did you ask to the dance?

Whom (did) you (ask)(to the dance) ?

***Whom* as object of preposition**

With whom were you dancing?

(**With whom**)(were) you (dancing) ?

Sometimes a sentence like the last one is phrased slightly differently.

Whom were you dancing with?

Notice that this sentence splits the prepositional phrase *with whom*.

Whom were you dancing **with**?

For this reason, these sentences are not considered good writing, even though they are fairly common speech.

Skill Exercise

Using *Who* and *Whom* in Questions

Choose the correct form of *who* and *whom* for each of these sentences by doing the following:

a. Mark the **verb**.

b. Tell whether the missing word is a subject, object of the verb, or object of a preposition by writing **SUBJ**, **OBJ VERB**, or **OBJ PREP** on the line before each sentence.

c. Write *who* or *whom* on the line in each sentence.

d. **Mark the subject** of the verb.

Remember to use the subject and object questions to find the subject and object.

| example |

__OBJ. VERB__ __Whom__ (are) you (seeking?)

_____ **1.** For _____ have you been waiting?

_____ **2.** _____ sent away for this recipe?

_____ **3.** With _____ has Breanna been studying

lately?

_____ **4.** _____ did he ask for directions?

_____ **5.** At _____ was that sarcastic comment

aimed?

_____ **6.** _____ voted for you for club president

besides your brother?

_____ **7.** For _____ did she purchase the copy of

Beowulf?

_____ **8.** _____ solved the murder first, Lord Peter

or his fiancée?

_____ **9.** _____ have you contacted regarding the

reunion?

_____ **10.** _____ broke off the engagement?

116 Beyond simple sentences

_____ **11.** _____ was most affected by this

announcement?

_____ **12.** _____ was Billy seeking after the rodeo?

_____ **13.** _____ brought the cookies?

_____ **14.** _____ did Dr. Hernandez hire as her

receptionist?

_____ **15.** With _____ does he plan to attend the

reception?

_____ **16.** _____ did you see in the shop?

_____ **17.** _____ here speaks Portuguese?

_____ **18.** For the last time, _____ did you meet in

the locker room?

_____ **19.** _____ is being sought for questioning,

Nedra or her roommate?

_____ **20.** For _____ were these laws written, the

people or the government?

JOINING MAIN CLAUSES

We have studied how to separate sentences. Now let's look at how they are joined.

Joining Main Clauses

Join main clauses into one sentence by using one of the following methods.

1. Comma plus conjunction
2. Semicolon   (;)

Though either of these methods is correct, the comma + conjunction method is the most common.

Joining Main Clauses with a Comma + Conjunction

Main clauses may be joined into one sentence with a **comma plus a coordinating conjunction**.

For example, the following sentences each contain a single main clause.

Separate sentences

Sam went into business. Barry joined the Army.

With a comma plus the conjunction *and* we can join them into a single sentence.

Main clauses joined with comma + conjunction

Sam went into business, **and** Barry joined the Army.

Notice that there is a main clause on each side of the connector — the comma + conjunction. The core idea of the first clause is *Sam – went* (subject – verb). The core idea of the second clause is *Barry – joined*.

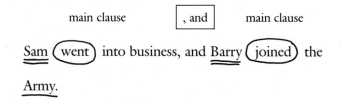

Coordinating Conjunctions — Conjunctions That Join Equals

Words that join equal sentence parts are called **coordinating conjunctions**. (Roughly translated, *coordination* is Latin for "joining equals.")

The most common coordinating conjunctions are listed below.

Coordinating Conjunctions

and	for
or	yet
but	so
nor	

Or and *nor* are sometimes used with the adjectives *either* and *neither*. *For*, *yet*, and *so* are not always used as conjunctions.

This is an important list to learn, especially *and*, *or*, *but*, and *nor*.

Words like *and* and *or* can join any equal sentence parts — two or more subjects, two or more verbs, or two or more main clauses — to each other. This fact can create punctuation problems.

Compare these sentences. This time the conjunction is *or*.

Main clauses joined with comma + conjunction

Jim might have gone to the Coho Club, **or** he might have walked home.

Verbs joined with conjunction

Jim might have gone to the Coho Club **or** walked home.

In the first sentence, there is a main clause on each side of the connector. Therefore, a comma must be used with it.

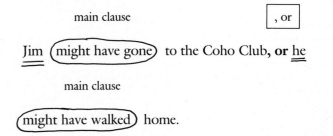

In the second sentence, the conjunction joins two verbs only, so there is no comma used with it.

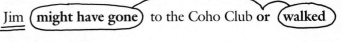

home.

Distinguish carefully between conjunctions that join main clauses and those that join only verbs or other sentence elements. Your punctuation will improve if you do.

Exercise 4

Joining Main Clauses with a Comma + Conjunction

Use a **comma + conjunction** to combine each of the following simple sentences into a compound sentence.
Then mark each **verb** and **subject** in your rewritten sentences.

example

A shawl was draped around her neck. A sash was tied at her waist.

A shawl (was draped) around her neck, and
a sash (was tied) at her waist.

1. The game was going badly. Brad left early.

_____

_____

2. Congress approved the appropriation bill by a large margin. The president vetoed it.

_____

_____

3. The plot was discovered months ago. There have been no arrests.

_____

_____

4. You could declare a major this semester. You could wait until your junior year.

_____

_____

5. The film was enjoyed by everyone in the group. It left Shelly strangely annoyed. (Use *yet.*)

_____

_____

6. The architects of Soviet policy are sane. They are intelligent. They possess an almost religious depth of purpose. (Use *and* to join this list of three main clauses.)

_____

_____

7. His purpose was clear. His language was not.

_____

_____

8. "Breaking with Moscow" is mistitled. Its author denies having broken with the city of his youth. (Use *for.*)

_____

_____

9. The colonel emerged from the cocoon of his own vision of things.

The view surprised him.

_____

_____

10. The letter could be printed as it is. It could be heavily edited.

_____

_____

Joining Main Clauses with a Semicolon

A **semicolon (;)** can also be used to join main clauses into one sentence. It is the only punctuation mark that *by itself* will join main clauses.

The following sentences are joined by semicolons.

Separate sentences

Last year I played intramural football. This year I might try soccer.

Joined by semicolon

Last year I played intramural football; this year I might try soccer.

Notice that again there is a main clause on each side of the semicolon. You can test that by looking for the subject and verb in each clause.

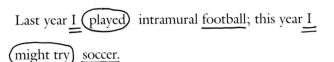

A semicolon cannot join a main clause to anything but a main clause. (We will look at semicolon errors in the next chapter.)

The semicolon is a special mark. Use it only when the clauses joined are similar in meaning, phrased similarly, or follow logically from one another. Because of this requirement, most main clauses cannot be joined by a semicolon.

In the example above, the semicolon was correct because the clauses expressed similar ideas phrased in similar ways. The clauses clearly belong together.

If you are not sure whether to use a semicolon in your writing, then the semicolon is probably incorrect. Join the clauses with a comma + conjunction, or punctuate them as separate sentences.

Exercise 5

Joining Main Clauses with a Semicolon

Of the following items, **choose the three** that could best be connected with semicolons.

Then **rewrite** each of the three items on the lines provided.

Finally, **mark each verb and subject** in your rewritten sentences.

example

The critics hated every word. The public loved it anyway.

The critics (hated) every word ; the public (loved) it anyway.

1. We approached the castle at last. A lone dog howled.

2. Each of the committees has submitted its report. Only yours has not been received.

3. The older brother wanted to rise to power. The younger was content with a humble government job.

4. The serious art of the city was magnificent. The recent restorations should help to justify its reputation.

5. One day they found themselves in a World War I pacifist gathering. Mario looked at his partner in surprise.

6. The Canadians found themselves with a problem. Relations with France have become dangerously strained.

A. Number: _____

_____

_____

B. Number: _____

_____

_____

C. Number: _____

_____

_____

Using a Semicolon with Words Like *However*

Semicolons are often used with words like *however*, *moreover*, and *therefore* to connect main clauses. This group is always followed by a comma. Taken together, the whole connector looks like this:

> **; however,**
> **; moreover,**
> **; therefore,**

The following sentence uses this kind of connector.

> Last year I played intramural football**; however,** this year I might try soccer.

Once again, there is a main clause on each side of the connector.

main clause

; however,

Last year <u>I</u> (played) intramural <u>football</u>**; however,** this

main clause

year <u>I</u> (might try) <u>soccer</u>.

Technically, words like *however* are called **conjunctive adverbs**. They fall into two groups — those that connect similar ideas and those that connect opposite ideas. For example:

Conjunctive Adverbs

Similarity	Opposition
besides	however
consequently	nevertheless
furthermore	
moreover	
therefore	

When you use these connectors, be careful to choose the one that expresses the logic of your sentence.

Exercise 6

Using Semicolons with Words Like *However*

Rewrite each of the following using a semicolon and one of the connectors from the list below.

> besides
> consequently
> furthermore
> moreover
> therefore
> however
> nevertheless

Follow each of the above words with a **comma**.

Then **mark each verb and subject** in your rewritten sentences.

Be sure to choose the connector that best expresses the relationship of ideas in the sentence.

example

We arrived at the vice chancellor's office by 4:30. She had already gone home.

We (arrived) at the vice chancellor's office by 4:30; however, she (had) already (gone) home.

1. The questions fairly tested our knowledge of the subject. They gave us a chance to show some writing skill.

   _____

   _____

   _____

2. The questions fairly tested our knowledge of the subject. No good student could answer them.

   _____

   _____

3. The new government rulings make that investment more expensive than in the past. You should consider other options.

   _____

   _____

4. The brown coat goes well with these slacks. It is all I can afford

right now.

_____

_____

5. Several ministers received threatening letters. Each spoke out against

the proposed Constitutional changes.

_____

_____

_____

PUNCTUATING MAIN CLAUSES IN PARAGRAPHS

Your work in this chapter has two benefits. First, it will help you to punctuate sentences correctly. College and business writing should be free of punctuation errors, and this goal by itself is worth your efforts.

But your work here has another important goal. One of the aims of good writing is to produce sentences that are strong, clear, pleasing, and readable. Combining clauses into sentences — and "un-combining" them — is a vital part of that process.

Should certain clauses be joined or separated? Only the writer can decide. As long as clauses are joined or separated correctly, there is no "textbook answer" to this question.

Nor should there be. Part of the fun of writing is in seeking your own solution to writing questions. This is how _your_ style develops and improves; this is how _your_ writing gets better.

The exercise below asks you to make decisions about combining sentences. Do the exercise carefully. Read the new sentences out loud and "listen" for the best solution. Don't be afraid to try several possibilities before settling on one of them.

Think of this exercise as a puzzle. Your goal is to please your "ear" by writing the most effective combination of short and long sentences possible. Of course, your work should be correct. But it can also be enjoyable. Have fun with it.

Exercise 7

Punctuating Main Clauses in Paragraphs

Use correct punctuation to **separate or join each main clause** in this paragraph. You may add conjunctions if you wish.

The house was silent Marcy lay awake for a long time the bright silent moon cast its silver light into the window and made a tangled blue-and-white design in the bedspread Marcy smoothed it with her hand the tortured pattern remained she wondered at her strange restlessness she was no doubt still thinking about Brad Palmer and his recent careless comment the incident had taken less than a minute Brad was certainly not an important member of her tight circle of friends what gave him the power to disturb her sleep with a word

Chapter Review

In this chapter you learned that

1. A **clause** is a group of words that contains a subject and verb.

2. A **main clause** is a clause that can stand alone as a complete sentence.

3. A **dependent clause** is a clause that cannot stand alone as a sentence because it contains words like *because* and *if* that connect them to something else.

4. A **complete sentence** is a group of words that contains at least one main clause.

5. Incomplete sentences, called **fragments**, are always wrong in college and professional writing.

6. Sentences must be separated by a **period**, **question mark**, or **exclamation point** and started with a **capital letter**.

7. Main clauses may be joined with
   a. A comma + coordinating conjunction (like *and*, *or*, *but*, or *nor*)
   b. A semicolon (;)

8. Sometimes a semicolon is used with a word like *however*, as a connector that looks like this — ; *however*,

The RELATED SKILL section showed you how to use *who* and *whom* in questions.

1. Use *who* (the subject form) for subjects.

2. Use *whom* (the object form) for objects of verbs and objects of prepositions.

Review Exercise 1

Define the following words:

1. Clause _____

_____

2. Main clause _____

_____

3. Dependent clause _____

_____

4. Simple sentence _____

_____

5. Sentence fragment _____

_____

Review Exercise 2

The following paragraphs are printed without punctuation. In addition, there is no capitalization except for names.

Using **end punctuation** and **capital letters**, separate each main clause into a simple sentence.

Then rewrite each paragraph on the lines provided.

A.   sentences for radio are usually short sometimes a phrase stands in place

of a whole sentence this makes radio writing different from college writing sentence fragments are incorrect in college writing radio writing is

much more informal it needs short sentences for a "punchy" effect

B.   these films show the suffering of the nation's coal miners they make a very powerful statement against the miners' harsh working conditions for this reason they have been banned by the government Colonel Rodriguez declared the mines in his country safe how then can these films be telling the truth the Colonel wants only accurate films shown in his country he thinks this makes him a good ruler what do you think

_____

_____

_____

_____

_____

_____

_____

_____

_____

_____

_____

Chapter 5 Writing Assignment

White a brief paragraph that uses **examples** to discuss a *good* **habit of a person you dislike**. Include several examples of sentences with more than one main clause in your paragraph.

   When you have made your final copy, **mark each verb, subject, object, and complement** of each *main* clause. Then make sure that all main clauses are correctly joined or separated.

Hints for Writing Paragraphs with Examples

   This paragraph is similar to the one you did for Chapter 4, except that here you are writing something good about a person you dislike.

   In all other respects, though, your work here will resemble your work in that chapter's paragraph. Use what you learned in doing that assignment to do this one well.

Before the rough draft:

1. Choose a person that you truly dislike. Your paragraph will be more interesting if you have strong feelings about this person.

2. Make a list of that person's good habits and select one of them for your paragraph.

3. Make a list of interesting stories that could be used as examples of this good habit. (Make this list as long as you can — your final essay will be better if you have a good list of stories to choose from.)

4. Select two stories from your list and mark the order in which to tell them.

5. For each story, make a short list of the events that make up that story.

6. Reread these lists and make any changes in them that you think will make your stories more effective.

Writing the rough draft:

1. Start your rough draft by writing an interesting opening sentence or two that mentions your subject and his or her good habit.

2. Then tell your first story, beginning with a sentence that starts "for example." Use your list of events to tell this story.

3. Now tell your second story, beginning with a sentence that starts with a phrase like, "On another occasion." Use your list of events to tell this story also.

4. Write a closing sentence that summarizes your feelings about this person. Include a statement about the good habit in your summary.

After the rough draft:

1. Do your best to correct any errors on this first copy.

2. Make any other changes you think will make your paragraph more interesting and readable.

3. Recopy your corrected paragraph on a clean sheet of paper and turn in all of your work.

6
Correcting common punctuation errors

Chapter Preview

This chapter will show you how to correct common mistakes like **run-on sentences** and **comma splice errors**.

In addition, a special RELATED SKILL section will show you how to use **correct fragments in paragraphs**.

Some punctuation errors occur more often than others. Many of these involve the punctuation of main clauses. These errors are:

Run-on sentences

Comma splices and other comma errors

Semicolon errors

Sentence fragments

RUN-ON SENTENCE ERROR

One of the most common punctuation errors is the **run-on sentence**. You have already seen several of them in Chapter 5. A run-on sentence occurs when two main clauses are written as one sentence with no punctuation between them.

The following is an example of a run-on sentence.

Run-on sentence (INCORRECT)

I never eat strong cheese the smell makes me sick.

When we mark this sentence, we discover that it contains two main clauses with no punctuation between them. (To help you see the two main clauses more easily, we have drawn a vertical line to mark the "breaking point" between them.)

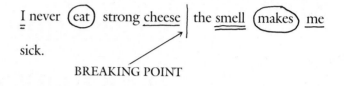

sick.

BREAKING POINT

Run-on sentences can be corrected by using any proper punctuation at the breaking point between the clauses. They can be separated with a period (or any other correct end punctuation), or they can be joined with a semicolon or comma + conjunction.

Two possible corrections of this run-on are shown below.

Corrected

I never eat strong cheese. **The** smell makes me sick.

I never eat strong cheese; the smell makes me sick.

Run-on sentences usually occur because a writer does not recognize that he or she has written two main clauses. The key to correcting run-on sentences, therefore, is in recognizing them.

Practice correcting run-on sentences by doing the following exercise. Then make sure your own writing is free of run-ons by using the techniques you have learned.

Exercise 1

Correcting Run-On Sentences

Mark each **verb**, **subject**, **object**, and **complement** in the following sentences.

Then **correct any run-on sentences** by placing correct punctuation (and capitalization) at the breaking point between main clauses. If any sentence is already correct, write **OK** in the margin.

The <u>book</u> (sold) for thousands. $\overset{T}{/}$he movie <u>rights</u> (went) for more.

OK   <u>Each</u> of the sweaters (was purchased) on sale at Formalda's Bargain

Basement.

1. The appointment can wait the letter must be finished.

2. The process is slow and takes a lot of patience.

3. The island was settled quickly the population swelled to several thousand in less than twenty years.

4. Would you read this now I need an answer.

5. Most people stop short of their ability others push themselves well beyond it.

6. The meat is fresh the salad bar is well stocked.

7. The truck was loaded with frozen fish and headed for Chicago supermarkets.

8. Movies bore him so do books and magazines.

9. Noelle wants to write professionally and shows a lot of promise.

10. Noelle wants to write professionally she shows a lot of promise.

11. The books are steamy the movies are even worse.

12. When did she arrive I must have missed her entrance.

13. Fantasies left him without an understanding of real relationships.

14. In this film the devil takes over the phone system and puts everyone on hold forever.

15. Ben's checkbook was lost the same evening.

16. The kiss lasted almost a minute and ended at the commercial.

17. We never noticed the peeling wallpaper or the musty odor in the closets.

133 Correcting common punctuation errors

18. The phone rang several times Sean answered it.

19. This cold medicine really works.

20. Her truck is painted white she drives it to Tacoma and back.

COMMA SPLICES

Another common punctuation error is the **comma splice**. A comma splice occurs when two main clauses — groups of words that could be separate sentences by themselves — are joined by a comma alone.

The following sentence contains a comma splice.

Comma splice (Incorrect)

Mona is not sick, she wants a vacation from work.

Notice that there are two main clauses in this sentence (*Mona – is* and *she – wants*) and no conjunction with the comma. This sentence could be marked as follows. (As before, a vertical line marks the "breaking point" between the main clauses.)

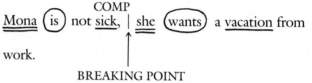

work.

BREAKING POINT

Like a run-on sentence, a comma splice can be corrected with any proper punctuation — end punctuation like the period, a semicolon, or a comma + conjunction.

Here are two methods of correcting the comma splice above.

Corrected

Mona is not sick**.** **S**he wants a vacation from work.

OR

Mona is not sick**,** **but** she wants a vacation from work.

Watch carefully for comma splices. A great many papers contain at least one.

Exercise 2

Correcting Comma Splices

Mark each **verb**, **subject**, **object**, and **complement** in the following sentences.

Then **correct all comma splices** by placing correct punctuation at the breaking point between main clauses. If any sentence is already correct, write **OK** in the margin.

examples

The book ~~sold~~ for thousands **;**/ the movie rights ~~went~~ for a lot more.

OK   This ~~sentence~~ is punctuated correctly, but that ~~one~~ is not.

1. The senator was nominated for a third term, but he did not run.

2. The senator was nominated for a third term, he did not run.

3. The bank balance is running low, our paychecks will not be deposited until Monday.

4. New cars are getting more expensive, they are also becoming harder to maintain.

5. I like her way of telling a story, do you?

6. The clothes are missing, the jewelry has not been touched.

7. They wanted to remember the lecture, so they taped it.

8. Janice enjoys chess, she plays regularly at the Third Avenue Kings and Queens.

9. The movie was *Little Caesar,* the character was Rico.

10. The slacks are hard to clean, the legs get mud-stained so easily.

11. This job takes know-how, stamina, and ambition.

12. The test was difficult, the essay assignment was easy.

13. Then the ball bounced into the stands, and Jimmy grabbed it on one bounce.

14. A salesman came to the door, gave her his business card, and asked for Mr. Blackmore.

15. The apartment above the hardware store is for rent, it has been vacant for three weeks.

135 Correcting common punctuation errors

16. The video won't be available for several weeks, the record is out now.

17. Wallace laughed at the jokes, and Marty sang along with the music.

18. Sandy left her notes at my apartment, she will need them tomorrow.

19. We found her playing in the playground, she was by the large slide.

20. Dr. Calabasa treated each patient, then he took the subway home.

OTHER COMMA ERRORS

Other errors can occur when using commas with coordinating conjunctions. Sometimes a comma is used where it shouldn't be, such as with a conjunction that joins only two verbs, not two main clauses.

Incorrect

Vanity Fair has been removed from the library, and was taken to storage.

Notice that this sentence contains one subject and two verbs, but only one main clause.

Incorrect

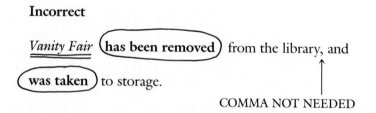

Since *and* joins only two verbs in this sentence, no comma is needed.

Corrected

Vanity Fair has been removed from the library and was taken to storage.

NO COMMA

At other times a comma is not used where it should be — with a conjunction that joins two main clauses.

Incorrect

Vanity Fair has been removed from the library and it is being stored.

This sentence contains two main clauses, one on each side of the vertical line.

Incorrect

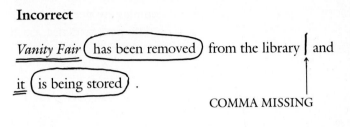

Vanity Fair has been removed from the library and it is being stored.

COMMA MISSING

Because two main clauses are being joined, a comma is needed with the conjunction *and*.

Corrected

Vanity Fair has been removed from the library, and it is being stored.

COMMA ADDED

This confusion arises because conjunctions like *and* can join either equal parts of one clause (like two subjects) or equal main clauses.

Let's look at these cases more closely.

One Clause or Two?

A sentence with two subjects and one verb has only one clause and is not punctuated with commas.

Two subjects and one verb — one clause

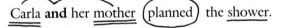

Carla **and** her mother planned the shower.

In the same way, a sentence with one subject and two verbs also has only one clause — and still no commas are needed.

One subject and two verbs — one clause

Carla planned the shower **and** chose the guests.

Even sentences with two subjects and two verbs have only one clause if both subjects "do" both verbs. Even here, no commas are needed.

Two subjects and two verbs — one clause

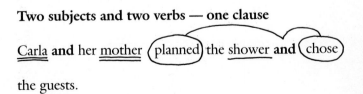

Carla **and** her mother planned the shower **and** chose the guests.

In this sentence, the two subjects, *Carla* and *mother*, act like one subject. Likewise, the two verbs, *planned* and *chose*, act like one verb. Because both subjects do both actions, the sentence contains one main clause, and no commas are needed.

The next sentence, on the other hand, has two subjects, two verbs, and two main clauses.

Two subjects and two verbs — two clauses

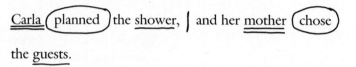

the guests.

Notice that in the sentence above each subject does only one action, and that there is a subject and verb on each side of the vertical line. Because **and** joins two main clauses, the comma is required.

All of this information can be summarized as follows.

One Clause or Two?

A sentence has **one clause** if it contains:

1. (Subject + subject) — verb

2. Subject — (verb + verb)

3. (Subject + subject) — (verb + verb)

A sentence has **two clauses** if it contains:

4. (Subject — verb) + (subject — verb)

Decide carefully whether a sentence contains one main clause or two before adding (or taking away) a comma with conjunctions like *and*.

Exercise 3

One Clause or Two Clauses?

Mark each **verb** and **subject** in the following sentences. Then tell whether each sentence has **one or two clauses**.

example

_____TWO_____ It (rained) all weekend, so they (canceled) the trip

until Thursday.

_____ **1.** She played a deaf composer in her first film and a

society matron in her next.

_____ **2.** The boys went fishing but caught nothing.

_____ **3.** The gate was damaged in last night's storm, so my

father fixed it.

_____ **4.** The house looked white and newly painted.

_____ **5.** The ship turned around, and it sailed home.

_____ **6.** The ship turned around and sailed home.

_____ **7.** I will be busy all weekend, but call me on Monday.

_____ **8.** Neither the coach nor the trainer saw the accident.

_____ **9.** Andrew and Sherman stood and announced their

engagements at the same time.

_____ **10.** The coat is too small for me, but the shirt fits nicely.

_____ **11.** She and I have attended college and worked to-

gether for the last three years.

_____ **12.** Sue and her father have just left for dinner and

a show.

_____ **13.** The explosion destroyed the building, but no one

was seriously injured.

_____ **14.** The explosion destroyed the building but injured no

one seriously.

_____ **15.** The medals were taken from the box and pinned

onto his chest.

_____ **16.** The medals were taken from the box, and the colo-

nel pinned them onto his chest.

_____ **17.** Another lark landed in the field and added its song

to the evening's music.

_____ **18.** The lamp flickered and went out.

_____ **19.** The lamp flickered, and its flame went out.

_____ **20.** The movie and the play shared a common fate.

The following exercise combines everything you have learned so far in this chapter.

Exercise 4

Correcting Errors with Compound Sentences

Correct any incorrect punctuation in the following sentences.
  If the sentence is incorrect, use the following abbreviations to tell which error the sentence contains.

> **CS** = Comma splice
>
> **RO** = Run-on sentence
>
> **CE** = Comma error (a comma must either be added or taken out)

If a sentence is already correct, write **OK** in the margin.

example   CS   Another delivery was scheduled for tomorrow. It should arrive in

the afternoon.

1. Have you solved problem seven, I haven't.

2. She works hard and she is honest.

3. Diving shops line Seaview Avenue, and most of the side streets.

4. American farm products are well advertised and attract a large market.

5. They called a special meeting of the council, the matter was presented

   in a closed-door session.

6. The store is closed the streets are dark.

7. Mrs. Quarrels called at last, and told her sister everything.

8. He is a cautious driver, the accident couldn't be his fault.

9. He is a cautious driver, so the accident couldn't be his fault.

10. The painting was expensive, it sold for $277,500.

SEMICOLON ERRORS

There are two more errors to note. One involves semicolons. When writers begin to use semicolons, they sometimes use them to join a main clause to a group of words that is not a main clause.

This practice, of course, is incorrect. Semicolons should be used to join main clauses only. (There are other uses of semicolons, but you will rarely encounter them.)

The following sentence contains this kind of semicolon error.

Semicolon error

Mischa discovered his true profession; at the Penwicker Staff Day Care Center.

The semicolon in this sentence joins a main clause (*Mischa – discovered – profession*) to a phrase. *At the Penwicker Staff Day Care Center* has no subject and no verb.

Mischa (discovered) his true profession; (at the

Penwicker Staff Day Care Center) .

SEMICOLON INCORRECT

Since no punctuation is needed to join the clause to this phrase, the semicolon should be removed.

Corrected

Mischa discovered his true profession at the Penwicker Staff Day Care Center.

SEMICOLON REMOVED

Avoid the temptation to use a semicolon where it "feels right" to do so. Instead, use the semicolon only when you are sure that it joins main clauses.

Exercise 5

Correcting Semicolon Errors

Some of the following sentences contain incorrect semicolons. Do the following for each one.

a. Mark each **verb**, **subject**, and **object** or **complement**.
b. Then tell whether the semicolon is correct by writing **YES** or **NO** on the line.
c. **Rewrite** any incorrect sentence, removing the semicolon.

<u>*NO*</u> The <u>Duchess</u> (entered) the <u>room</u>; in a blue satin ball gown.

The Duchess entered the room in a blue satin ball gown.

_____ 1. Is this your first time; at a formal dinner dance?

_____

_____

_____ 2. Half of the delegates to this year's convention have rented cars; this has eliminated some of the arguing over taxis.

_____

_____

_____ 3. Half of the delegates to this year's convention have rented cars; eliminating some of the arguing over taxis.

_____

_____

_____ 4. Roderigo walked on stage with a flourish; and flexed his muscles in several unique poses.

_____

_____

_____ 5. Most music students at Penwicker prefer rock to Bach; and dream of sweating magnificently for thousands of adoring fans.

_____

_____

_____ **6.** Bruno Pavlovski, on the other hand; would rather play his cello in Boston Common for tens of indifferent pigeons.

_____

_____

_____ **7.** We all seek the truth; some of us just look in more likely places.

_____

_____

_____ **8.** Stephan's books are all overdue; and lost, according to his latest explanation.

_____

_____

_____ **9.** Listening is more than polite silence; it is an active contribution to good conversation.

_____

_____

_____ **10.** Mother found father in the living room; a pair of cruise tickets to Jamaica in his hand.

_____

_____

SENTENCE FRAGMENTS

Every complete sentence must contain at least one main clause. Any sentence that doesn't contain at least one main clause is a **fragment**.

Fragments, whether intentional or not, are incorrect in college and professional writing.

There are two causes of sentence fragments.

1. Incorrect punctuation
2. Incorrect writing

Fragments from incorrect punctuation are easily corrected by changing the punctuation of the sentences. Fragments from incorrect writing must be corrected by rewriting.

Let's look at these fragments one at a time.

Correcting Fragments with Punctuation

One kind of fragment is the result of incorrect punctuation. Any misplaced period can result in a sentence fragment. For example, study the following sentence.

Fragment — Incorrect

Bill went to the store. And spent $100 on groceries.

PERIOD INCORRECT

Here a period was incorrectly added to a sentence that contains a subject and two verbs.

groceries.

Correctly punctuated, the sentence looks like this.

Corrected

Bill went to the store and spent $100 on groceries.

PERIOD REMOVED

If you have a tendency to write fragments, apply what you know about sentence structure to check all of your end punctuation.

Correcting Fragments by Rewriting

Some fragments are made, not by incorrect punctuation, but by incorrect writing. Sometimes a group of words that was intended to be a complete sentence lacks a subject, a verb, or both.

Long sentences are more often subject to this error than shorter ones. For example:

Another reason for the disintegration of the labor movement in the last half of the twentieth century.

This sentence has no verb, possibly because its length made it "feel complete" to the writer. It consists of a noun and four adjectives.

Another reason (for the disintegration) (of the labor movement) (in the last half) (of the twentieth century.)

This error could be corrected in any of several ways. You could, for example, add a subject and verb at the beginning, or a verb and a complement or an object at the end.

Corrected (1)

This is another reason for the disintegration of the labor movement in the last half of the twentieth century.

Corrected (2)

Another reason for the disintegration of the labor movement in the last half of the twentieth century is the growing affluence of many union members.

In the first sentence, the core of the main clause is *this – is – reason* (subject – verb – complement). In the second, the core of the main clause is *reason – is – affluence.*

Of course, there are many other ways to rewrite this sentence as well.

Exercise 6	Recognizing Complete Sentences and Fragments

Tell which of the following are complete sentences and which are fragments by writing **sentence** or **fragment** on the line.

Rewrite any fragment so it is a complete sentence.

examples

Sentence _____ The emperor was assassinated in 277 B.C.

_____

_____

Fragment _____ For an important test.

We arrived for an important test.

_____

_____ **1.** An old forgotten book.

_____

_____

_____ **2.** Over twenty thousand clay soldiers were buried

with China's first ruler.

_____

_____

_____ **3.** She bought the perfume on an impulse.

_____

_____

_____ **4.** As good as anyone else.

_____

_____

_____ **5.** The answer was correct.

_____

_____

_____ **6.** For the third time this semester.

_____

_____

_____ **7.** Lupe received a perfect math score for the third time

this semester.

_____

_____

_____ **8.** Hoping for a better grade.

_____

_____

_____ **9.** A good computer system.

_____

_____

_____ **10.** Jerry studied last night.

_____

_____

Exercise 7

Correcting Fragments

Rewrite each of the following fragments in two different ways. Then place an **X** next to the version you prefer.

Note that some can be corrected by repunctuating the sentence, while others must be rewritten.

1. The promotion recently foretold by a fortune gypsy. From

    Hyde Park.

    A. _____

    _____

    B. _____

    _____

2. Each of the twins was sent floating down the river in a basket. And

    was found by a servant of the old count.

    A. _____

    _____

    B. _____

    _____

3. A discovery of importance in the field of food production. And an

    idea for saving many starving children.

    A. _____

    _____

B. _____

_____

4. Another dozen Rembrandts-to-be were on display. Along the warm pavements of Berkeley Street. Their paintings were on display. Also.

A. _____

_____

B. _____

_____

5. A set of pictures left at the photo developer for too long. He picked them up only last month.

A. _____

_____

B. _____

_____

6. The market closes in just a few minutes. Just time for a few items.

A. _____

_____

B. _____

_____

7. One of several members of the local drinking society on vacation at the Sunset Health. And Rejuvenation Spa.

A. _____

_____

B. _____

_____

8. Each motorcycle was worth more than most Asian automobiles with bucket seats. A lot more.

A. _____

_____

B. _____

_____

9. She could be the next news reporter on Eyewitness Action Central News on the local independent television station. Could be an excellent photographer as well.

A. _____

_____

B. _____

_____

10. A close encounter with a partially conscious loan officer at the Penwicker County Savings and Loan. A good time was had by all.

A. _____

_____

B. _____

_____

RELATED SKILL   CORRECTING FRAGMENTS IN PARAGRAPHS

It is more difficult to find and correct fragments in paragraphs than in separately printed sentences.

Remember — every complete sentence must have at least one main clause. Look at each "sentence" in a paragraph carefully to understand its structure. If you can find subjects and verbs and tell the difference between a main clause and a dependent clause, you can correct fragments wherever they appear.

Correcting Fragments in Paragraphs

Correct all fragments in the following paragraph. Then **rewrite** the paragraph on the lines below.

The boarding house had a good reputation. This meant a lot in the thirties. During the Great Depression. It sat on Forest Avenue. Near the entrance to McKinley Park. The boarding house was a big old house. Very friendly. I started living there in 1936. I moved north from St. Louis. My job required me to commute to the Loop. The Loop is downtown Chicago. Every morning I rode the Howard "L." Got on near Forest and Henderson. It took me to the old Goldblatt's store. I didn't make much money, but I worked. In the evenings I went back to the boarding house. It was a lot safer than a lot of places. And besides, the jazz clubs weren't very far away. Got good entertainment that way. Anyway, I survived. And did pretty well, too.

_____

_____

_____

_____

_____

_____

_____

_____

_____

_____

_____

_____

_____

Chapter Review

In this chapter you learned that

1. A **run-on sentence** is an error in which two main clauses are incorrectly joined with no punctuation between them.

2. A **comma splice** is an error in which two main clauses are incorrectly joined with only a comma between them.

3. **Commas** must be used with conjunctions to join two main clauses, but not to join two parts of one clause, such as two verbs.

4. **Semicolon errors** result when a semicolon joins a main clause to a group of words that is not a main clause.

5. **Fragments** can be caused by incorrect punctuation or incorrect writing.

In the RELATED SKILL section you learned how to **correct fragments in paragraphs** by making sure each sentence has at least one main clause.

Review Exercise

Correct all punctuation errors in the following paragraph. If a sentence is incorrect, use the following abbreviations to tell which error the sentence contains.

CS	=	Comma splice
RO	=	Run-on sentence
CE	=	Comma error (a comma must either be added or taken out)
SE	=	Semicolon error
FR	=	Fragment

Then **rewrite** the corrected sentences on the lines below.

Many of the wildlife pests have interesting histories. Three bird pests are pigeons; house sparrows, and starlings, they were all deliberately imported to this country. Great flocks of starlings have darkened the sunset in many cities. Because of their great numbers. Starlings are reverse commuters they feed in the fields by day, and spend the nights in the city. In many areas starlings push bluebirds from their nests and they have even ousted desert birds from their nests in Southwestern cactus.[1]

_____

_____

_____

_____

_____

_____

_____

_____

_____

_____

_____

_____

[1] Adapted from "Elect Tarzan Mayor" by Christopher Nyerges, © *New York Times*, July 23, 1979.

Chapter 6 Writing Assignment

Write a paragraph that explains, step-by-step, how something is done. Your subject this time is **how to be attractive to people you wish to date.**

When you have made your final copy:

a. Mark each **verb**, **subject**, **object**, and **complement**.
b. Make sure that all **main clauses** are correctly joined or separated.

Hints for Writing Process Paragraphs

This should be an interesting paragraph to write. Be honest, but also have fun with it.

The strength of a process paragraph is in the soundness of its advice and the clarity of its directions. Take care, therefore, in the planning stages ("before the rough draft"). If your plan is a good one, the paragraph will have its best chance to succeed.

Before the rough draft:

1. Make a preliminary list of the steps you think make up this process.

2. Now edit this list — add steps, take steps out, change the order of what you have written — so that its final form represents your best thoughts on this subject.

3. Recopy your list of steps and add a good example for each step.

Writing the rough draft:

1. Start your rough draft by writing a sentence or two that tells what the process is and why you are going to write about it.

2. Then discuss each item on your list one by one. Start your first step with a word or phrase like *first*.

3. Briefly discuss your example for each step.

4. Write a closing sentence that tells how successful the reader will be if he or she follows your advice.

After the rough draft:

1. Do your best to correct any errors on this first copy. Be especially careful to correct all errors in the punctuation of main clauses.

2. Make any other changes you think will make your paragraph more interesting and readable.

3. Recopy your corrected paragraph on a clean sheet of paper and turn in all of your work.

153 Correcting common punctuation errors

7
Using dependent clauses

Chapter Preview

This chapter will show you

1. How to find **dependent clauses** used as adjectives, adverbs, and nouns.

2. How to **punctuate dependent clauses** in sentences.

3. How to **combine sentences** to create dependent clauses.

In addition, a special RELATED SKILL section will help you learn to use the tip-off words *who* and *whom* correctly.

DEPENDENT CLAUSES

You saw in Chapter 5 that main clauses are clauses that can stand alone as sentences. Remember that dependent clauses are those clauses that cannot stand alone. Instead, they act like parts of a sentence. In this chapter we will examine *how* dependent clauses function as sentence parts.

Though we'll look at dependent clauses one at a time, remember that all dependent clauses function in much the same way: To supply additional information for a main clause.

Dependent clauses are groups of words that can take the place of subjects, objects, adjectives, and adverbs in a sentence. But unlike phrases, dependent clauses always contain within them a subject and a verb.

SUBJECT —	VERB —	**Object**
(dependent clause)		(dependent clause)
Adjectives	**Adverbs**	**Adjectives**
(dependent clause)	(dependent clause)	(dependent clause)

There are three kinds of dependent clauses:

> Adjective clauses
> Adverb clauses
> Noun clauses

Adjective clauses (sometimes called **relative clauses**) act like one-word adjectives by describing nouns and pronouns.

Adverb clauses act like one-word adverbs by describing verbs.

Noun clauses act like one-word nouns. Noun clauses can be subjects, objects of all kinds (objects of verbs, objects of prepositions), and complements.

Although dependent clauses contain a subject and a verb, they cannot stand alone as sentences. This is because dependent clauses are introduced by **tip-off words** that connect them to the main clause.

Let's look at dependent clauses one at a time.

ADJECTIVE CLAUSES

Adjective clauses (sometimes called **relative clauses**) act like one-word adjectives.

Adjective clauses can appear any place in a sentence that a one-word adjective can occur. They can describe any noun or pronoun in a sentence.

Adjective clauses always answer one of the adjective questions.

> Which?
> What kind?
> How many?
> Whose?

In addition, each adjective clause starts with a **tip-off word** or a phrase that includes a tip-off word.

Compare the following sentences.

The essay for my geology class needs work.

The essay that I wrote for my geology class needs work.

The main idea of the first sentence is *essay – needs – work* (subject + verb + object). *For my geology class* is an adjective phrase describing *essay*.

The essay (for my geology class)(needs) work.

The main idea of the second sentence is the same as the first, *essay – needs – work*. *That I wrote for my geology class* is also an adjective because it too describes the subject *essay*.

The essay **that I wrote for my geology class** (needs)

work.

**Adjective
question:**   *Which essay?*
Answer: *That I wrote for my geology class*

That I wrote for my geology class is a clause because it contains a subject and a verb — *I wrote*. It is therefore an adjective clause. Notice that it begins with the tip-off word *that*.

that I (wrote) for my geology class

Tip-Off Words for Adjective Clauses

A **tip-off word** is a word that

1. Shows that a dependent clause is coming, and

2. Connects the dependent clause to the rest of the sentence.

That is the tip-off word for the sentence above. It announces the start of the dependent clause, and it connects the clause to *essay*. (*That* is a pronoun that takes its meaning from *essay*.)

Notice that *that* also acts as the object of the verb *wrote*.

Adjective clause

that I (wrote) for my geology class

Even though *that* is the object of the verb *wrote*, it is moved to the beginning of the adjective clause for emphasis. Written in normal word order, the clause would look like this.

Adjective clause (in normal word order)

I (wrote) **that** for my geology class

All tip-off words for adjective clauses are like this one — a pronoun or adjective that

1. Takes part in the clause, and

2. Refers back to a word that the clause describes.

Use the following list of tip-off words when doing the exercises in this section.

Tip-Off Words for Adjective Clauses

Pronouns	Adjective
who	whose
whom	
which	
that	

Who (subject form) and *whom* (object form) refer only to people. *Whose* is the adjective form of *who* or *whom*. It may refer to people, animals, or things. *That* refers only to animals and things, never to people. *Which* may refer to animals or things.

Hidden Tip-Off Words

In Chapter 2, you saw that the subject *you* in a command can be hidden.

Hidden subject *you*

Come after eight o'clock.

(You) Come after eight o'clock.

You is left out of the sentence, but "understood" to be there.

In the same way, the tip-off words *that* or *which* may also be "hidden" — left out of the sentence, but understood to be there.

Hidden tip-off word *that*

I knew everything he was going to say.

I knew everything **(that)** he was going to say.

Whether *that* is printed in the sentence or not, we treat the sentence as though it were present. Hidden tip-off words are common in adjective and noun clauses, and you will discover them in your own writing.

Marking Sentences with Adjective Clauses

Adjective clauses are marked like adjective phrases. The words of the clause are grouped — this time by a **long bracket** — and an **arrow** shows which word it describes.

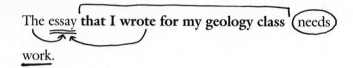

We recommend that you mark dependent clauses first, before marking the rest of the sentence. Otherwise you might mistake the verb in the dependent clause for the main verb of the sentence.

Because dependent clauses should be marked first, we need to revise the sentence marking order you first saw on page 93.

Sentence Marking Order (Revised)

1. **Group dependent clauses** with long brackets.

2. **Group remaining prepositional phrases** with parentheses.

3. Mark the **verb**, **subject**, and **object** or **complement**.

4. Starting at the beginning of the sentence, draw **arrows** to show what each adjective and adverb word, phrase, or clause, describes.

NOTE: **Do not mark a phrase within another phrase.** (Treat the largest phrase as one word, no matter what other phrases it contains.)

Examples of Adjective Clauses

To help you find adjective clauses more easily, here are more sentences that contain them.

Mr. Handleman, **who knows your father**, is waiting for you.

Mr. Handleman, **whom you met last winter**, is in town for the board meeting.

I studied the readings **that were assigned for today**.

We just met the writer **whose novel you are reading**.

The first adjective clause, *who knows your father*, describes the subject, Mr. Handleman. Here is how this sentence looks when marked completely:

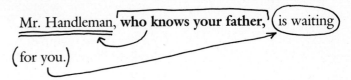

Notice that the tip-off word *who* is also the subject of *knows*, the verb in the dependent clause.

Adjective clause

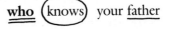

The second adjective clause, *whom you met last winter*, also describes the subject, Mr. Handleman.

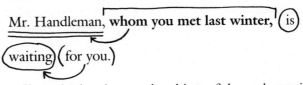

Notice that the tip-off word *whom* is now the object of the verb *met* in the dependent clause.

Adjective clause

The third sentence contains the adjective clause *that were assigned for today*.

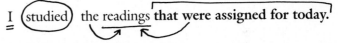

The tip-off word *that* is the subject of the verb *were assigned*.

Adjective clause

The final sample sentence contains the adjective clause *whose novel you are reading*.

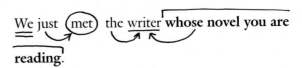

Here the tip-off word is *whose*, an adjective that describes *novel*, the object of *are reading*. Once more, the tip-off word is brought to the beginning of the clause.

whose novel you are reading

In the above examples, we have written and marked the adjective clauses separately. This is to show you which tip-off words are subjects and which are objects.

In your own marking, however, you need only mark sentences as we have done, by grouping the entire clause and showing what word it describes.

Exercise 1

Finding Adjective Clauses

A. **Mark each sentence completely.** (In the following sentences the adjective clauses have been printed in **boldface** type.)

example

A messenger **on whom you can rely** will be sent .

1. Julio saw a painting **that he likes very much.**

2. A man **who looks like your father** was in the bank today.

3. My sociology class, **which I needed in order to graduate this semester**, was just canceled.

4. They devised a plan **on which everyone could agree**.

5. She wrote a paper **that might be published.**

6. The afternoon shift, **which I hate**, is being given even more work next week.

7. They always gave him anything **that he wanted.**

8. The couch **that you liked so much** is on sale at Jackson's.

9. Napoleon, **whom Frenchmen still admire**, conquered most of Europe.

10. Courses **that require a lot of reading** are bad for my grade-point average.

B. **Mark each sentence completely.** (In these sentences, the adjective clauses have NOT been printed in boldface type.)

| **example** | Workers who join the strike could be disciplined . |

1. Professor Black, who lectured here last year, will return in June.

2. All donations that we receive are tax-deductible.

3. The finance committee, which approved your loan, just sent this letter.

4. Don't say anything that you might regret later.

5. The boxes that you need will be delivered tomorrow.

6. The wines that they produce are noted for their fragrance.

7. Buckworth has written another book that will get most of its sales from college English classrooms.

8. Mackie hatched a plot that cannot fail.

9. The page on which he wrote the first draft of the poem is now worth several thousand dollars.

10. We introduced her to Inspector Daley, who wants to write best sellers.

Punctuating Adjective Clauses

Adjective clauses are sometimes separated from the rest of the sentence according to the "Interrupter Rule," and sometimes they are not.

The Interrupter Rule

Punctuate any sentence interrupter by separating it from the rest of the sentence with commas.

> Interrupter, ************************************ .
> *************** , interrupter, *************** .
> ********************************* , interrupter.

When to apply the Interrupter Rule depends on two things:

1. The position of the clause in the sentence

2. The kind of information the clause contains

Either of these conditions can cause the Interrupter Rule to be applied.

Punctuating Adjective Clauses by Position

The normal position of an adjective clause is after the word it describes. Adjective clauses follow adjective phrases that describe the same word.

Normal Position of Adjective Clauses

Adjective – NOUN – Adjective phrases – **Adjective clause**

The following sentence, for example, contains both an adjective phrase and an adjective clause.

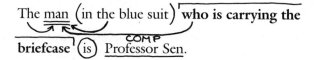

Adjective clauses will rarely be found out of normal position. As a result, most adjective clauses will be punctuated according to the kind of information they contain.

Punctuating Adjective Clauses by Kind of Information

Adjective clauses contain either **"needed"** or **"extra"** information.

"Needed" Adjectives

Adjective information is "needed" if it is required to

1. Identify the word it describes, or

2. Narrow down a larger group to a smaller one.

Any adjective information that is not "needed" is "extra."

Knowing whether an adjective clause contains "needed" or "extra" information is the key to punctuating it.

Punctuating Adjective Clauses

Any adjective clause that contains *"extra" information* should be separated from the rest of the sentence with commas.

Do not separate adjective clauses that contain "needed" information.

Adjective clauses that contain "extra information" are sometimes called **non-restrictive relative clauses**.

The following sentence shows how they are punctuated. Notice that Uncle Frank has already been identified by name. Therefore, the adjective clause contains "extra" information and should be punctuated with commas.

"Extra" adjective clauses — commas required

Uncle Frank**, for whom my brother works,** hires his
└────── COMMAS ──────┘

relatives whenever possible.

************** **, interrupter,** ************** .

"Needed" adjective clauses (sometimes called **restrictive relative clauses**) are never separated from the rest of the sentence with commas.

Clause "needed" to identify — no commas

The man **for whom my brother works** hires his
└────── NO COMMAS ──────┘

relatives whenever possible.

Notice that the man is not identified, so the adjective clause is needed for identification.

The following sentence contains an adjective clause needed to narrow down a group — in this case from "all people" to the smaller group "people who have too much money."

Clause "needed" to narrow a group — no commas

People **who have too much money** are always
└────── NO COMMAS ──────┘

welcome at the Coho Club.

Notice that, according to the sentence, only the smaller group is always welcome.

HINT: Adjective clauses that start with the tip-off word *which* always contain "extra" information. Adjective clauses that start with the tip-off word *that* always contain "needed" information.

Exercise 2

Punctuating Adjective Clauses

A. In these sentences, the adjective clause is printed in **boldface** type.

    a. On the line tell whether the adjective clause contains **NEEDED** or **EXTRA** information.

    b. **Punctuate** each sentence correctly.

example

    __EXTRA__ The Stanley Steamers, **who play in a semi-pro league,** have a large local following.

_____ 1. It's hard to find a novel **that doesn't contain a lot of violence.**

_____ 2. Lung cancer **which threatens every smoker** can now be cured in some cases.

_____ 3. Grass **that roots quickly** was planted on the hill.

_____ 4. Maiden-grass **which roots quickly** was planted on the hill.

_____ 5. The passengers **who followed the steward's instructions** were not injured.

_____ 6. The student **who sits in the back** has taken this course before.

_____ 7. Mr. Conley **who sits in the back** has taken this course before.

_____ 8. For several minutes we watched a balloon **that was rising through the clouds.**

_____ 9. The band welcomed Ensign Jones **who was recently commended for bravery**.

_____ 10. Venus and Mars **which are the two closest planets to Earth** can both be seen in the western sky tonight.

B. In these sentences, the adjective clause is NOT printed in boldface type.
  a. Mark each adjective clause and draw an **arrow** to the word it describes.
  b. Tell whether it contains **NEEDED** or **EXTRA** information.
  c. Punctuate each sentence.

_____ 1. Courses that teach nothing useful are not popular here.

_____ 2. Our basketball team which won its last five games meets its toughest rival this weekend.

_____ 3. The last two messages which you must not have received explained the dean's recent action.

_____ 4. Dr. Ramos who teaches only at night cannot meet with anyone before 7:30 P.M.

_____ 5. *The Broken Bed* which received every nomination possible for a musical opens here in September.

_____ 6. The revolutionary zeal that drove him never abated.

_____ 7. Ms. Frost rehired the supervisors who were laid off last month.

_____ 8. Restaurants that offer coupons are doing well.

_____ 9. The Silesian trade mission which Dr. Ruben has organized just opened for business in December.

_____ **10.** We need a research laboratory that specializes in

microbiology.

ADVERB CLAUSES

Adverb clauses act like one-word adverbs. They describe verbs and always answer one of the adverb questions.

> When?
> Where?
> Why?
> How?
> Under what condition?

In addition, all adverb clauses begin with tip-off words.
Compare the following sentences.

> Rita entered graduate school last fall.
>
> Rita entered graduate school because she wanted a Master's degree in business.

The core of the first sentence is _Rita – entered – school_ (subject + verb + object). _Last fall_ is an adverb phrase describing the verb _entered_.

The main idea of the second sentence is the same as the first, _Rita – entered – school. Because she wanted a Master's degree in business_ is also an adverb because it too describes the verb _entered_.

Adverb question:	Entered _why?_
Answer:	_Because she wanted a Master's degree in business_

Because she wanted a Master's degree in business is a clause because it contains a subject and a verb — _she wanted_. It is therefore an adverb clause. Notice that it begins with the tip-off word _because_.

Tip-Off Words for Adverb Clauses

Like those for adjective clauses, adverb clause tip-off words show that an adverb clause is coming. However, they do *not* take part in the clause. Their job is purely to join the adverb clause to the verb it describes. For this reason, adverb clause tip-off words are called conjunctions (words that join).

Unlike coordinating conjunctions (words that join equals), adverb clause tip-off words are **subordinating conjunctions** because they join unequals. ("Sub-ordinate" means "lesser (*sub*) in rank or order." Subordinating conjunctions are simply conjunctions used to create subordinate — or dependent — clauses.)

Because is the tip-off word for the adverb clause in the last example.

Adverb clause

because <u>she</u> (wanted) a Master's degree in business

Each adverb clause tip-off word is like this one. It

1. Joins the adverb clause to the action it describes and

2. Tells us the logic of that relationship.

In this case, the relationship is one of *reasons* — the adverb clause tells why the action "entered" occurred.

Other tip-off words for adverb clauses include the following.

Tip-Off Words for Adverb Clauses (Subordinating Conjunctions)

When?

after	just after
as	just before, etc.
as soon as	since (meaning *after*)
before	until
even after	when
before, etc.	whenever while

Where?

where	wherever

Why?

because	so (meaning *so that*)
in order that	so that
since (meaning *because*)	

How?

as	as though
as if	

Under what condition?

although	if
as long as	though
even if	unless
even though	whether

This list is not complete, but it does contain most of the common tip-off words and phrases. Use it to help you do the exercises in this section. Adverb clause tip-off words are never "hidden."

Marking Sentences with Adverb Clauses

An adverb clause is marked like an adjective clause — with a **long bracket** and an **arrow** to the word it describes.

Rita (entered) graduate school **because she wanted a Master's degree in business.**

As with adjective clauses, we recommend that you mark dependent adverb clauses first, before marking other parts of the sentence. Use the sentence marking order printed on page 158 to help you mark sentences that contain adverb clauses.

Examples of Adverb Clauses

Here are some more sentences that contain adverb clauses.

> Franklin arrived **just before I did.**

> The infection can be stopped **if it is treated soon.**

The first sentence contains an adverb clause that tells "when." Here's how the sentence looks when marked completely.

Adverb clause telling *when*

Franklin (arrived) **just before I did.**

Notice that the tip-off words *just before* establish the adverb relationship.

Adverb clause

just before I (did)

The second sentence contains an adverb clause telling *under what condition.*

Adverb clause telling *under what condition*

The infection (can be stopped) **if it is treated soon.**

Here the tip-off word *if* announces what the condition is.

Adverb clause

if it (is treated) soon

Exercise 3

Finding Adverb Clauses

A. In the following sentences the adverb clauses are printed in **boldface type.**

a. **Mark each sentence completely.**

b. Then tell which **adverb question** the adverb clause answers.

example

Burst when? **As soon as she sat down,** the audience (burst) (into applause.)

_____ 1. He always says things like that **when he lectures.**

_____ 2. Sandra will call **after she finishes work.**

_____ 3. **Because the presentation was delayed,** Mr. Pritchard cut short his speech.

_____ 4. The purchase will take place **whether you approve or not.**

_____ 5. **If you release the choke,** the engine will start.

_____ 6. Mary spoke out **because she had to.**

_____ 7. We can leave **whenever you wish.**

_____ 8. Reporters were not allowed on the field **until after the plane landed.**

_____ 9. They lost their deposit **because they changed their plans.**

_____ 10. Salesmen, **when they speak too fast,** always make me suspicious.

B. In these sentences, the adverb clause has NOT been printed in bold-face type.

    a. Mark each sentence completely.

    b. Then tell which **adverb question** the adverb clause answers.

example

Writes when? My daughter (writes) as often as she can.

_____ **1.** The product can be improved if they find more investors.

_____ **2.** These reservations were made several weeks before the hotel opened.

_____ **3.** Even though she is seventy-one, Mattie will enter college in the fall.

_____ **4.** Before Juan left town, he visited St. Cecilia's again.

_____ **5.** Although Mr. Wesniewski sold his property on Arrow Lake, he still visits his friends there.

_____ **6.** They found the cat when they looked near the garbage can.

_____ **7.** I read several of those books because they were assigned in Humanities Seminar.

_____ **8.** Martin accepted the invitation so that he could meet her parents.

_____ **9.** The prosecutor waited until the witness arrived.

_____ **10.** As soon as you find the receipt, return the suitcase to the store.

Punctuating Adverb Clauses

Adverb clauses are sometimes separated from the rest of the sentence according to the "Interrupter Rule," and sometimes they are not.

Though some adverb clauses contain "extra" information, most of the time adverb clauses are punctuated by position.

The normal position of an adverb clause is after the clause whose verb it describes. This usually places adverb clauses at the end of the sentence.

Normal Position of Adverb Clauses

VERB – Adverb – Adverb phrases –**Adverb clause**

The following sentences, for example, contain an adverb clause in its normal position.

Adverb clause in normal position

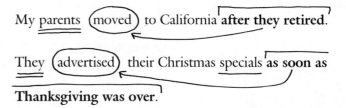

My parents (moved) to California **after they retired.**

They (advertised) their Christmas specials **as soon as Thanksgiving was over.**

Out-of-position adverb clauses are punctuated according to the Interrupter Rule.

Punctuating Adverb Clauses by Position

Any adverb clause that is *out of normal position* should be separated from the rest of the sentence with commas.

The most common place for out-of-position adverb clauses is at the beginning of the sentence. Adverb clauses that begin a sentence ("introductory position") are always separated with commas.

The following sentence contains an introductory adverb clause.

Introductory adverb clause — COMMA NEEDED

After they retired, my parents moved to California.

COMMA

As soon as Thanksgiving was over, the stores

COMMA

advertised their Christmas specials.

Interrupter, ******************************** .

Like other adverbs, adverb clauses can easily be moved to other places in the sentence. When they are, they must be punctuated like interrupters.

Out-of-position adverb clause — COMMAS NEEDED

My parents, **after they retired,** moved to California.

└───── COMMAS ─────┘

The stores, **as soon as Thanksgiving was over,**

└──────── COMMAS ────────┘

advertised their Christmas specials.

************** , **interrupter,** ************** .

Punctuating Adverb Clauses by Kind of Information

As a rule, adverb clauses in normal position are not separated with commas.

Adverb clause in normal position — NO COMMAS

My parents moved to California **after they retired.**

NO COMMA

They advertised their Christmas specials **as soon as**

NO COMMA

Thanksgiving was over.

There is one exception, however — adverb clauses beginning with words like *although* always contain "extra" information.

Punctuating Adverb Clauses Beginning with "Although"

Adverb clauses that begin with tip-off words like *although* always are punctuated like interrupters, even when they are in normal position.

The following sentence, for example, contains such a clause.

Adverb clause beginning with _although_ — COMMA REQUIRED

Your questions will be answered tomorrow, **although**

↑
COMMA

many of them have been discussed before.

By definition, clauses that start with _although_ contain information that is not important enough to change the action of the main clause. Therefore, "although" clauses contain the adverb version of "extra" information and should be punctuated as interrupters.

Exercise 4

Punctuating Adverb Clauses

A. In the following sentences the adverb clauses have been printed in **boldface** type.

 a. **Punctuate** each of the following sentences correctly.

 b. If you add commas, tell whether the adverb clause is **out of normal position** or contains **extra information** by writing **OUT** or **EXTRA** on the line.

 c. If a sentence is already correctly punctuated, write **OK** on the line.

example

_____OUT_____ **Until he registered for Dr. Sherman's class,** James had never been exposed to eighteenth-century art.

_____ 1. She spoke for workers' rights all her life **because she believed in the trade union movement.**

_____ 2. We did well on the test **although we had little time to study for it.**

_____ 3. **As you read this essay** notice how the writer explains each of his reasons in order.

_____ 4. **When Mark begins his serve** he bounces the ball twice and takes a long, deep breath.

_____ 5. The manufacturers could have increased production **if more capital had been available.**

_____ 6. **If more capital had been available** the manufactur-ers could have increased production.

_____ 7. We should return early **whether we wish to or not**.

_____ 8. The machinery droned on **as we spoke**.

_____ 9. **As we spoke** the machinery droned on.

_____ 10. You'll find the keys **wherever the cat left them**.

B. In the following sentences the adverb clause has NOT been printed in **boldface** type.

    a. **Punctuate** each of the following sentences correctly.

    b. If you add commas, tell whether the adverb clause is **out of normal position** or contains extra information by writing **OUT** or **EXTRA** on the line.

    c. If a sentence is already correctly punctuated, write **OK** on the line.

_____ 1. It can't hurt if you can't feel it.

_____ 2. Simon speaks as though he is practicing for the U.S. Senate.

_____ 3. The task as you know is difficult.

_____ 4. The baby's first automatic smile occurs more often as he responds to the people around him.

_____ 5. As he responds to the people around him the baby's first automatic smile occurs more often.

_____ 6. You should be careful when you are away from home about the security of your cash.

_____ 7. This electronics book was outdated before it was published.

_____ 8. Ever since we sold the farm I have missed the smell of black earth.

_____ 9. Because the dockworkers are on strike your ship-

ment will probably be delayed another couple of

weeks.

_____ 10. The planet is lighter although it is several times

larger than its neighbor.

NOUN CLAUSES

Noun clauses act like nouns in a sentence. They can be anything nouns can be — subjects, objects of all kinds, and complements. You can discover what job a noun clause is doing in a sentence by asking the subject and object questions.

Subject question: Ask "who?" or "what?" and then say the verb.

Object question: Say the verb (*or* preposition), and then ask "whom?" or "what?"

All noun clauses contain a subject and verb and begin with a **tip-off word** (or a phrase containing a tip-off word).

Compare the following sentences.

I heard the answer.

I heard that the test is tomorrow.

I heard what you said.

In each sentence the main subject and verb are *I – heard*. Each verb is followed by an object that answers the object question *heard what?*

The first sentence has a one-word object. The next two have noun clauses as objects.

I (heard) the answer.

Object question: Heard *what?*
Answer: *Answer*

I (heard) **that the test is tomorrow.**

Object question: Heard *what?*
Answer: *That the test is tomorrow*

175 Using dependent clauses

I (heard) **what you said.**

**Object
question:**   Heard *what?*
Answer: *What you said*

That the test is tomorrow and *what you said* are noun clauses. Each contains a subject and verb (*test – is* and *you – said*), and each begins with a tip-off word (*that* and *what*).

Noun clauses

that the test (is) tomorrow

what you (said)

Tip-Off Words for Noun Clauses

Like all tip-off words, tip-off words for noun clauses show that a dependent clause is coming. Some (pronouns and adjectives) take part in the dependent clause, while others (subordinating conjunctions) do not.

Conjunctions as Noun Clause Tip-Off Words

The most common noun clause tip-off word is *that* (used as a conjunction). In the noun clause *that the test is tomorrow, that* is a conjunction that acts as a tip-off word.

Noun clause

that the test (is) tomorrow

A list of subordinating conjunctions used as noun clause tip-off words appears in the box that follows. (Recall that subordinating conjunctions are simply conjunctions used to create subordinate — or dependent — clauses.)

Tip-Off Words for Noun Clauses
Group 1: Conjunctions

how	that
when	
where	
why	
whether	

Note that some phrases like *certain that* and *happy that* introduce dependent clauses that act as complements.

He was **certain that Ben was a native Hawaiian**.

Object
question: Was *what?*
Answer: *certain that Ben was a native Hawaiian*

You can mark sentences containing these clauses as follows:

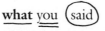

Pronouns and Adjectives as Noun Clause Tip-Off Words

Pronouns and adjectives can also act as noun clause tip-off words. Unlike conjunctions, these words always have a function within the dependent clause.

In the noun clause *what you said*, *what* is a pronoun that acts as a tip-off word. Notice that, like all tip-off words, *what* has been moved to the beginning of the noun clause.

Noun clause

Written in normal word order, the clause would look like this.

Noun clause (in normal word order)

you (said) **what**

A list of pronouns and adjectives used as noun clause tip-off words appears in the following box.

Tip-Off Words for Noun Clauses
Group 2: Pronouns and Adjectives

who	whoever
whom	whomever
what	whatever
which	whichever

Recall that the object form of *who* is *whom.* Choose the correct form of these words based on how they are used in the dependent clause. *Who* should be used for subjects and complements, and *whom* should be used for objects.

You will see these tip-off words in the examples and exercises that follow. Use these lists to help you work in this section.

Hidden Tip-Off Words

Earlier in this chapter, you saw that the adjective tip-off words *that* or *which* may be "hidden" — left out of the sentence, but understood to be there.

In the same way, the noun clause tip-off word *that* can be hidden in a sentence. For example:

Hidden tip-off word *that*

I heard the test is tomorrow.

I heard **(that)** the test is tomorrow.

Whether *that* is printed in the sentence or not, we treat the sentence as though it were present.

Marking Sentences with Noun Clauses

A noun clause is marked like other dependent clauses, with a **long bracket** and a mark to show how it is used. Since noun clauses are used as subjects, objects, and complements, they are usually **underlined**.

I (heard) ⌐**that the test is tomorrow**.⌐

I (heard) ⌐**what you said**.⌐

Punctuating Noun Clauses

Noun clauses receive the same punctuation as one-word nouns — usually none.

Noun Clauses as Indirect Quotations

The most common use of noun clauses is in **indirect quotations**. Indirect quotations report a speaker's words, rephrased slightly. The usual tip-off word for indirect quotations is *that*.

Her assistant said **that she would be in the office later today**.

(Speaker's exact words: *I will be in the office later today.*)

Said is the main verb of this sentence. What the speaker said appears in the noun clause.

Sentences like these, by the way, are usually simple in construction. This one is the equivalent of a four-word sentence. The whole noun clause acts like a one-word object.

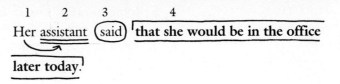

Her assistant (said) 'that she would be in the office later today.'

Quotations will be discussed in detail in Chapter 16.

Finding Noun Clauses

A. In the following sentences the noun clauses have been printed in **boldface** type.

1. **Mark** each sentence completely.

2. Place an **X** in the margin of any sentence that contains an indirect quotation.

example

Jennifer (said) '**that she would get the scholarship**.'

1. **How much you revise your work** is your decision.

2. Then he mentioned **that the exam schedule had been changed.**

3. **That you are an honorable man** is well known.

4. We can plan the meeting for **whenever you are free.**

5. **However Stan gets to the game** is his decision.

6. Cynthia told them **whatever they wanted to hear.**

B. In the following sentences the noun clauses have NOT been printed in boldface type.

1. **Mark** each sentence completely.

2. Place an **X** in the margin of any sentence that contains an indirect quotation.

example

I (suppose) 'that you want to borrow my book again.'

1. How much your uncle owned is still in question.

2. Hank saw why the ship was rocking so much.

3. After the barbeque Sheree's father announced that he would retire before the summer.

4. They offered her whatever salary she wanted.

5. Johnson hoped that everything had gone well at the interview.

6. Allan said that the clothes in this store are too expensive.

RELATED SKILL   USING *WHO* AND *WHOM* IN DEPENDENT CLAUSES

Choosing between *who* and *whom* as a tip-off word in dependent clauses is a special problem.

The subject form *who* must be used if the tip-off word is the subject of the verb in the dependent clause.

Mr. Handleman, **who knows your father**, is waiting for you.

Dependent clause

The object form *whom* must be used if the tip-off word is an object.

Mr. Handleman, **whom you met last winter**, is in town for the board meeting.

Dependent clause

Notice that, written in normal word order, the clause in the last sentence would look like this.

Dependent clause

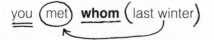

No matter how these words are used in speech, good college and professional writers always use *who* and *whom* correctly.

Using *Who* and *Whom* in Adjective Clauses

A. Write the correct form of the tip-off words **who** and **whom** on the line in each of the following sentences.

Then tell **what job** *who* or *whom* does in the dependent clause.

example

DeRon, ___*who*___ answered the phone, is visiting from Alabama.

subject of verb answered

1. The man _____ made the offer no longer works here.

_____

2. Here is a politician _____ I respect.

_____

3. A resident _____ saw the robbery has been interviewed.

_____

4. Ms. Wilson is a researcher with _____ I work.

_____

5. The mayor, for _____ I voted, has recently changed his position on every major issue.

_____

6. Inspector Kelly, _____ you know, is speaking at noon in the Penwicker Auditorium.

_____

7. Professor Brannigan will always help students _____ ask for his assistance.

_____

8. The report finally went to Margaret, for _____ it was origi-

nally intended.

_____

9. The hairdresser _____ my sister recommended does very

good work.

_____

10. Jenkins, the supply driver _____ received the commen-

dation, was rewarded with an extra week's vacation.

_____

B. **Correct any errors** in the use of **who** and **whom** in the following
sentences.

   1. Several reporters who you know well are attending the luncheon.

   2. Several reporters who know you well are attending the luncheon.

   3. An actress whom Kelly once represented is now working the New

   York stage.

   4. We didn't know anyone who we could ask.

   5. Several young women who entered the competition have since

   withdrawn under protest.

   6. A high official, whom declined to be named, made the announce-

   ment this morning.

   7. I notified the manufacturer who issued the original warranty.

   8. Bobby Maxwell, who saw the letter, would not comment on

   its contents.

   9. The teachers who you remember are all retired.

   10. Each of the tenants who I have spoken to is willing to sign

   the petition.

FRAGMENTS FROM DEPENDENT CLAUSES

Dependent clauses (or parts of sentences that contain dependent clauses) are sometimes incorrectly punctuated as separate sentences. When they are, a fragment is created. As you learned in Chapter 6, fragments are always incorrect in college and professional writing.

The following sentence contains this kind of fragment.

Fragment from dependent clause — incorrect

We ought to drive slowly. **Until we get to a gas station**.

↑

PERIOD INCORRECT

Until we get to a gas station is an adverb clause. Notice that it starts with the tip-off word *until*. Therefore, it cannot stand alone as a separate sentence.

Correct this fragment by changing the punctuation between the fragment and the rest of the sentence and removing the capital letter on *until*.

Corrected

We ought to drive slowly **until we get to a gas station**.

↑

PERIOD REMOVED

Notice that if the adverb clause had been written first, it would still have to be in the same sentence with *ought*, the verb it describes.

Fragments from dependent clause — incorrect

Until we get to a gas station. We will have to drive slowly.

↑

PERIOD INCORRECT

Corrected

Until we get to a gas station, we ought to drive slowly.

↑

COMMA ADDED

When correcting fragments in your own writing, watch especially for dependent clauses and make sure to use commas where necessary.

Exercise 6

Correcting Fragments from Dependent Clauses

Correct any incorrect punctuation in the following sentences. If an item is already correctly punctuated, write **OK** in the margin.

My brother earns extra money by working at the thrift store. ~~Even~~ ‸even
though all of his classes are in the early morning and late evening.

1. I cannot give you a good reason. Why Valentia deliberately endangered herself.

2. Several men who work for the county. Have been using publicly owned construction equipment.

3. The crow waited. Something rustled nearby.

4. You can have. Whatever you want.

5. If the constitution is not approved. Two of the political parties will go underground.

6. The rangers reacted quickly. As soon as they received the call. One of them was on his way to the campsite.

7. An exercise program was rerun. Because the station manager requested it.

8. A few of her patients were tested when they came in. Others had to be recalled.

9. All of the tapes that you hold in your hand. Belong to the radio station.

10. Several theories about the origin of Venus have been advanced. That take as evidence the earth's oldest written documents.

11. The checks were just delivered. The box was placed on her desk.

12. I did not see him. Because he was not there. You cannot convince me otherwise.

13. I did not see him. He was not there. You cannot convince me otherwise.

14. She looked at the birth records. After she finished with the county marriage certificates. She took notes regarding both and left.

15. She took a job in Chicago. Because her brother lived nearby.

16. The pony pranced around the ring. Until she received a signal from her trainer.

17. The dream came at midnight. When I fell asleep. It was the usual frightening one.

18. A car passed us on the freeway. As soon as I saw the driver's face. I knew where she was going.

19. The heart operation was successful. If Mr. Conklin will watch his diet from now on. He should live a long and happy life.

20. When you look at me like that. I melt. Because I cannot forget about last summer.

COMBINING SENTENCES TO CREATE DEPENDENT CLAUSES

All first drafts contain unnecessary words. You can combine sentences to make your writing less wordy and therefore easier to read. For example, the following sentences can be combined so that one is an adjective clause within the other.

Separate sentences

Carlos Ramirez owns his own grocery business.
He sponsors a Little League team for the neighborhood children.

Either of these clauses can be made dependent on the other. The question is, which sentence should be the dependent clause and which should be the main clause?

The answer depends on which clause the author considers more important. *The most important information should always go in the main clause.*

Two of the possibilities are printed below.

Sentences combined — emphasis on Little League team

Carlos Ramirez, who owns his own grocery business, sponsors a Little League team for the neighborhood children.

OR

Sentences combined — emphasis on grocery store business

Carlos Ramirez, who sponsors a Little League team for the neighborhood children, owns his own grocery business.

Though these sentences contain the same information, they emphasize different ideas. Be careful to put the idea you consider most important in the main clause of the sentences you create.

Exercise 7

Combining Sentences to Create Dependent Clauses

Combine each of the following into a sentence containing at least one dependent clause.

Make sure that your new sentences are punctuated correctly.

1. Dana had a bad dream last week. She has not slept well since.

_____

_____

_____

2. The game is not going well. Our team is losing a lot more slowly than usual.

_____

_____

_____

3. The new police promotion list mentions Sergeant Farrarro. He worked with the Sno Kings youth gang.

_____

_____

_____

4. The new group of colors is used in this cosmetic. They have been developed by Westlake Laboratories. We believe that they are absolutely nontoxic to the skin.

_____

_____

_____

5. The Punic Wars were eventually won by the Romans. The reason is that the Romans had better generals.

_____

_____

_____

Chapter Review

In this chapter you learned that

1. **Dependent clauses** are clauses that act as adjectives, adverbs, or nouns.

2. Dependent clauses always contain a **subject and verb**.

3. Dependent clauses always begin with a **tip-off word** that connects the clause to the rest of the sentence.

4. **Normal position** for adjective and adverb clauses is after the words they describe.

5. **The Interrupter Rule** says that you should punctuate any sentence interrupter by separating it from the rest of the sentence with commas.

6. **Punctuate** the following according to the Interrupter Rule:
   a. **Adjective clauses** containing "extra" information
   b. **Adverb clauses** that are **out of normal position**, especially introductory adverb clauses
   c. **Adverb clauses** that start with words like *although*

187 Using dependent clauses

7. **"Extra" information** is adjective information that is not needed to
   a. **Identify** the word it describes, or
   b. **Narrow down** a larger group to a smaller one

8. **Noun clauses** do not receive special punctuation.

In the RELATED SKILL section you learned about *who* and *whom* as tip-off words.

1. Use *who* when the tip-off word is the **subject** of the verb in the dependent clause.

2. Use *whom* when the tip-off word is an **object** within the dependent clause.

Review Exercise 1

Mark each sentence in the following paragraphs completely.

Often the old thinkers knew what they were talking about. One of the early Greeks thought that the world was made of super-small particles. The "atom" was the name that he gave to one of these particles. Another Greek thinker had an even more radical idea. People who disagree should seek truth before victory. Both of these ideas were originally rejected by those who heard them. Today they are widely held.

When these great men lived, the world was younger, fewer ideas were written down, and few people remembered the thoughts of previous generations. Those early thinkers were guided only by their own ideas. Today the history of thought lies before us. When we don't know whether an idea is true, we can read what others have said or written about it. Because the early philosophers started with less, their accomplishments are greater than ours. Our ideas may be more developed, but the early thinkers had those ideas first.

Review Exercise 2

Correct any incorrect punctuation in the following paragraph. NOTE: The only errors in this exercise involve dependent clauses.

After the smoke cleared. Luke looked at the floor around him. He could not believe, what had happened. Idle smoke drifted from a long gun, that now lay hot against his leg. The men who murdered his wife lay dead. Luke's reactions were faster. Than his thoughts. When the words were spoken his hand had already moved. Sheriff Granger whose ears were good even if his mind was weak would no doubt walk in shortly.

Review Exercise 3

The following paragraph is composed mainly of simple sentences. Use sentence combining and editing to **create some sentences with two main clauses** and **some sentences with a main clause and a dependent clause**.

I want to tell you about something that happens. It happens a lot lately. I imagine my father. At those times I see him as a boy of nine. What I mean is he is standing on a dark spot in this flat Illinois land. He is near a railroad crossing. It is night. It is hot. Summer here is dreadful and windless. The air clots and settles close to the ground. Also the sky floats farther away than at other times of the year. The sky is smeared thick with stars. It is baseball season.

_____

_____

_____

_____

_____

Chapter 7 Writing Assignment

Write a paragraph that explains in a step-by-step way how something is done. Your subject this time is **how to be a bad roommate**. Include several dependent clauses in your paragraph.

When you have made your final copy

1. **Mark each verb, subject, object**, and **complement** of each *main* clause. (You do not have to mark any dependent clauses.)

2. Make sure that

   a. All **main clauses** are correctly joined or separated.
   b. All **dependent clauses** are correctly punctuated.

Hints for Writing Process Paragraphs

This paragraph, like the last one, should be interesting if you write honestly about what you know to be true. Take time in the planning stage to gather good material. Your paragraph will have its best chance of success if you do.

Before the rough draft:

1. Make a preliminary list of the steps you think make up this process.

2. Now edit this list — add steps, take steps out, change the order of what you have written — so that its final form represents your best thoughts on this subject. (Your paragraph will be more interesting if you give good time to this step.)

3. Recopy your list of steps and add a good example for each step.

Writing the rough draft:

1. Start your rough draft by writing a sentence or two that tell what the process is and why you are going to write about it.

2. Then discuss each item on your list one by one. Start your first step with a word or phrase like *first*.

3. Briefly discuss your example for each step.

4. Write a closing sentence that tells how successful the reader will be if he or she follows your advice.

After the rough draft:

1. Do your best to correct any errors on this first copy. Be especially careful to correct all errors in the punctuation of main clauses.

2. Make any other changes you think will make your paragraph more interesting and readable.

3. Recopy your corrected paragraph on a clean sheet of paper and turn in all of your work.

U N I T
III

Two complex phrases

The chapters in this unit will show you how to use and punctuate two common, but complex, phrases. These phrases have rather technical names. They are

Verbal phrases

Appositive phrases

Because both kinds of phrases present students with important punctuation problems, we will take a little time to show them to you.

Chapter 8 will show you how to find verbals and verbal phrases in sentences. Chapter 9 will show you how verbal phrases are punctuated. Chapter 10 will show you how to find and punctuate appositives and appositive phrases.

8
Using verbals and verbal phrases

Chapter Preview

This chapter will show you how to find **verbals** and **verbal phrases** in sentences.

As the name implies, **verbals** are related to verbs. Verbals are NOT verbs, but they are made from verbs. *Running* is an example of a verbal. *Running,* in itself, is NOT a verb, but it is made from the verb *run.*

Verbal phrases are built around verbals. *Running to the store,* for example, is a verbal phrase.

Verbal phrases are quite common. They can be used as nouns (that is, as subjects, objects, and complements), as adjectives, and as adverbs. When verbal phrases are used as adjectives and adverbs, they are often punctuated in a special way.

VERBALS

Verbals are NOT verbs, but they are made from verbs. There are three kinds of verbals:

1. **-*Ing* words,** like *seeing*

2. **Infinitives,** like *to see*

3. **Past participles,** like *seen*

Verbals cannot be verbs by themselves. The following sentences, for example, are incorrect because they contain no verb:

> **Incorrect**
>
> I **seeing** the ball.
>
> I **to see** the ball.
>
> I **seen** the ball.

Verbals, like *seeing,* cannot be verbs by themselves. But verbals can be used in a variety of other ways, as you will soon see.

Let's look more closely at the three kinds of verbals and the phrases built around them. We will start with -*ing* words.

-*ING* WORDS

-*Ing* words are made by adding -*ing* to words like *run, see, go, play, read,* and the like. The following are examples of -*ing* words.

Verb	-*Ing* word
run	running
see	seeing
go	going
play	playing
read	reading

Sometimes the final letter of the verb is doubled or a final *e* is dropped. (For rules on spelling *-ing* words, see Chapter 18.)

-Ing words are sometimes called **present participles** (when used as adjectives) or **gerunds** (when used as nouns). We will call them simply *-ing* words, however.

Uses of *-Ing* Words

-Ing words are very common in writing. They can be used as

> Nouns
> Adjectives
> Adverbs

Let's look at some examples.

-Ing words as nouns

Dancing is fun.

Subject question:	*What* is (fun)?
Answer:	*Dancing*

Dancing (is) fun.

My sister likes **dancing**.

Object question:	Likes *what?*
Answer:	*Dancing*

My sister (likes) **dancing**.

-Ing words as adjectives

My sister's **dancing** teacher lives in Oakland.

Adjective question:	*What kind of teacher?*
Answer:	*Dancing* teacher

My sister's **dancing** teacher (lives) (in Oakland.)

-*Ing* words as adverbs

She spends her weekends **dancing**.

Adverb question: Spends *how?*
Answer: *Dancing*

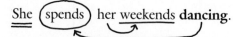

She (spends) her weekends **dancing**.

-*Ing* words can also be used with helping verbs to make verb phrases. You have seen this many times in previous chapters.

-*Ing* words in verb phrases

My sister is **dancing** in the chorus.

My sister (is dancing) (in the chorus.)

None of these uses should surprise you. You have encountered many -*ing* words in previous chapters. As you have seen, the subject, object, adjective, and adverb questions will help you see how -*ing* words are used.

The exercise below will help you find -*ing* words in simple sentences. If you can find -*ing* words, you can find and punctuate -*ing* phrases. Remember that punctuating -*ing* phrases is one of our goals in this unit.

Exercise 1

-*Ing* Words

A. **Mark the following sentences completely.** (To help you, the -*ing* words are printed in **boldface**.)

example

Johnnie (got) a **running** start.

1. Alan has been **fighting** again.

2. **Gossiping** is common among my relatives.

3. Good base **running** is the mark of an experienced baseball player.

4. **Matchmaking** is Fecundia's second favorite hobby.

5. Pine Coastal Community College is still **offering** scholarships.

6. Her first love is still **swimming.**

7. Pablo is still **taking dancing** classes.

8. This watch needs **winding**.

9. Good **reading** builds good minds.

10. Good **reading** skills build good minds.

B. **Mark the following sentences completely**. (The *-ing* words are not printed in boldface.)

1. Theodore does the washing on Thursdays.

2. Another nonworking copier was installed in Accounting.

3. Sometimes breathing is difficult for Mrs. Nanchez.

4. She has a lingering disease.

5. Politicking is a growth industry in this department.

6. Mr. Perez is running for city councilman.

7. Biron was found sleeping.

8. Alice is hiking regularly.

9. Hiking always interested Alice.

10. Alice was always interested in hiking.

-ING PHRASES

Now let's take a look at some verbal phrases — phrases built around verbals. The first kind of verbal phrase is the *-ing* phrase. *-Ing* phrases are common in sentences.

NOTE: *Verbal* phrases are not *verb* phrases. Though the names are similar, these two should not be confused. Verbals can never be verbs, and verbal phrases can never be verb phrases.

Structure of Verbal Phrases

A **verbal phrase** is a verbal + any words connected to it. What words can be connected to verbals?

1. Verbals can be described by **adverbs**.

Example: Running *slowly*

Adverb question: Running *how?*
Answer: *Slowly*

2. Verbals from action verbs can have **objects**.

Example: Running the *store*

Object
question: Running *what?*
Answer
(one word):   *Store*

3. Verbals from linking verbs can have **complements**.

Example: Being a *father*

Object
question: Being *what?*
Answer
(one word):   *Father*

The diagram below may help you picture verbal phrases.

VERBAL	—	**Object** or
(-*Ing* word)		**Complement**
|		|
Adverbs		Adjectives

The following verbal phrase, for example, has both an object and an adverb. (The verbal is printed in **boldface** type.)

running the store efficiently

Object
question: Running *what?*   *Store*
Adverb
question: Running *how?*   *Efficiently*

Notice that the verbal is always the key word in a verbal phrase. The verbal doesn't describe other words in the phrase — other words describe it, complete it, or receive its action.

For comparison, look at the following phrase. It is NOT a verbal phrase, even though it contains a verbal.

NOT a verbal phrase

the running water

This is not a verbal phrase because the verbal, *running,* is not the key word in this phrase.

the running water

The key word is *water. Running* is an adjective describing it.

Notice that because prepositional phrases act as adjectives and adverbs, prepositional phrases can appear within verbal phrases.

looking **in the library**

Adverb		
question:	*Looking where?*	
Answer:	*In the library*	

Here the phrase *in the library* describes *looking*. Therefore, it is part of the verbal phrase.

The following exercise will help you recognize *-ing* phrases. Remember that an *-ing* phrase is an *-ing* word + any words connected to it.

Exercise 2

Recognizing *-Ing* Phrases

Tell which of the following are *-ing* verbal phrases and which are not by writing **YES** or **NO** on the line. Then place **square brackets** [   ] around each verbal phrase.

examples

____YES____ [Writing the paper on time]

____NO____ Another writing assignment

_____ 1. Answering letters

_____ 2. The basketball court

_____ 3. At the basketball court

_____ 4. Playing at the basketball court

_____ 5. A skiing instructor

_____ 6. Skiing with the instructor

_____ 7. Playing tennis this afternoon

_____ 8. A playing child

_____ 9. Watching the game

_____ 10. Finding the answers

_____ 11. A jogging book

_____ 12. A book on jogging

_____ 13. Jogging in the morning with my wife

_____ 14. Yesterday

_____ 15. Smiling proudly

_____ 16. Drawing incorrect conclusions

201 Using verbals and verbal phrases

_____ **17.** Painting the bathroom

_____ **18.** Another excellent painting

_____ **19.** Working at the bank

_____ **20.** A good working arrangement

-Ing Phrases in Sentences

Now let's look at how *-ing* phrases are used in sentences. Like *-ing* words, *-ing* phrases can be

> Nouns (subjects, objects, and complements)
> Adjectives
> Adverbs

-Ing Phrases as Nouns

-Ing phrases can be used as nouns. This means they can be subjects, objects, and complements. Once you find the *-ing* phrases in a sentence, the subject and object questions will show you which ones are used as subjects, objects, and complements.

Here are some examples of these uses, first with simple *-ing* words, and then with phrases based on these words.

Subject

Dancing is fun.

Dancing at the Zig-Zag Club is fun.

Object

My sister likes **dancing**.

My sister likes **dancing on weekends**.

Marking *-ing* Phrases

-Ing phrases are marked with

1. **Square brackets** [   ] to group the phrase
2. An **underline** or **arrow** to show what the phrase does in the sentence.

As always, we will not mark smaller phrases within larger ones. We are interested in the verbal phrase itself, not the smaller phrases it contains.

202 Two complex phrases

Any word or phrase connected to the verbal is part of the verbal phrase and should be bracketed with the verbal phrase.

$$\Big[\text{Looking in the library}\Big]$$

Here are some marked sentences containing *-ing* words and phrases used as nouns.

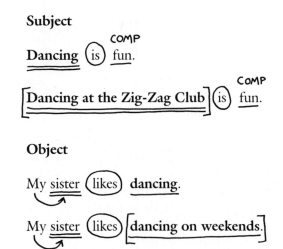

Subject

Dancing ⟨is⟩ fun. `COMP`

[Dancing at the Zig-Zag Club] ⟨is⟩ fun. `COMP`

Object

My sister ⟨likes⟩ dancing.

My sister ⟨likes⟩ [dancing on weekends.]

While *-ing* phrases can also be used as nouns in other ways (for example, as objects of prepositions and subjects inside dependent clauses), studying these uses will take us beyond what we want to do in this unit.

If you learn to recognize those phrases that act as subjects, objects, adjectives, and adverbs, you will be well prepared for the punctuation lessons that follow.

-Ing Phrases as Adjectives and Adverbs

-Ing phrases are often used as adjectives and adverbs. Once you find the *-ing* phrases in a sentence, the adjective and adverb questions will show you which ones are used in these ways.

The following sentence contains an *-ing* phrase used as an adjective describing the subject.

-Ing phrase as adjective

My sister, **dancing in the chorus**, was noticed by Mr. Birnbock.

Adjective question: *Which* (or *what kind of*) sister?
Answer: *Dancing in the chorus*

My sister, [dancing in the chorus,] ⟨was noticed⟩ ⟨by Mr. Birnbock.⟩

The next example contains an *-ing* phrase used as an adverb to describe the verb.

-*Ing* phrase as adverb

My sister spends her weekends **dancing in the chorus**.

Adverb
question: Spends *how?*
Answer: *Dancing in the chorus*

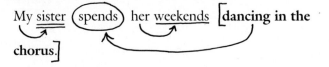

Marking Sentences Completely

We can now revise our recommended order for marking sentences to include verbal phrases.

Because verbal phrases contain words that can be confused for the verb of the sentence, we recommend that you now mark them before looking for the main verb of the sentence.

Sentence Marking Order (Revised)

1. **Group dependent clauses** with long brackets.

2. **Group remaining verbal phrases** with square brackets.

3. **Group remaining prepositional phrases** with parentheses.

4. Mark the **verb**, **subject**, and **object** or **complement**.

5. Starting at the beginning of the sentence, draw **arrows** to show what each adjective and adverb word or phrase describes.

Exercise 3

Finding *-Ing* Phrases

Mark each of the following sentences completely. Do not mark phrases within other phrases. (To help you, the *-ing* phrases have been printed in **boldface** type and the exercise has been divided into two sections, one containing *-ing* phrases that function as nouns, the other as adjectives and adverbs.

example

[**Returning to the base**] (was) an adventure.
                                    COMP

Nouns

1. **Smoking cigarettes** could damage her health.

2. I do not enjoy **doing housework**.

3. **Studying harder** is a large part of Jason's game plan.

4. The subject of this chapter is **finding verbal phrases**.

Adjectives and Adverbs

5. Senator Black, **answering all questions**, eventually spoke about the rumors of his bad health.

6. Martin spent three years **searching for his mother**.

7. The alarm unit **protecting the house** was damaged in the storm.

8. **Written at the last minute**, the story had to be revised.

9. She works at Anderson Mills **answering sales letters**.

10. Jim discovered the dog **rummaging through the garbage can**.

11. The rest of their friends arrived **wearing Captain Kirk masks**.

12. General Abrams spends his evenings **playing with his children**.

Exercise 4

Finding *-Ing* Phrases

Mark each of the following sentences completely. Do not mark phrases within other phrases. (In this exercise, the *-ing* phrases have NOT been printed in boldface type.)

1. Playing football could lead to serious injuries.

2. Playing football, Jackie injured his left shoulder.

3. Nature enjoys disobeying the rules.

4. Dr. Blitzkrieg was found raiding the refrigerator.

5. My roommate usually eats standing up.

INFINITIVES AND INFINITIVE PHRASES

Infinitives are made by adding the word *to* to the present tense form. The present tense form includes words like *run, see, go, play, read,* and the like. (Present tense verbs are discussed in Chapter 11.)

Verb	Infinitive
run	to run
see	to see
go	to go
play	to play
read	to read

Verb phrases starting with *have* and *be* also have infinitive forms.

Verb	Infinitive
have run	to have run
be seeing	to be seeing

Notice that these infinitives also start with the word *to*.

NOTE: Infinitives are not verbs; and can never be part of a verb phrase.

Infinitive Phrases

Phrases can be built around infinitives just as they can around *-ing* words. An **infinitive phrase**, like any verbal phrase, includes the infinitive + any words or phrases connected to it.

1. Infinitives can be described by **adverbs**.

Example: To run *slowly*

Adverb question: To run *how?*
Answer: *Slowly*

2. Infinitive forms of action verbs can have **objects**.

Example: To run the *store*

Object question: To run *what?*
Answer (one word):   *Store*

3. Infinitive forms of linking verbs can have **complements**.

Example: To be a *father*

**Object
question:** To be *what?*
**Answer
(one word):** *Father*

The diagram below may help you picture infinitive and other verbal phrases.

$$\text{VERBAL} — \text{Object or}$$

VERBAL — **Object** or
(Infinitive) **Complement**
| |
Adverbs Adjectives

Uses of Infinitives and Infinitive Phrases

Infinitives and infinitive phrases, just like *-ing* words and phrases, can be used as

Nouns

Adjectives

Adverbs

Let's look at some examples, first with simple infinitives, and then with infinitive phrases.

Subjects

To dance is her desire.

**Subject
question:** *What* is (her desire)?
Answer: *To dance*

To dance in the chorus is her desire.

**Subject
question:** *What* is (her desire)?
Answer: *To dance in the chorus*

Objects

My sister likes **to dance.**

**Object
question:** Likes *what?*
Answer: *To dance*

My sister likes **to dance on stage**.

**Object
question:** Likes *what?*
Answer: *To dance on stage*

Adjectives

A desire **to dance** drove my sister to the stage.

**Adjective
question:** *What kind of* desire?
Answer: A desire *to dance*

A desire **to dance in the chorus** drove my sister to the stage.

**Adjective
question:** *What kind of* desire?
Answer: A desire *to dance in the chorus*

Adverbs

My brother lives **to eat**.

**Adverb
question:** Lives *why?*
Answer: *To eat*

My brother lives **to eat hamburgers with mayonnaise**.

**Adverb
question:** Lives *why?*
Answer: *To eat hamburgers with mayonnaise*

Marking Infinitives

Mark both infinitives and infinitive phrases like other verbal phrases — with

1. **Square brackets [   ]** to group the phrase
2. An **underline** or **arrow** to show what the phrase does in the sentence.

Once more, we will not mark smaller phrases within larger ones. We are interested in the verbal phrase itself, not the smaller phrases it contains.

Subjects

Objects

Adjectives

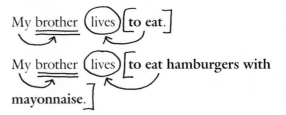

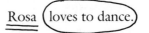

Adverbs

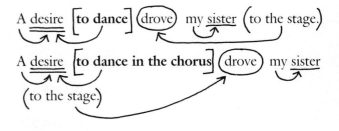

Infinitives and Verb Phrases

Infinitives are not verbs. Notice that an infinitive can never be part of a verb phrase since *to* is not a helping verb. In sentences like the following, the infinitive is almost always an object or a complement.

NOT

Rosa (loves to dance.)

Ought is a common verb with infinitives. (*Ought* is not a helping verb, but the old past tense of the verb *owe*. The new past tense is *owed*.)

Miguel (ought) [to relax.]

The following exercises will help you find infinitives and infinitive phrases. Use the sentence marking order on page 204 to guide you.

Exercise 5

Finding Infinitives and Infinitive Phrases

Mark the following sentences completely. Do not mark phrases within other phrases. (To help you, the infinitives and infinitive phrases have been printed in **boldface** type and the exercise has been divided into two sections, one containing *-ing* phrases that function as nouns, the other as adjectives and adverbs.

Be prepared to tell which question each infinitive phrase answers.

example

Congress (acted) [to prevent war] .

Nouns

1. The checkbook refuses **to balance**.

2. Fatilda likes **to laugh**.

3. I wanted **to be seen**.

4. Robin prefers **to play**.

5. Aram will try **to arrange for a loan**.

6. **To answer the mail** takes too much time.

Adjectives and Adverbs

7. Meta has no desire **to get married**.

8. The need **to work** overwhelmed Barry.

9. It is good **to travel**.

10. She soon found the will **to continue**.

11. Christie went on vacation **to rest**.

12. The computer was bought **to help the secretarial staff with word processing**.

13. **To breathe easier**, she took several more pills.

14. Donna sings **to express her love of beauty**.

15. The need **to love** lives in all of us.

Exercise 6

Finding Infinitives and Infinitive Phrases

Mark each of the following sentences completely. Do not mark phrases within other phrases. (In this exercise, the verbal phrases have not been printed in boldface type.)

Be prepared to tell which question each infinitive phrase answers.

1. She refused to give up.

2. She refused to give up her place in line.

3. To eat is to live.

4. Dr. Rosario ought to enroll.

5. Henri's plan is to investigate.

6. Karin wants to travel.

7. The boss wanted to leave early today.

8. To ride the bus costs seventy-five cents now.

9. The outside of the house really needs to be painted.

10. Ben prefers to eat rare meat.

BONUS. One way to relax is to meditate.

PAST PARTICIPLES AND PAST PARTICIPLE PHRASES

Past participles are the last type of verbal we will study. They are made in a variety of ways. The most common is to add *-ed* or *-d* to the present tense form. The present tense form includes words like *run, see, go, play, read,* and the like. (Present tense verbs are discussed in Chapter 11.)

Verbs that add *-ed* or *-d* to make the past tense and past participle are called **regular verbs**. For example:

Verb	Past Tense	Past Participle
accept	accepted	accepted
amuse	amused	amused
ask	asked	asked
awaken	awakened	awakened
arrange	arranged	arranged
calculate	calculated	calculated
dance	danced	danced
displease	displeased	displeased
edit	edited	edited
elect	elected	elected
farm	farmed	farmed
hire	hired	hired
injure	injured	injured
like	liked	liked
look	looked	looked
organize	organized	organized

Verb	Past Tense	Past Participle
pass	passed	passed
petrify	petrified	petrified
plan	planned	planned
play	played	played
record	recorded	recorded
revise	revised	revised
seal	sealed	sealed
treat	treated	treated
wreck	wrecked	wrecked

Regular verbs are discussed in greater detail in Chapter 12.

The following shows past tense and past participle forms of many common irregular verbs. **Irregular verbs** make the past tense and the past participle in a variety of ways. For example:

Verb	Past Tense	Past Participle
become	became	become
buy	bought	bought
drink	drank	drunk
find	found	found
hurt	hurt	hurt
run	ran	run
see	saw	seen
send	sent	sent
sing	sang	sung
stand	stood	stood
stick	stuck	stuck
swear	swore	sworn
swing	swang	swung
teach	taught	taught
write	wrote	written

Irregular verbs are discussed in greater detail in Chapter 13. Use both of the lists above while doing exercises in this chapter.

Past Participle Phrases

Phrases can be built around past participles just as they can around *-ing* words. A **past participle phrase**, like any verbal phrase, includes the past participle + any words or phrases connected to it.

Unlike other verbal phrases, past participle phrases contain only past participles and adverbs. (Because they show an action being received, past participles don't have objects or complements.)

Past participle phrases

Sent **slowly**

Adverb question:	Sent *how?*
Answer:	*Slowly*

Seen **last night**

Adverb question:	Seen *when?*
Answer:	*Last night*

Uses of Past Participles and Past Participle Phrases

Past participles, like *-ing* words, can be used as nouns, adjectives, and adverbs.

Past participle as subject

The **deceased** lived in this town.

Subject question:	*Who* lived?
Answer:	*Deceased*

Past participle as object

We saw three **drunks** on Twelfth Street.

Object question:	Saw *who?*
Answer:	*Drunks*

Past participle as adjective

These **frozen** dinners are almost edible.

Adjective question:	*What kind of* dinner?
Answer:	*Frozen*

Past participle as adverb

These dinners were served **frozen**.

Adverb question:	Were served *how?*
Answer:	*Frozen*

213 Using verbals and verbal phrases

In addition, past participles can also be used with helping verbs to make verb phrases. You have seen this many times in previous chapters.

Past participles in verb phrases

She was **seen** by Mr. Birnbock.

Keep in mind, though, that past participles, like all verbals, are NOT verbs and cannot be used by themselves as verbs.

Most past participle phrases are used as **adjectives**, though some are used as **adverbs**.

Past participle phrase as adjective

These dinners, **frozen since January**, are almost edible.

**Adjective
question:** *What kind of* dinners?
Answer: *Frozen since January.*

Past participle as adverb

Many people live **frozen into unhappy jobs.**

**Adverb
question:** Live *how?*
Answer: *Frozen into unhappy jobs.*

Marking Past Participle Phrases

Mark past participle phrases like other verbal phrases — with

1. **Square brackets** [   ] to group the phrase
2. An **underline** or **arrow** to show what the phrase does in the sentence.

Once again, we will not mark phrases within other phrases.

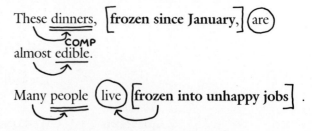

The following exercise will help you find past participles and past participle phrases. Use the sentence marking order on page 204 to guide you.

Exercise 7

Past Participles and Past Participle Phrases

A. Mark the following sentences completely. (To help you, the past participles are printed in **boldface**.)

example

The trip, [**planned** yesterday,] (was **postponed**) (until tomorrow.)

1. Three **drunks** emerged **unhurt** from the **wrecked** car.

2. Her **sworn** statement was **recorded** by the police.

3. The **injured** were **treated** at Bessemer Hospital.

4. **Written at the last minute**, the story was later **revised**.

5. He found a dollar **stuck to the floor of the cafeteria**.

B. Mark the following sentences completely. (The past participles are NOT printed in boldface.)

1. He examined the statue found at the Indian burial site.

2. Mrs. Corvallis, amused by his sense of humor, accepted his invitation to lunch.

3. Displeased with her low scores, Bennie asked for a tutor.

4. At this school honesty is an accepted practice.

5. The mine shaft was sealed by the engineers hired by Ms. White.

Exercise 8

Finding Verbal Phrases in Paragraphs

Mark each sentence of the following paragraphs completely. Do not mark phrases within other phrases.

Running breathlessly through the light rain, Arlene Laboheme turned right at the Katz Diner sign and fled into the alley. A distant streetlight revealed a ragged brick surface and dozens of trash cans overflowing with restaurant rubbish. Arlene covered her nose to avoid the rising smell of rotting leftovers. Then rushing forward, she hid behind a large pile of boxes.

Footsteps slapped against the pavement in the street ahead of her. They approached, grew louder, and then stopped. Arlene heard speech, muffled by the distance and the rain. The footsteps retreated, and she breathed deeply again. Arlene wondered when she would be free of these men and their questions. Avoiding them was becoming a full-time job. Perhaps it was time to do something.

A wicked plan began forming in Arlene's mind. Arlene began to smile.

Chapter Review

In this chapter you learned that

1. A **verbal** is a word made from a verb.

2. The three **types of verbals** are
   a. **-Ing words,** like *seeing*
   b. **Infinitives,** like *to see*
   c. **Past participles,** like *seen*

3. **Verbals** can be used as
   a. **Nouns**
   b. **Adjectives**
   c. **Adverbs**

4. In addition, **-Ing words** and **past participles** can be used in **verb phrases.**

5. Verbal phrases
   = VERBAL + adverbs + objects (and adjectives)

6. The **object and adverb questions** will find objects and adverbs within verbal phrases.

7. **Verbal phrases** can be used as
   a. **Nouns**
   b. **Adjectives**
   c. **Adverbs**

Review Exercise 1

Write the verbal forms of the following verbs. If necessary, use the list of principal parts in the Appendix to help you.

example

	-Ing word	Infinitive	Past Participle
write	*writing*	*to write*	*written*

1. sing _____ _____ _____

2. arrange _____ _____ _____

3. see _____ _____ _____

4. run _____ _____ _____

5. plan _____ _____ _____

6. elect _____ _____ _____

7. stand _____ _____ _____

8. farm _____ _____ _____

9. pass _____ _____ _____

10. buy _____ _____ _____

11. teach _____ _____ _____

12. awaken _____ _____ _____

13. find _____ _____ _____

14. edit _____ _____ _____

15. calculate _____ _____ _____

16. petrify _____ _____ _____

17. swing _____ _____ _____

18. dance _____ _____ _____

19. organize _____ _____ _____

20. become _____ _____ _____

Review Exercise 2

Mark each of the following sentences completely.

example

This page, typewritten on a Smith Corona, was identified by Mr. Chan.

217 Using verbals and verbal phrases

1. Professor Sanchez, visiting from Mexico, spoke to our Spanish class.

2. To be a better linebacker, Roger is lifting weights.

3. The spaghetti, frozen to the screen door, looks like bad art from Andy Warhol's gastric period.

4. We could not stop Mr. Lin from chasing her into the street.

5. Alan found happiness writing speech textbooks.

6. Tsin stepped carefully up the worn stairs.

7. She gave the check to her singing coach yesterday.

8. I hope to do better on this test.

9. The new snow, melting in the streets and sidewalks, reminds me of my youth.

10. Earning this scholarship helped to keep me in school.

11. The clicking of the starter motor was the first sign of trouble.

12. Laretha had a strong urge to answer that smart remark.

13. The struggle, prolonged for many years, finally ended in an ineffective truce.

14. Socialists roamed the land looking for easy recruits.

15. They finally found him digging for gold in Utah.

16. The short book was split between the readers in equal portions.

17. Neither man could bear to look.

18. Alberta let her hair down at last.

19. Standing in the open doorway, Stuart looked in shock at the destruction in the front yard.

20. No one saw the plane flying in through the fog.

Review Exercise 3

This well-written paragraph contains sentences that are more complicated than many you have seen so far. Nevertheless, they use only the elements you have already studied.

For that reason, this exercise is a good review of sentence structure. If you can mark these sentences correctly, you have learned enough to analyze the structure of any sentence you will normally encounter in college work — your own or anyone else's.

Mark each sentence in this paragraph completely. Work slowly and carefully, and do your best. When you are finished, check your work.

NOTE: The last sentence contains missing words, marked by three dots. Mark this sentence as though the dots were not there.

Much good has come into American life since my childhood that makes things easier and nicer for almost everybody, but much has also been lost, and the shabby substitutes have deprived us of good and modest pleasures. It seems to me, to name a simple few, we are less for the loss of the climbing sweet pea, the elm tree, and jogging in place could be a violation of the pleasure of walking in the woods or just walking downtown.

A major loss in American life . . . is the boarding house, completely replaced now by the ugly, cold motel.[1]

[1]From *Memoir of a New Orleans Boarding House* by Lillian Hellman, From *The NY Times*, May 21, 1980.

Chapter 8 Writing Assignment

Write a paragraph that explains in a step-by-step way how something is done. Your subject this time is **how to succeed in school if you have a full-time job.** Include several examples of verbal phrases in your paragraph.

When you have made your final copy

1. **Mark the verb, subject, object, and complement** of each *main* clause. (You do not have to mark any dependent clauses.)

2. Place square brackets around each **verbal** phrase.

3. Finally, make sure that
   a. All **main clauses** are correctly joined or separated.
   b. All **dependent clauses** are correctly punctuated.

Hints for Writing Process Paragraphs

This paragraph deals with an important problem, one that many students face. Your writing will be most interesting if your advice is good and useful. Take time in the planning stage to make sure this is so, and your paragraph will have its best chance of success.

Before the rough draft:

1. Make a preliminary list of the steps you think make up this process.

2. Now edit this list — add steps, take steps out, change the order of what you have written — so that its final form represents your best thoughts on this subject. (Your paragraph will be more interesting if you do not rush through this step.)

3. Recopy your list of steps and add a good example for each step.

Writing the rough draft:

1. Start your rough draft by writing a sentence or two that tells what the process is and why you are going to write about it.

2. Then discuss each item on your list one by one. Start your first step with a word or phrase like *first*.

3. Briefly discuss your example for each step.

4. Write a closing sentence that tells how successful the reader will be if he or she follows your advice.

After the rough draft:

1. Do your best to correct any errors on this first copy. Be especially careful to correct all errors in the punctuation of main clauses.

2. Make any other changes you think will make your paragraph more interesting and readable.

3. Recopy your corrected paragraph on a clean sheet of paper and turn in all of your work.

c h a p t e r

9

Punctuating verbal phrases

Chapter Preview

This chapter will show you

1. When to **punctuate verbal phrases** in sentences.

2. How to apply the **Interrupter Rule.**

In addition, a special RELATED SKILL section will help you avoid an error called **"dangling phrases."**

PUNCTUATING DESCRIPTIVE VERBAL PHRASES

As you saw in the last chapter, verbal phrases can be used as nouns, adjectives, and adverbs.

Verbal phrases used as nouns (that is, as subjects, objects, and complements) require no special punctuation. But **descriptive verbal phrases** often do.

Descriptive phrases are those used as adjectives and adverbs. They are called "descriptive phrases" because they describe nouns, pronouns, and verbs. Descriptive verbal phrases are not part of the core of the sentence — the subject – verb – object.

SUBJECT	—	VERB	—	Object
Adjectives		**Adverbs**		**Adjectives**
(descriptive verbal phrases)		(descriptive verbal phrases)		(descriptive verbal phrases)

Like descriptive dependent clauses, descriptive verbal phrases are sometimes separated from the rest of the sentence with commas according to the Interrupter Rule, and sometimes they are not.

The Interrupter Rule

Punctuate any sentence interrupter by separating it from the rest of the sentence with commas.

Interrupter, ******************************** .

************** , interrupter, ************** .

******************************** , interrupter.

When to apply the Interrupter Rule depends on two things.

1. The position of the phrase in the sentence

2. The kind of information the phrase contains

Either of these conditions can cause the Interrupter Rule to be applied.

Punctuating Verbal Phrases by Position

The normal position of adjective verbal phrases is following the nouns or pronouns they describe, as shown in the following diagram.

Normal Position of Adjective Phrases

Adjective – NOUN – Prepositional phrase – **Verbal phrase**

The following sentence, for example, contains all of these elements.

The woman (in the blue dress) [using the copy
machine] (smiled.)

Notice that the adjective phrases are listed with the verbal phrase last.
Adverb verbal phrases are usually found after the main clause whose verb they describe, as the following chart shows.

Normal Position of Adverb Phrases

VERB – Adverb – Prepositional phrase – **Verbal phrase**

The following shows all of these elements.

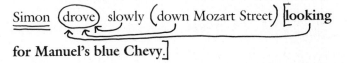

Simon (drove) slowly (down Mozart Street) [looking
for Manuel's blue Chevy.]

When adjective and adverb verbal phrases are moved to other positions in the sentence, the Interrupter Rule is applied.

Punctuating Verbal Phrases by Position

Any verbal phrase that is *out of normal position* should be separated from the rest of the sentence with commas.

The most common place for out-of-position verbal phrases is at the beginning of the sentence ("introductory position"). **Introductory verbal phrases** are always set off by commas. Both adjective and adverb phrases can appear in introductory position.

The following sentence contains an introductory verbal phrase. In this case the verbal is an infinitive.

Introductory verbal phrase

To finish the project on time, Mrs. Washington has been working late.

The phrase *to finish the project on time* describes the verb *has been working*. It is an adverb phrase out of its normal position.

Introductory verbal phrase — COMMA NEEDED

To finish the project on time, Mrs. Washington has been working late.

COMMA

Interrupter, ******************************* .

Notice that verbal phrases used as nouns are not descriptive. Therefore, they are not punctuated as interrupters, even when they begin a sentence. Compare these sentences.

To work as a nurse was Selma's only desire.

To work as a nurse, Selma sacrificed for many years.

The first sentence contains a verbal phrase used as a subject. The second contains an introductory verbal phrase used as an adverb.

Verbal phrase as subject

Descriptive verbal phrase

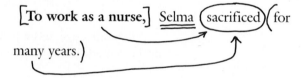

The first sentence requires no punctuation; we do not normally place commas between the subject and the verb.

Verbal phrase as subject — NO COMMA

To work as a nurse was Selma's only desire.

NO COMMA

The second sentence, on the other hand, needs a comma between the introductory verbal phrase and the rest of the sentence.

Descriptive verbal phrase — COMMA NEEDED

To work as a nurse, Selma sacrificed for many years.

COMMA

Watch for these situations in the exercises that follow and in your own writing.

Exercise 1

Punctuating Introductory Verbal Phrases

A. All of the verbal phrases in the following sentences are printed in **boldface** type. Some are descriptive verbal phrases, and some are not.

1. Draw an **arrow** from each descriptive verbal phrase to the word it describes.

2. Then supply **commas** to punctuate introductory verbal phrases.

3. If a sentence needs no additional punctuation, write **OK** in the margin.

example

To rescue the children, we cut several holes in the roof of

the building.

1. She imagined Rosemary **arriving at the station**.

2. **To see her brother this summer** Debra will have to go to the farm.

3. **Hoping to be considered for a promotion** Martin has registered in

night courses at Penwicker College.

4. A man **answering that description** works at the restaurant.

5. **Stuck in the elevator** Professor Fowler used the time to

grade papers.

6. **Looking at his hand** the boy noticed a small paper cut.

7. **Finding all that money** was just luck.

8. **Getting help from the French artillery** General Washington

launched his assault against Yorktown.

9. We watched Lisa's balloon **rising through the clouds.**

10. **To buy the farm** my family borrowed from three banks.

B. The verbal phrases in the following sentences are NOT printed in boldface type. Some are descriptive verbal phrases, and some are not.

1. **Mark each descriptive verbal phrase** and draw an **arrow** to the word it describes.

2. Then supply **commas** to punctuate introductory verbal phrases.

3. If a sentence needs no additional punctuation, write **OK** in the margin.

1. To develop a strong heart you should exercise regularly.

2. Being published is Marcus's foremost dream.

3. Almost unknown today James K. Polk was one of our strongest presidents.

4. Brad attends school to meet women.

5. Returning from the Toshito Electronics reception Roger and Nivea walked quietly together.

6. Smiling wickedly they left the others to themselves.

7. Queen Zenon found herself waiting by the banks of the Nile.

8. Unknown to his coworkers Ambrose is a legend in the lawn bowling leagues.

9. They found a row of cabs standing idle.

10. Finding a new car necessary Wanda and Wilbur pooled their resources and bought one.

Punctuating Verbal Phrases by Kind of Information

Like adjective clauses, adjective verbal phrases are also punctuated based on the kind of information they contain. Some adjective verbal phrases contain information that is "needed."

"Needed" Adjectives

Adjective information is "needed" if it is required to
1. Identify the word it describes, or
2. Narrow down a larger group to a smaller one.

Phrases that do not contain "needed" information are "extra."

To show the difference between "needed" and "extra" verbal phrases, we punctuate them differently.

Punctuating Verbal Phrases by Kind of Information

Any adjective verbal phrases that contain *"extra" information* should be separated from the rest of the sentence with commas.

Do not separate verbal phrases that contain "needed" information unless they are out of normal position.

"Extra" verbal phrases are punctuated according to the Interrupter Rule.

The following sentence contains a verbal phrase used as an adjective.

"Extra" adjective verbal phrase

Mrs. Brown, **running the projector,** was injured last night.

Notice that the words it describes, *Mrs. Brown*, has already been identified by name. Therefore, the verbal phrase contains "extra" information and should be punctuated with commas.

"Extra" adjective verbal phrase — COMMAS REQUIRED

Mrs. Brown, **running the projector,** was injured last night. ↑   ↑
└──── COMMAS ────┘

"Needed" verbal phrases, on the other hand, are not separated from the sentence with commas.

Verbal phrase "needed" to identify — NO COMMAS

The woman **running the projector** is paid by the hour.
↑   ↑
└── NO COMMAS ──┘

In this sentence, the verbal phrase *running the projector* describes *woman* and also points out which woman the writer is talking about. The verbal phrase is "needed" for identification and is not separated with commas.

The following sentence contains a verbal phrase that narrows down a group — in this case, from the large group "all women" to the smaller group "women looking for work."

**Verbal phrase "needed" to narrow down a group —
NO COMMAS**

Women **looking for work** are applying in Moorpark.

└─ NO COMMAS ─┘

Notice that, according to the sentence, only the smaller group is applying in Moorpark.

Exercise 2

Punctuating "Extra" Verbal Phrases

A. In the following sentences the adjective verbal phrases are printed in **boldface** type.

1. Draw an **arrow** from the verbal phrase to the word it describes.

2. Tell whether the verbal phrase is **NEEDED** or **EXTRA**.

3. Add **commas** where necessary.

Remember that only verbal phrases containing "extra" information should be punctuated as interrupters.

If you think any of these sentences could be punctuated either way, be prepared to defend the punctuation you decided to use.

example

___EXTRA___ Our baseball team, **playing tomorrow**, observed a

ten o'clock curfew.

_____ 1. Juno **trying to get a better grade** stayed in the library every evening.

_____ 2. The pants **standing in the corner** need to be washed.

_____ 3. Marybeth **discovering new skills** has decided on a new career.

_____ 4. The soloist **playing in tonight's concert** has never performed the Brahms second sonata before.

_____ 5. Zeta Melbourne **playing in tonight's concert** has performed the Brahms second sonata only once before.

_____ 6. Mrs. VanDerKellen **watching the fireworks** was as delighted as her children with the display.

_____ 7. Melba served lunch to the ladies **canning tomatoes in the basement**.

_____ 8. The prince spoke the words **written for him by the archbishop**.

_____ 9. The old family dog **resting by the fire** looks as retired as Grandpa **sleeping in a chair beside him**.

_____ 10. Several of the governors **invited to the reception** have publicly refused to attend.

B. In the following sentences the adjective verbal phrases are NOT printed in boldface type.
1. **Mark each verbal phrase** and draw an **arrow** to the word it describes.
2. Tell whether the verbal phrase is **NEEDED** or **EXTRA**.
3. Add **commas** where necessary.

_____ 1. John paying for his first car had to work all last summer.

_____ 2. They surveyed the damage to the sled broken in the storm.

_____ 3. The tree bending in the storm has stood there for many years.

_____ 4. These four candidates hearing of Senator Black's withdrawal had no comment.

_____ 5. All of the candidates hearing of his decision had no comment.

_____ 6. Dr. Abbott rushed to the emergency ward was suffering from chest pains.

_____ 7. Herman playing well scored three of the goals himself.

_____ 8. The team playing best will win.

_____ 9. The dog was frightened by my uncle pounding loudly on the kitchen table.

_____ 10. Ron burned the letters mentioning his uncle.

RELATED SKILL   AVOIDING "DANGLING PHRASES"

Some adjective phrases describe a word that does not appear in the sentence. These phrases are called **dangling phrases** because they aren't attached to anything.

Dangling phrases are often comic without intending to be.

Sentence with dangling phrase — INCORRECT

Walking down the street, the sandwich tasted good.

In this sentence, the adjective phrase *walking down the street* appears to describe *sandwich*.

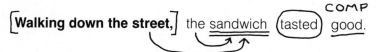

But can a sandwich walk? Of course not. *Walking down the street* is a dangling phrase because the person who did the walking does not appear in the sentence.

There are often many ways to correct these errors. Here is one way.

CORRECTED

Walking down the street, Joe enjoyed the sandwich.

This time, *walking down the street* describes *Joe*, who was doing the walking.

Most dangling phrases appear at the beginning of the sentence. Watch for them in your writing. Dangling phrases occur more often than you might expect and should always be corrected.

Skill Exercise 1

Finding Dangling Phrases

Each of the following sentences contains a verbal phrase printed in **boldface** type.

1. **Draw an arrow** from the verbal phrase to the word it describes.
2. If the phrase is a dangling phrase, write **YES** on the line next to the sentence; if not, write **NO.**
3. **Correct and rewrite** each sentence that contains a dangling phrase.

example

_____YES_____ **Coming to Florence,** it is a beautiful city.

Coming to Florence, I found a beautiful city.

_____ 1. **Writing in several languages,** Dr. Salamar is often published.

_____

_____

_____ 2. **Traveling west through Kansas,** the best road is I-70.

_____

_____

_____ 3. **Worn out by his lecturing,** the class was thoroughly bored.

_____

_____

_____ **4. Turning now to our West Coast satellite pic-**

ture, this is the current weather.

_____

_____

_____ **5. To transfer next year,** Breanna will start applying

now.

_____

_____

_____ **6. Charging across the lawn,** the garden hose lay

directly in Brenda's way.

_____

_____

_____ **7. Basically opposed to marriage,** the event

caught us all by surprise.

_____

_____

_____ **8. Running the restaurant as best she can,** the

chili is nevertheless inedible.

_____

_____

_____ **9. Having made up her mind,** Sharlott found the

task easier to carry out.

_____

_____

_____ **10. Having made up her mind,** the task was easy to

carry out.

_____

_____

FRAGMENTS FROM VERBAL PHRASES

Every complete sentence must contain at least one main clause. Any sentence that doesn't contain at least one main clause is a **fragment**. As you learned in Chapter 6, fragments are always incorrect in college and professional writing.

One kind of fragment is the result of incorrectly punctuating a verbal phrase (or a group of words that contains a verbal phrase) as a complete sentence.

The following sentence contains this kind of fragment.

Fragment from verbal phrase — INCORRECT

Mario is working at North's Market. **To learn the grocery business.**

PERIOD INCORRECT

The verbal *to learn* is not a verb, and the phrase *to learn the grocery business* is not a complete sentence.

Correct this fragment by changing the punctuation between the fragment and the rest of the sentence and removing the capital letter on *to*.

CORRECTED

Mario is working at North's market **to learn the grocery business.**

PERIOD REMOVED

Notice that if the verbal phrase had been written first, it would still have to be in the same sentence with *is working,* the verb it describes.

Fragment from verbal phrase — INCORRECT

To learn the grocery business. Mario is working at North's Market.

PERIOD INCORRECT

CORRECTED

To learn the grocery business, Mario is working at
North's Market.

COMMA ADDED

Let's look at another one.

Fragments — INCORRECT

The gentlemen **playing cards**. Have been in that game
for two days.

PERIOD INCORRECT

Here both "sentences" are fragments. The first has a noun, *gentlemen*, and
an adjective verbal phrase, *playing cards*. The second has a verb, *have been*,
and adverbs, but no subject.

Notice that *gentlemen* is the real subject of *have been*. Correct this sentence
by removing the period after *cards* and changing *Have* to *have*.

CORRECTED

The gentlemen **playing cards** have been in that game
for two days.

PERIOD REMOVED

Marking this sentence will show these relationships more clearly.

The gentlemen [**playing cards**] (have been) (in that
game) (for two days.)

When correcting fragments in your own writing, watch especially for verbal phrases used as adjectives and adverbs and make sure to use commas
where necessary.

Exercise 3

Correcting Fragments from Verbal Phrases

Correct any incorrect punctuation in the following. If an item is already
correctly punctuated, write **OK** in the margin.

example

To be believed completely. , *he* ~~He~~ would tell any lie.

1. Finding his first route blocked by house plants. Simon stumbled into

   the dining room by mistake.

2. A window stood open. To let in the afternoon air.

3. Steadman left to attend graduate school. It was his goal all along.

4. The cattlemen's desire to protect open land. Ultimately resulted, surprisingly, in an even faster closing of the only grazing range in the north county.

5. I heard a morning thrush. Singing to attract a mate.

6. The cultural exchange produced excellent results. Several students agreed to return the following year.

7. The regulation was intended. To reduce paperwork. It seems to be working.

8. A set of armor kept in the museum basement. Once belonged to the Black Prince of Wales.

9. The show first aired in 1967. Only to be removed after a two-week run.

10. They applied a titration technique. To remove all excess Xenium required three applications.

11. The Indian applied healing leaves. To soothe the wounds of his friend.

12. Falling after many years. The old elm shattered the wooden picnic table beneath it.

13. Several coats of paint, specially chosen by Mr. Hamadi. Were applied to the weathered outside of the house.

14. His glasses, pinching the bridge of his nose. Left broad red marks on his skin.

15. Standing in a pool of water. The truck could not be started.

235 Punctuating verbal phrases

16. Three cells stood open. To allow the cleaning crew to do their work. They were finished by noon.

17. Your silence, speaking for you, is not as eloquent as your speech. We are waiting for your side of the story.

18. To hear the speaker more easily and get a clear view of the main parade platform. We left the house earlier this year and found a better place to stand.

19. Mr. Longbow was a full-blooded Apache. Descended from a brother of Geronimo himself.

20. George placed his name in nomination. By submitting a petition with the required number of signatures.

COMBINING SENTENCES TO CREATE VERBAL PHRASES

The first version of a piece of writing usually contains unnecessary words. This is normal, since the purpose of this first draft is simply to get the idea down on paper. Nevertheless, wordy sentences are hard to read and should therefore be "tightened" (made more concise) by revising and editing before a final draft is prepared.

We can make writing less wordy by combining sentences to create verbal phrases. In this way we eliminate words that aren't needed and combine the rest into tighter, more readable sentences.

Uncombined — WORDY

Mr. Bramble was looking for his gradebook. He discovered his lost answer sheets instead.

Combined

Mr. Bramble, **looking for his gradebook**, discovered his lost answer sheets instead.

Here's another example:

Uncombined — WORDY

Jack received the message. Then he phoned his wife.

After receiving the message, Jack phoned his wife.

These sentences have been combined by creating verbal phrases. Sentence combining is an excellent way to eliminate unnecessary words. It also allows the writer to show which ideas are more important than others.

Notice, for example, that in the second example receiving the message is less important than phoning Jack's wife. We know this because the main clause is *Jack phoned his wife. After receiving the message* is an adverb phrase. Therefore, it is less important than the main part of the sentence.

Of course, the best way to phrase a group of sentences is a matter of individual taste. That's what makes one person's writing style different from another's. But to create your best sentences, you should consider more than one way of phrasing your ideas, especially if they are wordy.

Exercises like the following will help you think about all of your sentence options. Do them in a spirit of discovery. Rewriting sentences is like working a puzzle to find the best solution. Play with these sentences until you find a version that sounds good to you.

Exercise 4

Combining Sentences to Create Verbal Phrases

Combine each of the following items to create at least one descriptive verbal phrase. Be sure that the verbal phrase is punctuated correctly.

example

Maxim went to the rear of the railroad car. ~~He wanted~~ to relax in the lounge.

Maxim went to the rear of the railroad car to relax in the lounge.

1. Ron entered college in 1985. His goal was to become a corporate lawyer.

   _____

   _____

2. The student is raising his hand. He has discovered the solution to problem seventeen.

   _____

   _____

3. The Athenians only pretended to believe the Dorian promises. They were doing this because of their distrust.

_____

_____

4. Most of the first line of defenders was killed. They were attacked by charging elephants.

_____

_____

5. The bell hung from an iron spring on the back porch. It rang intermittently in the wind.

_____

_____

6. Someone finally repaired the old rocker. It was broken by the children.

_____

_____

7. The program was ranked highly in the ratings. It was canceled anyway.

_____

_____

8. The deficit has not been reduced in twelve years. It was supposed to be temporary.

_____

_____

9. Mrs. Cagney funded the project herself. She was responding to pleas of the conservationists in her district.

_____

_____

10. The paintings are a recent acquisition. They have been displayed at the Abrahms Gallery.

_____

_____

11. Samuel Beckett was born in Ireland. He spent many years in Paris.

_____

_____

12. An attendant saw the robbery. The attendant was working alone at the Gasexx station.

_____

_____

13. The report was recently filed with the district alcohol commission. It was reported almost immediately in the press.

_____

_____

14. Their cat purrs constantly. She must be looking for attention.

_____

_____

15. The television station released a list of its owners. This action was in response to critics.

_____

_____

Chapter Review

In this chapter you learned that

1. **Descriptive verbal phrases** are those used as adjectives and adverbs.

2. **Normal position** for descriptive verbal phrases is after the words they describe.

3. **The Interrupter Rule** says that you should punctuate any sentence interrupter by separating it from the rest of the sentence with commas.

4. **Punctuate** the following descriptive verbal phrases according to the Interrupter Rule.
   a. **Out-of-position** verbal phrases, especially **introductory** verbal phrases.
   b. Verbal phrases containing **"extra" information.**

5. **"Extra" information** is adjective information that is not needed to
   a. **Identify** the word it describes, or
   b. **Narrow down** a larger group to a smaller one.

In the RELATED SKILL section you learned that **"dangling phrases"** are

1. Phrases that describe a word not in the sentence

2. ALWAYS incorrect

Review Exercise 1

1. **Punctuate the descriptive verbal phrases** in each of the following sentences.

2. **Tell why** you chose the punctuation you used by writing one of the following on the line.
   a. **INTRO** if you add commas because the phrase is introductory
   b. **EXTRA** if you add commas because the phrase contains "extra" information
   c. **OK** if the sentence is already correctly punctuated

Be careful not to punctuate verbal phrases used as nouns.

examples

EXTRA The Phoenix Corporation **,** backed by several

wealthy investors **,** began operation earlier this year.

_____ To recall the cars was their only option.

_____ 1. Rhyming constantly Louella amused all of her clients at the answering service.

_____ 2. These anti-aging ingredients developed in France can be found in no other skin cream.

_____ 3. Taking the train Sylvester still arrived several hours earlier.

_____ 4. Taking the train gave Sylvester time to relax before the ceremony.

_____ 5. The budget agreement announced only yesterday guarantees operating money for the company through next spring.

_____ 6. We welcome the kind of effort made by Senator Patrillo.

_____ 7. Several Thanksgiving turkeys were found escaping through the back gate.

_____ 8. Changing the baby presented several challenges to Elmer.

_____ 9. Discovering the source of his good luck Juan wrote his aunt a letter of thanks.

_____ 10. Strong winds coming out of Canada chilled the northern Montana grazing lands.

_____ 11. Admitting defeat was never one of Marcus's strong points.

_____ 12. Running out of control Kurt stumbled near the finish line and lost.

_____ **13.** Joe tossed the offer in the trash basket to keep it

from being discovered.

_____ **14.** Wendy looking lost asked directions of several pas-

sersby without success.

_____ **15.** The town stopped growing to prevent a takeover by

real estate speculators.

_____ **16.** To prevent a takeover by real estate speculators the

town stopped growing.

_____ **17.** The trumpet player standing on the left of the stage

is the better of the two.

_____ **18.** To eat at the Meat Wagon Truck Stop and Diner is

a surprisingly good treat.

_____ **19.** To win the lottery the two brothers bought a great

many tickets.

_____ **20.** I spoke to the chocolate fairy hoping for an

Easter surprise.

Review Exercise 2

Correct any errors in punctuation of verbal phrases in the following
sentences.

Sunning herself Sondra was at peace. The warm sun shining brightly beat

hard and warm on her brown back. Her golden hair falling carelessly across

her eyes shaded her from the bright glare. She had forgotten school entirely.

Her friend Carolyn had just departed after a delightful afternoon. Her mind

was at rest.

Then Sondra thought of Brad Palmer. She had not seen Brad in several days. Surely he would call soon. Smiling she thought of all his sweet words and relaxed. No thought could disturb her now. So what if her history research paper stubbornly refused to write itself? She could forgive it. To preserve the present mood she could forgive anything.

Across town in Carolyn's single apartment the phone rang loudly. No one moved to answer it. Humming nervously in a phone booth on the street below Brad Palmer held a receiver to his ear and waited.

Review Exercise 3

Edit the following paragraphs by combining sentences wherever possible **to create verbal phrases.** When you are finished, make sure your new verbal phrases are punctuated correctly.

In grade school Jesse always did well in math. He could multiply before many students could add. In high school he showed skill in physics as well. He won first place in three science fairs. Jesse was graduating from college. He wanted to do serious work in science. His friends discouraged him. They said he would end up this way. He would end up mixing pesticides in fifty-five gallon drums for some chemical company. They argued that no one from the neighborhood had ever made it in that world.

But Jesse's mind was made up. Once that happened, it could not be changed. Later his friends were no longer arguing. They were cheering. Today Jesse works in a small town. The town is surrounded by the Arizona desert. Yesterday the papers made an announcement. Jessie had discovered a new element. The phone has been ringing all day. It brought him the news.

The Nobel Prize committee would like to see him.

Chapter 9 Writing Assignment

Write a paragraph that **compares two high school teachers** — one who is effective as a teacher and one who is not. In your comparison, tell a **story** about each teacher that shows the point you are trying to make.

When you have made your final copy

1. Mark the **verb**, **subject**, **object**, and **complement of each main clause**.

2. Next, make sure that
   a. All **main clauses** are correctly joined or separated.
   b. All **dependent clauses** and **verbal phrases** are correctly punctuated.
   c. Your paragraph contains **no fragments**.

Hints for Writing Comparison Paragraphs

Comparisons are most effective when the writer gives the same kind of information about each subject. For example, the writer should compare the price of one machine with the price of another, not the price of one with the speed of another.

Comparisons are also effective when the information is presented in the best order. For this paragraph, choose an order that places the most interesting story last.

As usual, both of these goals are best met by making good use of the planning time — the time before the rough draft.

Before the rough draft:

1. Make a preliminary list of the teachers you *may* write about.

2. Now edit this list until you find the two teachers — one who is effective and one who is not — that would be the most interesting to read about.

3. Make a list of all the stories you *may* tell about these two teachers.

4. Now select two stories — one about each teacher — that would make the best reading. (Your paragraph will be more interesting if you spend sufficient time on these first four steps.)

5. For each story, make a short list of the events that make up that story.

6. Reread these lists and make any changes in them that you think will make your stories more effective.

Writing the rough draft:

1. Start your rough draft by writing an interesting sentence or two that names the teachers and tells the reader you are going to compare them. Using your own words, say that they are different in their effectiveness.

2. Then discuss the first teacher. Start with a sentence that names the teacher and tells how effective that teacher was. Use your first list of events to tell your story about this person.

3. Next discuss the second teacher. Start with a sentence that names the teacher and tells how effective that teacher was. This sentence should begin with the phrase "On the other hand," followed by a comma. Use your second list of events to tell your story about this person.

4. Write a closing sentence or two that
   a. Names both teachers again.
   b. Tells what you gained from having been taught by each of them.

After the rough draft:

1. Do your best to correct any errors on this first copy. Be especially careful to correct all errors in punctuation.

2. Make any other changes you think will make your paragraph more interesting and readable.

3. Recopy your corrected paragraph on a clean sheet of paper and turn in all of your work.

c　h　a　p　t　e　r

10
Appositives and appositive phrases

Chapter Preview

This chapter will show you

1. How to find **appositives** and **appositive phrases**.

2. When to **punctuate appositives** in sentences.

In addition, a special RELATED SKILL section will help you use pronouns in appositives and appositive phrases.

APPOSITIVES

Sometimes a noun is followed by another noun that repeats and explains it.

> My sister **Mary** is a registered nurse.
>
> We interviewed one student, **Benjamin.**

The noun *Mary* repeats and explains the subject *sister.* (Notice that *sister* is not capitalized; *sister Mary* is therefore not a name.)

> My sister **Mary** (is) a registered nurse.

In the same way, the noun *Benjamin* repeats and explains the object, *student.*

> We (interviewed) one student, **Benjamin**.

Nouns like *Mary* and *Benjamin* that repeat and explain other nouns are called **appositives.** Appositives are very common. Much writing, including much of your writing, contains them.

    Notice that in the first sentence, the appositive is not separated with commas, while in the second sentence it is. One of the reasons we are studying appositives is to punctuate them correctly. (We will look closely at the punctuation of appositives later in this section.)

Marking Appositives

Though appositives, strictly speaking, are nouns and not adjectives, we will mark them like adjectives because of the way they act. Mark appositives as follows.

1. **Underline** the appositive and write **APP** over it.

2. Draw an **arrow** from the appositive to the noun it explains.

The appositive in the above examples would be marked like this.

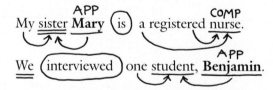

> My sister **Mary** (is) a registered nurse.
>
> We (interviewed) one student, **Benjamin**.

The following exercise will help you practice finding appositives.

Exercise 1

Finding Appositives

Some of these sentences contain appositives and some do not.

    Mark each sentence completely. (Keep in mind that not all appositives are punctuated with commas.)

APP
Her father, Ben Watson, came to this town in 1947.

1. My cousin Hannah will graduate from college next year.

2. He has read his favorite book, *Longshot*, ten times.

3. She spoke to her friend Emma last Tuesday.

4. His dog Frank even goes to class with him.

5. The right answer could not be found.

6. She is still using an old word processing program, Wordstar.

7. Johann's least favorite composer, Brahms, will be the subject of tomorrow's exam.

8. Ellery spoke to the witness yesterday.

9. The janitor Harrison was no help either.

10. Allen's autobiographical book *Walter* was recently published.

APPOSITIVE PHRASES

Because appositives are nouns, they can be accompanied by adjectives or adjective phrases.

> We visited Ann's sister, **a registered nurse**.

The appositive *nurse* repeats and explains the noun *sister*, the object of the verb. In this case, the appositive *nurse* is described by two adjectives, *a* and *registered*.

a registered **nurse**

When appositives are accompanied by adjectives, the whole group of words is called an **appositive phrase**.

> **Appositive phrase**

> We visited Ann's sister, **a registered nurse**.

Here's another example.

> Mr. Clemons, **a man from the State Department**, will speak today.

In this sentence *a man from the State Department* is an appositive phrase describing the subject *Mr. Clemons*. Notice that the appositive *man* is described by two adjectives, one of which is a prepositional phrase.

a **man** (from the State Department)

Marking Appositives and Appositive Phrases

Appositive phrases are marked like appositives, except that the phrase is grouped. To mark appositive phrases

1. Group the appositive phrase with **parentheses**.

2. **Underline** the appositive and write **APP** over it.

3. Draw an **arrow** from the appositive to the noun it explains.

The sample sentences can be marked as follows.

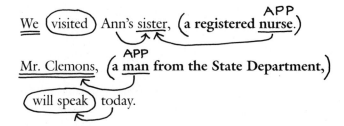

We (visited) Ann's sister, (a registered nurse.)

Mr. Clemons, (a **man** from the State Department,) (will speak) today.

Notice that, as always, the smaller phrase inside the larger one is not marked.

Exercise 2

example

Finding Appositives and Appositive Phrases

Mark each sentence completely.

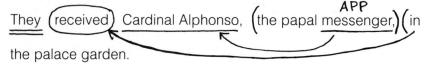

They (received) Cardinal Alphonso, (the papal messenger,) (in the palace garden.

1. The Shadow Warriors, a local street gang, have recently joined with the Snow Kings in a neighborhood cleanup drive.

2. Michael's brother, a medical technician, has promised to pay his tuition this semester.

3. His brother the medical technician has promised to pay Michael's tuition this semester.

4. One of the advertisements was placed by my uncle the writer.

5. Only one thing, poverty, prevented him from being rich.

6. A detective by nature, Mr. Swanson immediately reconsidered the events of last night.

7. The new Shakespeare biography, *In a Fine Frenzy,* has been well reviewed in the New York press.

8. We recently bought one of the better accounting programs, ProRate.

9. His brother Ben wrote it.

10. Professor Amber, a geologist from Hawaii, will lecture on volcano formation.

RELATED SKILL   USING PRONOUNS AS APPOSITIVES

As you have learned, the personal pronouns and the pronoun *who* change form depending on how they are used. This applies especially to pronouns used as appositives.

Using Pronouns as Appositives

Use the **subject form** for all appositives following

1. Subjects
2. Complements

Use the **object form** for appositives following

1. All objects

Appositive following subject

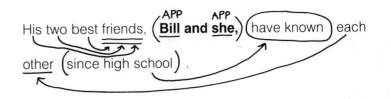

Appositive following object

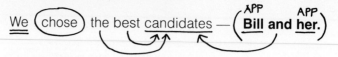

Appositive following complement

In the first example, the subject form *she* is used because the appositive repeats the subject. In the second example, the object form *her* is used because the appositive repeats an object, in this case, the object of the verb.

In the final example, the subject form *she* is used because the appositive repeats the complement, which "equals" the subject.

The following chart lists the subject and object forms of these pronouns.

Forms of Pronouns

Subject Form	Object Form
I	me
you	you
he	him
she	her
it	it
we	us
they	them
who	whom

Skill Exercise 1

Using Pronouns as Appositives

Correct any pronoun errors in the following sentences.

example

The hypnotist's subjects, Jennifer and ~~me~~ I, were asleep in minutes.

1. The soup was prepared by the fraternity's best cooks, Bill and I.

2. A solution was provided by the best chemistry student in the class — she.

3. These are the new class officers, Mr. Macy, Mr. Penwicker, and she.

4. Two young women, her and Ms. Pariah, used the tickets instead.

5. Both patients, Henry and he, recommended Dr. Patrick.

6. In return for my good advice, they donated ten dollars to a needy charity — I.

7. To her most loyal fans, Dr. Calistoga and he, she left part of her estate.

8. The only remaining soldiers, we of the 29th Cavalry, wish to report an action involving the enemy.

9. The battle was reported by its only remaining soldiers, we three.

10. The rain fell on the entire class, but especially on our coordinators, Melanie and he.

PUNCTUATING APPOSITIVES AND APPOSITIVE PHRASES

Like dependent clauses and descriptive verbal phrases, appositives are sometimes punctuated according to the Interrupter Rule, and sometimes they are not.

The Interrupter Rule

Punctuate any sentence interrupter by separating it from the rest of the sentence with commas.

Interrupter, ******************************** .

**************** , **interrupter,** ************** .

******************************** , **interrupter.**

As usual, when to apply the Interrupter Rule depends on two things:

1. The position of the phrase in the sentence

2. The kind of information the phrase contains

Either of these conditions can be reason to apply the Interrupter Rule.

Punctuating Introductory Appositives

Most appositives will appear in one of two places.

1. Immediately following the word they describe (their normal position)
2. **Introductory** position

Like introductory verbal phrases, introductory appositives are punctuated according to the Interrupter Rule.

Punctuating Appositive Phrases by Position

Any appositive phrase that is *out of normal position* should be separated from the rest of the sentence with commas.

Introductory appositive phrases are always separated with commas.

Introductory appositive phrase

A master dramatist, Shakespeare understood theater well.

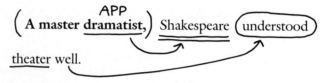

theater well.

Interrupter, ******************************** .

Punctuating Appositives Containing "Extra" Information

Appositives are also punctuated with commas when they contain "extra" information.

Like adjective clauses and verbal phrases, appositives are also punctuated based on the kind of information they contain. Some appositives contain information that is "needed," and some do not.

"Needed" Adjectives

Adjective information is "needed" if it is required to

1. Identify the word it describes, or
2. Narrow down a larger group to a smaller one.

Information that is not "needed" is "extra." To show the difference between "needed" and "extra" appositive phrases, we punctuate them differently.

Punctuating Appositive Phrases by Kind of Information

Any appositive phrase that contains "extra" information should be separated from the rest of the sentence with commas.

Most appositives, in fact, contain "extra" information about the words they describe. For this reason, most appositives are separated from the rest of the sentence with commas.

Let's look at some examples.

Appositive containing "extra" information — COMMAS REQUIRED

Chuck Water's latest film, *Riptide*, is about an aging scuba diver.
↑ ↑
COMMAS

*************** , **interrupter,** *************** .

In this sentence, the film has already been identified — a person can have only one latest film. Therefore, the appositive *Riptide* contains "extra" information and is separated from the rest of the sentence with commas.

Appositive containing "extra" information — COMMAS REQUIRED

Mrs. Jackson, **one of the theology faculty,** is traveling

└────── COMMAS ──────┘

in Ethiopia this spring.

*************** , **interrupter,** *************** .

Here, the subject is identified by name. Once more, the appositive contains "extra" information and is separated from the rest of the sentence with commas.

Appositives that do contain "needed" information should not be separated from the rest of the sentence.

**Appositive containing "needed" information —
NO COMMAS**

My friend **the actor** is now working in New York.

↑   ↑

NO COMMAS

In this sentence, the appositive *the actor* is needed to tell us which friend the writer is talking about. The information identifies the subject, and therefore commas are not used.

Notice that in the following sentence, punctuation will depend on the number of aunts that Julie has.

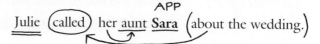

If Julie has more than one aunt, the word *Sara* is needed for identification.

**Appositive containing "needed" information —
NO COMMAS**

Julie called her aunt **Sara** about the wedding.

↑   ↑

NO COMMAS

But if Julie has only one aunt, the appositive contains "extra" information. If only one aunt exists, she does not need further identification.

**Appositive containing "extra" information —
COMMAS REQUIRED**

Julie called her aunt, **Sara,** about the wedding.

↑   ↑

COMMAS

Exercise 3

Punctuating Appositives and Appositive Phrases

A. The appositives in the following sentences are printed in **boldface** type.

    1. Punctuate the appositive or **appositive phrases**.

    2. Tell why you chose the punctuation you used by writing one of the following on the line.

        a. INTRO if you add commas because the appositive is introductory.

        b. EXTRA if you add commas because the appositive contains "extra" information

        c. OK if the sentence is already correctly punctuated

EXTRA A new dress material **,** **Plexicloth** **,** was used in this stunning creation.

_____ 1. He placed the order with his only uncle **Bill**.

_____ 2. The cause of the conflict **a disagreement over land reform** was soon forgotten.

_____ 3. The gun **a battered .38** was recovered from the lake.

_____ 4. He said the social welfare system punishes its beneficiaries **the poor**.

_____ 5. A recent law **the Rand-Tartley Reform Act** is presently under congressional review.

_____ 6. Jamaal is studying the proton **a subatomic particle**.

_____ 7. **A poet of sorts** he wants to have its name changed to something more pleasing.

_____ 8. Consequential Insurance **our auto insurance company** waits three months and then pays its claims promptly.

_____ 9. She ended the set with her best saloon song **a slow version of "Torchie."**

_____ 10. I finally got the whole story from my friend **the hot-shot lawyer**.

B. The appositives in the following sentences are NOT printed in bold-face type.

  1. **Punctuate each appositive or appositive phrase** correctly.
    NOTE: Some sentences contain more than one appositive.

2. **Tell why** you chose the punctuation you used by writing one of the following on the line.

   a. **INTRO** if you add commas because the appositive is introductory

   b. **EXTRA** if you add commas because the appositive contains "extra" information

   c. **OK** if the sentence is already correctly punctuated

_____ 1. A student of history Samuelson recalled the incident easily.

_____ 2. Carelessness his greatest virtue offset vindictiveness his worst fault.

_____ 3. My cousin the garage mechanic will fix the car for me.

_____ 4. My cousin a garage mechanic will fix the car for me.

_____ 5. The band Asleep at the Wheel will hold a concert this weekend.

_____ 6. Old and In the Way a local rock group will join them.

_____ 7. They are promoting the Tart-Haftley Act another attempt to restrict immoral activity by congressmen.

_____ 8. She is in trouble in her worst course French.

_____ 9. His mother Mary will attend with him.

_____ 10. Of his three sisters his sister Fran will not attend.

COMBINING SENTENCES TO CREATE APPOSITIVES

Using appositives is a good way to give your sentences variety and make them interesting.

To get more appositives into your writing, look for ways to combine sentences when you edit your rough drafts.

Uncombined sentences

English is one of the Germanic languages. English also contains many French and Latin words.

Combined sentences

English, **one of the Germanic languages,** also contains many French and Latin words.

By combining these two sentences, the weaker words are removed, and the most important information is saved. The writing is "tighter" (more concise) and easier to read as a result.

Notice that the writer chose to use the second of the two original sentences as the main clause of the revised version. The main clause of a sentence is always its most important idea.

If she had wished, she could have made the first original sentence the main clause of her revision. It is up to the writer to place the emphasis where she or he thinks it belongs.

Of course, not all sentences are improved by combining. As always, use your own judgment. But do consider sentence combining opportunities. Most writing, student and professional, can be improved by the kind of tightening that sentence combining provides.

Exercise 4

Combining Sentences to Create Appositives

Combine each of the following groups of sentences to create at least one appositive. Make sure that the appositive is punctuated correctly.

example

Dr. Kane , ~~is~~ a candidate for city attorney. , ~~He~~ will be speaking at the college on Wednesday.

Dr. Kane, a candidate for city attorney, will be speaking at the college on Wednesday.

1. One senator even appeared in the commercials. The senator was Henry White.

_____

_____

2. The fraud was eventually uncovered. It was a scandal involving military recruitment.

_____

_____

3. The local review officer had been bribing high school students to enlist. The officer was named Sergeant Raggs.

_____

_____

4. The dream centered around Ben's childhood hero. In his youth he idolized King Arthur.

_____

_____

5. The wood of that tree burns very well. I'm talking about the heart ash.

_____

_____

6. Mrs. Steed works at the ministry. She told me about this job.

_____

_____

7. We entered Penwicker because of its political anesthetics department. Penwicker has one of the finest political anesthetics department in the country.

_____

_____

_____

8. The academic gown is worn on Regent's Day. Regent's Day is a traditional holiday of the college.

_____

_____

9. Simple revenge is a common motive for murder. It was in the Marietta case also.

_____

_____

10. Marcus received no help from the tribunes. The tribunes were named Polonius and Claudianus.

_____

_____

Chapter Review

In this chapter you learned that

1. **Appositives** are nouns that repeat and explain other nouns in the sentence.

2. **Appositive phrases** are appositives with adjectives connected to them.

3. The **normal position** of appositives and appositive phrases is immediately after the word they describe.

4. **Introductory appositives** are punctuated according to the Interrupter Rule.

5. **Appositives containing "extra" information** are punctuated according to the Interrupter Rule.

In the RELATED SKILL section you learned about

Pronouns as appositives

a. Use **subject form** for appositives following subjects and complements.

b. Use **object form** for appositives following all objects.

Review Exercise 1

Correct any punctuation errors with appositives and verbal phrases in the following paragraph.

Luke Sutton sat alone in a far corner of the saloon. Apparently waiting for someone he drank his beer slowly. A quiet man Luke was quiet now. Several years had passed since the Civil War the major conflict of his generation. Luke had returned to Wyoming two years ago. He had come to Hightower the county of his birth and discovered his burned-out homestead. He knew his wife had been killed in his absence. He had rebuilt and kept his peace. Now he watched for clues to the secret, held by everyone in town but him. Keeping his silence had cost him many sleepless nights. But today all would be right. Today Ben Farber the town drunk had agreed to talk to him. Today Luke would be paid for his trouble in his favorite coin the truth.

Review Exercise 2

Edit the following paragraph by combining sentences to make appositives. Then **rewrite** your new sentences on the lines below.
When you are finished, make sure your new sentences are punctuated correctly.

Jamie Johnson was one of the best high school basketball players in the city. Jamie Johnson has returned to Chicago. After failing to be drafted by the NBA, Jamie played with the Marshalls until last year. The Marshalls are a local semipro team. Then he went to Italy for a season. Now he is back. One of his father's friends is named Charles Leonard. Charles Leonard owns Mao Tse Duck. This is a successful and popular restaurant. Mr. Leonard wants to teach Jamie the restaurant business. Jamie likes Mr. Leonard and thinks this is a good opportunity. He has seen too many friends destroyed by a deadly combination. The combination is a pipeful of coke and a headful of NBA dreams. Jamie wants something better for himself. He would rather have a stomachful of food and a future full of work he can count on.

_____

_____

_____

_____

_____

_____

_____

_____

_____

_____

_____

_____

_____

_____

Review Exercise 3

This exercise is similar to the previous one, but a little more difficult.

Edit the following paragraphs by combining sentences wherever possible **to create appositives and verbal phrases**. Try several ways to edit each group of sentences. The best solution may not be the first one you try.

Then **rewrite** your finished sentences on the lines provided.

When you are finished, make sure your new sentences are punctuated correctly.

Shakespeare's sonnets were probably written between 1588 and 1597. They detail a striking story. It is one of friendship and betrayal. The Earl of Southampton was a young lord of Elizabethan England. He became the poet's friend. The friendship became devotion. This devotion was probably felt on both sides.

At about the same time Shakespeare took a mistress. The mistress was a dark, beautiful woman. He loved her at first, but her strong sensuality soon repelled him. Her sensuality was initially appealing to him. Still he could not break free from her.

Neither relationship ended well. The mistress discovered the rich young earl. This is the earl who was Shakespeare's friend. She turned the earl's attention away from the poet.

Both of them betrayed the poet. But he was trapped by the pleasures he had shared with his mistress. He could not let go of her. Shakespeare also remembered the friendship he had shared with the earl. The poet would not let go of him. This was a horrible, painful situation. It nevertheless produced some of the greatest poems in the English language.

_____

_____

_____

Chapter 10 Writing Assignment

Write a paragraph that **compares two former boyfriends or girlfriends** (or, if you wish, two former friends), by telling **one important way they were different**. In your comparison, tell one story about each boyfriend or girlfriend that shows the points you are trying to make.

When you have made your final copy

1. Mark the **verb, subject, object, and complement of each main clause**.

2. Next, make sure that
   a. All **main clauses** are correctly joined or separated.
   b. All **dependent clauses**, **verbal phrases**, and **appositive phrases** are correctly punctuated.
   c. Your paragraph contains **no fragments**.

Hints for Writing Comparison Paragraphs

This paragraph can be both colorful and serious at the same time. It will be the most effective if you choose people who are opposite each other in some extreme way. Then select good stories, stories that are interesting in themselves.

Have a sense of humor about the people you are writing about, but don't let the reader think you dislike either of them. Remember, these are people you cared about at one time. The reader will like your paragraph better if you like your subjects despite their humorous differences.

Before the rough draft:

1. Make a preliminary list of the boyfriends or girlfriends you *may* write about.

2. Now edit this list until you find the two that would be the most interesting to read about.

3. Next, make a second list that includes all of the ways in which these two were different. Don't skimp in making this list — you are making the single most important decision of the paper.

4. Choose one of these differences for your paragraph.

5. Make a third list of all the stories you *might* tell about these two people that relates to this difference.

6. Now select two stories — one about each person — that would make the best reading.

Writing the rough draft:

1. Start your rough draft by writing an interesting sentence or two that
   a. Mentions each person
   b. Tells the reader you are going to compare them
   c. Mentions the difference that you are going to discuss

2. Then discuss the first person. Start with a sentence that mentions the person and tells what he or she was like. Then tell the story you chose about that person.

3. Next discuss the second person. Start with a sentence that mentions the person and tells how he or she is different from the first person. This sentence should begin with the phrase "On the other hand," followed by a comma. Then tell the story you chose about that person.

4. Write a closing sentence or two that
   a. Mentions both people
   b. Tells what you gained from having had two such different people in your life

After the rough draft:

1. Do your best to correct any errors on this first copy. Be especially careful to correct all errors in punctuation.

2. Make any other changes you think will make your paragraph more interesting and readable.

3. Recopy your corrected paragraph on a clean sheet of paper and turn in all of your work.

U N I T
IV

Verbs

In this unit you will study three common verb problems.

One problem involves verbs that add -s endings (like *see* and *sees*). In speech these endings are often dropped, which can lead to difficulty in writing. Verbs that add -s (**present tense verbs**) are discussed in Chapter 11.

Another problem involves verbs that add -ed endings (verbs like *walk* and *walked*). Many speakers also drop this ending, which leads to difficulty in writing. Verbs that add -ed (**regular verbs**) will be discussed in Chapter 12.

A final difficulty is in choosing between verb forms like *saw* and *seen* in sentences. These forms (called the **past tense** and **past participle**) are often made in unusual ways, which is why verbs like *see* are called **irregular verbs**. Irregular verbs will be discussed in Chapter 13.

11
Verbs that add -s

Chapter Preview

This chapter will show you how to find and correct **errors with present tense verbs** (verbs that add -s) and the verbs **was** and **were**.

In addition, a RELATED SKILL section will help you find and correct these errors in sentences with **more than one clause and with verbal phrases**.

NOTE: The chapters in this Unit can be worked by any student who has completed Unit 1.

  For students who have completed Units 2 and 3, the RELATED SKILL section contains exercises that rely on knowledge of that material as well.

PRESENT TENSE VERBS

A present tense verb shows an action happening now or an action that often happens.

Action happening now

I **see** your brother in the store.

Action that often happens

Uncle Jerry **tells** good stories.

Forms of Present Tense Verbs

Except for the verb *to be*, all present tense verbs have two forms. The first is the **basic form**. The second is the **-s form**.

Present Tense Verb Forms

Basic Form	-s Form
run	runs
call	calls
dress	dresses
apply	applies

Notice that some verbs add *-s*,

run	runs
call	calls

some add *-es*,

dress	dresses

and some that end in *-y* change the *y* to *i* before adding *-es*.

apply	applies

You can find the rules for spelling these forms correctly in Chapter 18, Spelling.

Subject-Verb Agreement

"Agreement" in sentences means matching the form of one word to the form of another.

As you know, present tense verbs have more than one form, and the subject determines which form is correct. The basic form is used with some subjects, and the *-s* form is used with other subjects.

Matching verb forms to subjects is called **subject-verb agreement**. Subject-verb agreement is not always followed in speech, but in college and professional writing it is required.

In this chapter you will learn the **Present Tense Rule**, which tells you which verb form to use with each personal pronoun subject. Then you will learn **pronoun substitution**, a way to convert every subject to a personal pronoun that has the same meaning as the original subject. By using pronoun substitution, you can apply the Present Tense Rule to sentences with subjects that are not personal pronouns.

NOTE: The chapters in this Unit, including this one, can be worked by any student who has completed Unit 1.

For students who have also completed Units 2 and 3, the RELATED SKILL section contains exercises that rely on knowledge of that material as well.

THE PRESENT TENSE RULE

The Present Tense Rule tells when present tense forms should be used. It is your guide to subject-verb agreement.

Present Tense Rule

For one-word present tense verbs and those that start a verb phrase

1. Use the *-s* form when the subject is *he*, *she*, or *it*.

2. Use the basic form in all other cases.

This rule also applies to the past tense forms *was* and *were*.

The Present Tense Rule is the basic rule of subject-verb agreement. It will always tell you which present tense verb to use if the subject is a personal pronoun. (Later you will see how to make all subjects into personal pronouns.)

Remember that the Present Tense Rule applies only to one-word verbs and the first word in a verb phrase. The rule does not apply to verb phrases like *would see*, since *would* is not a present tense verb. In phrases like *would see*, the basic form (*see*) is always used.

The following shows how the present tense rule is applied to the verbs *to run* and *to dress*.

Present Tense Forms of *To Run*

Singular	**Plural**
I run	we run
you run	you run
he **runs**	
she **runs**	they run
it **runs**	

Present Tense Forms of *To Dress*

Singular	**Plural**
I dress	we dress
you dress	you dress
he **dresses**	
she **dresses**	they dress
it **dresses**	

Notice that the *-s* form is used only with the subjects *he, she,* and *it*.

Exercise 1

Present Tense Verbs with Pronoun Subjects

Using the Present Tense Rule, write the **correct form of the verb**.

example To fall   It *falls*   .

1. To work   I   _____ .

2. To reply   You _____ .

3. To ask   He   _____ .

4. To remind   They _____ .

5. To force   She _____ .

6. To smile   We   _____ .

7. To confess   He   _____ .

8. To pass   It   _____ .

9. To arrange   You   _____ .

10. To write   I   _____ .

11. To interview   They   _____ .

12. To sit   He   _____ .

13. To see   She   _____ .

14. To enroll   We   _____ .

15. To subscribe   It   _____ .

16. To marry   She   _____ .

17. To tell   He   _____ .

18. To cut   They   _____ .

19. To sympathize   I   _____ .

20. To choose   He   _____ .

Exercise 2

Present Tense Verbs with Pronoun Subjects

Using the Present Tense Rule, complete the following simple sentences by writing **any correct pronoun subject** from the following list.

I	we
you	you
he	they
she	
it	

Notice that each pronoun is the start of a sentence. Therefore, use a capital letter.

example

   She _____ remembers.

1. _____ answers.

2. _____ rings.

3. _____ find.

4. _____ chooses.

5. _____ protect.

6. _____ wake.

7. _____ eats.

8. _____ relies.

9. _____ play.

10. _____ drives.

11. _____ search.

12. _____ classify.

13. _____ hopes.

14. _____ fixes.

15. _____ thank.

16. _____ bleaches.

17. _____ bind.

18. _____ mashes.

19. _____ dig.

20. _____ becomes.

Subjects and Verbs Connected by *And*, *Or*, *But*, or *Nor*

Some sentences have more than one subject or verb connected by *and*, *or*, *but*, or *nor*. You studied some of these sentences in Chapter 1. Sentences like these must be treated carefully when applying subject-verb agreement.

1. When two or more subjects are connected by *and*, the subjects combine and act like *they*.

Subjects joined by *and*

He and she (= they) **see**.

Present Tense
Rule: *they see*

2. On the other hand, when two or more subjects are connected by *but*, *or*, or *nor*, the verb agrees with the subject nearest to it.

Subjects joined by *or*

Either he or **they see**. (Present Tense Rule: *they see*)
NEAREST SUBJECT

Either they or **he sees**. (Present Tense Rule: *he sees*)
NEAREST SUBJECT

Notice that in the above sentences, when the subjects were reversed, the verb changed.

3. When two or more verbs are connected by *any* connecting word, each verb must agree with the subject.

Verbs joined by *and*

She **works** and **plays**.

Present Tense
Rule: *she works*
               she plays

Exercise 3

Subjects and Verbs Connected by *And, Or, But,* or *Nor*
Using the Present Tense Rule, write the **correct form of the verb.**

| **example** | To fall | It or they _*fall*_____ . |

1. To work   You and I _____ .

2. To reply   You and he _____ .

3. To ask   You or he _____ .

4. To remind/   He _____ and _____ .
   to tell

5. To force   Neither she nor you _____ .

6. To smile   Neither you nor she _____ .

7. To confess   He and she _____ .

8. To pass   Either he or she _____ .

9. To arrange/   You _____ or _____ .
   to plan

10. To write   You and I _____ .

11. To interview   Neither they nor he _____ .

12. To sit/to sing   He _____ and _____ .

13. To see   They and she _____ .

14. To enroll   Not we, but you _____ .

15. To subscribe   It and you _____ .

16. To marry   She and he _____ .

17. To tell   He or she _____ .

18. To cut   They and he _____ .

19. To sympathize   They and I _____ .

20. To choose/   He neither _____ nor _____ .
      to advise

Exercise 4

Subjects and Verbs Connected by *And, Or, But,* or *Nor*

Using the Present Tense Rule, complete the following simple sentences by writing **any combination of correct pronoun subjects** chosen from the following list.

I	we
you	you
he	they
she	
it	

Use capital letters when a pronoun starts a sentence.

example

You _____ and *she* _____ remember.

1. Either _____ or _____ answers.

2. Either _____ or _____ ring.

3. Not _____ , but _____ find.

4. _____ and _____ choose.

5. _____ or _____ protect.

6. _____ or _____ wakes.

7. Neither _____ nor _____ eats.

8. _____ and _____ rely.

9. Not _____ , but _____ play.

10. Not _____ , but _____ drives.

11. _____ and _____ search.

12. _____ or _____ classify.

13. Neither _____ nor _____ hopes.

14. Either _____ or _____ fix.

15. _____ and _____ thank.

16. Not _____ , but _____ bleaches.

17. Not _____ , but _____ bind.

18. _____ or _____ mashes.

19. _____ or _____ dig.

20. _____ and _____ become.

To Be and *To Have*

The verbs *to be* and *to have* have irregular present tense forms. *To be* has irregular past tense forms as well.

Both of these verbs are common in speech and writing. In addition, they are important helping verbs. We will therefore study them carefully.

To Be

The present tense forms of *to be* are *am*, *is*, and *are*. Its past tense forms are *was* and *were*.

Present Tense Forms of *To Be*

Singular	Plural
I am	we are
You are	you are
he **is**	
she **is**	they are
it **is**	

279 Verbs that add *-s*

Past Tense Forms of *To Be*

Singular	Plural
I **was**	we were
you were	you were
he **was** she **was** it **was**	they were

Notice that even though *to be* doesn't have regular present tense forms, it is like other verbs in one respect. The *-s* form *is* is used with *he, she,* and *it*.

Notice also that *be* is not a verb by itself, even though it is sometimes used that way in speech.

Incorrect

I **be**

Corrected

I **am**

To Have

The verb *to have* has two present tense forms — *have* and *has*.

Present Tense Forms of *To Have*

Singular	Plural
I have	we have
you have	you have
he **has** she **has** it **has**	they have

Notice that here again, the *-s* form *has* is used with the subjects *he, she,* and *it*.

Exercise 5

To Be and **To Have** with Pronoun Subjects

Using the Present Tense Rule, write the **correct form of the verb** in parentheses.

| example | To be (present tense)   It _____*is*_____ . |

1. *To be*   (present tense)   I   _____ .

2. *To have*   (present tense)   You   _____ .

3. *To be*   (present tense)   He   _____ .

4. *To be*   (present tense)   They _____ .

5. *To have*   (present tense)   She   _____ .

6. *To be*   (past tense)   We   _____ .

7. *To be*   (past tense)   He   _____ .

8. *To be*   (present tense)   It   _____ .

9. *To have*   (present tense)   You   _____ .

10. *To have* (present tense)   I   _____ .

11. *To be*   (present tense)   They _____ .

12. *To be*   (present tense)   He   _____ .

13. *To have* (present tense)   He   _____ .

14. *To be*   (present tense)   We   _____ .

15. *To be*   (past tense)   It   _____ .

16. *To be*   (present tense)   She   _____ .

17. *To have* (present tense)   He   _____ .

18. *To be*   (present tense)   They _____ .

19. *To have* (present tense)   I   _____ .

20. *To be*   (past tense)   He   _____ .

Exercise 6

To Be and **To Have** with Pronoun Subjects

Using the Present Tense Rule, write **any correct pronoun subject** chosen from the following list.

281 Verbs that add -*s*

I   we
you   you
he   they
she
it

Notice that each pronoun is the start of a sentence. Therefore, use a capital letter.

example   _____She_____ is.

1. _____ am.

2. _____ is.

3. _____ or _____ is.

4. _____ and _____ were.

5. _____ are.

6. _____ and _____ are.

7. _____ or _____ are.

8. _____ was.

9. _____ or _____ was.

10. Neither _____ nor _____ was.

11. _____ was.

12. _____ were.

13. _____ and _____ were.

14. _____ or _____ were.

15. _____ has.

16. Neither _____ nor _____ has.

17. _____ and _____ has.

18. _____ have.

19. _____ and _____ have.

20. Not _____ , but _____ have.

THE PRESENT TENSE RULE IN SENTENCES

Now that you can choose between the basic form and the *-s* form of present tense verbs, it is time to practice with longer sentences.

First we will study sentences with personal pronouns as subjects. Then we will study sentences with noun subjects by learning how to convert every noun into a personal pronoun with **pronoun substitution**.

Sentences with Pronoun Subjects

Sentences with personal pronoun subjects are the easiest to work with, so we will begin with them. The sentences in these exercises all have one-word verbs and personal pronoun subjects — *I, you, he, she, it, we,* or *they.*

Notice that the Present Tense Rule always applies to these sentences.

Exercise 7

Using Present Tense Verbs with Pronoun Subjects

Each of these sentences contains a blank line where a present tense verb belongs.

a. Mark the **subject** of each verb.

b. **Write the correct present tense form** of the verb in parentheses on the line.

Be sure to follow the Present Tense Rule. Be careful — some of these sentences have more than one subject.

example

She and I _*watch*_ late movies on TV.
(to watch)

1. We _____ in the all-Greek glee club.
   (to sing)

2. I usually _____ to work on photography projects.
   (to prefer)

3. He and I frequently _____ in the morning.
   (to run)

4. Not I, but she _____ a job at the Computer Center.
   (to want)

5. We really _____ or _____ very little about the
   (to know)   (to understand)
   moons of Jupiter.

6. It _____ its own way home.
   (to find)

7. They _____ and _____ every piece of mail.
   (to read)   (to answer)

8. He _____ his work has improved.
   (to find)

9. Neither she nor I _____ to play baseball.
   (to like)

10. It _____ from place to place during the winter.
           (to wander)

11. In the shed she _____ her canned vegetables.
                        (to store)

12. We _____ to the office manager.
          (to report)

13. He _____ or _____ to her every night.
         (to call)   (to talk)

14. He and she often _____ into Chicago to visit her high
                        (to go)

school friends.

15. It _____ and _____ patience.
       (to require)   (to teach)

16. They _____ and _____ new workers each month.
       (to interview)   (to hire)

17. She _____ several new workers each month.
        (to hire)

18. I _____ often with my roommate about his fear of tests.
     (to joke)

19. Neither we nor they _____ her with her homework during
                   (to help)

exam week.

20. We _____ *One of the Best* every Thursday night.
       (to watch)

    Now let's work with the same kind of sentences, only with *to be* and *to have* as verbs.

Exercise 8

Using *To Be* and *To Have* with Pronoun Subjects

Each of the sentences in this exercise contains a blank line where a verb belongs.

a. Mark the **subject** of each sentence.

b. **Write the correct form** of the verb in parentheses on the line — either the **present tense** or *was* or *were*.

If necessary, use the charts on pages 279 and 280 to help you. Be careful — some of these sentences have more than one subject.

example

She ___*is*___ one of the candidates for treasurer.
     (to be)

1. He and I _____ in town for just this weekend.
          (to be)

2. She _____ and _____ an excellent employee.
      (to be)   (*was* or *were*)

3. They _____ one of the finest examples of Indian beadwork
       (to have)

in the Southwest.

4. He _____ in the market for a BMW.
   (*was* or *were*)

5. It _____ time for another evaluation.
   (*to be*)

6. You and I _____ not the best coaches for this team.
   (*to be*)

7. She _____ only a few minutes and _____ in
   (*to have*)   (*to be*)

   a hurry.

8. You _____ already a candidate for the promotion.
   (*was* or *were*)

9. Neither he nor they _____ ever critical of my efforts.
   (*to be*)

10. Neither they nor he _____ enough quarters for the
    (*to have*)

    washing machines.

Exercise 9

Correcting Present Tense Verbs with Pronoun Subjects

Each of the sentences in this exercise contains a present tense verb.

a. Mark the **verb** and **subject** of each sentence.

b. Then **correct** any incorrect verb forms.

c. If the sentence contains no errors, write **OK** in the margin.

If necessary, use the charts on pages 279 and 280 to help you. Be careful
— some of these sentences have more than one subject or verb.

examples

works
She (work) every Saturday.

ok   He and I (find) this class challenging.

1. We washes and dry dishes every evening.

2. I hates last minute work.

3. You and he finds his humor refreshing.

4. Most evenings she and I walks by the lake after supper.

5. Usually they teaches that course in the spring.

6. He do his homework in the morning and work in the evening.

7. I knows your need for an evening babysitter.

8. It look like another boring weekend.

9. They always takes their youngest daughter with them to the island.

285 Verbs that add -*s*

10. Either he or she report all the results to the chief surgeon in person.

11. He and she comes late to school on Fridays.

12. The rest of the week she ride with her sister in the truck.

13. They usually arrive from Boston and stays a week.

14. I sometimes hears moans from the locked room in the back of

the house.

15. You and he vote the same way in every election.

16. She never ring the bell or knock on the door.

17. She just come on in.

18. We always looks for him in the library.

19. It make a list of those documents and record it.

20. I want your help with the report.

Exercise 10

Correcting *To Be* and *To Have* with Pronoun Subjects

Each of the sentences in this exercise contains a form of *to be* or *to have*.

a. Mark the **verb** and **subject** of each sentence.

b. Then **correct** any incorrect form of *to be* or *to have*.

c. If the sentence contains no errors, write **OK** in the margin.

If necessary, use the charts on pages 279 and 280 to help you. Be careful — some of these sentences have more than one subject or verb.

example

She (*be*) my best teacher.
is

1. We and you is on her list of available applicants.

2. She have a copy in her desk.

3. He be luckier than most people and have a good mind besides.

4. You and I am nowhere near a solution to problem twelve.

5. They never have enough room in this sorority house for a large party.

6. We usually has dinner at seven.

7. You and she has a color television in your room.

8. She be the wife of the Roman governor and have much power.

9. It were hard enough without Byron's help.

10. In the evening she and I was waitresses.

11. Either she or we have several examples in stock.

12. Neither we nor she were in his upper division course.

13. He have an answer for everything and be ready for anything.

14. She have a decision and are happy with it.

15. You and I was wrong.

16. In his desk he have extra paper.

17. Neither they nor you was on time.

18. We were at the door for at least ten minutes.

19. He be the one for the team.

20. Both he and she has a book with the wrong answers in it.

Finding the Pronoun Substitute for the Subject

You now know how to apply the Present Tense Rule to sentences with personal pronouns as subjects. The next step is to apply the rule to sentences with nouns and other kinds of pronouns as subjects.

In order to do that accurately, we need to learn a technique called **pronoun substitution**.

Pronoun substitution will turn any subject into a personal pronoun. With pronoun substitution, correcting subject-verb agreement will never be more complicated than it is in the exercises you have just done.

Every subject or group of subjects can be turned into a personal pronoun that means the same thing as that subject.

If the noun *cars*, for example, is used as a subject, it could be turned into the personal pronoun *they* without changing the meaning.

Several racing **cars** (crashed) at Altamont last week.

They (crashed) at Altamont last week.

We say that *they* is the **pronoun substitute** for *cars*.

Pronoun substitute: *cars* = *they*

287 Verbs that add *-s*

We can show the pronoun substitute when we mark sentences by writing it over the subject.

Several racing *they* **cars** (crashed) at Altamont last week.

Notice that only *they* will substitute for *cars*. None of the other personal pronouns — *I, you, he, she, it,* or *we* — will work.

All subjects have personal pronoun substitutes. If the subject is a pronoun like *someone*, for example, the personal pronoun substitute is *he or she*. (We say "he or she" because we don't know whether the subject is a man or a woman.)

he or she **Someone** in a red sedan (is watching) me.

Recall that two or more subjects joined by *and* act like one subject, and the pronoun substitute is always *they*.

they **Mike and Clara** (met) last spring at the Fish-out-of-

Water Dance.

On the other hand, if the subject is two or more subjects joined by *but, or,* or *nor*, each subject has its own pronoun substitute.

he *she* Either **Marcus** or **Melissa** (can help) you.

This is because the verb, as you have learned, must agree with the nearest subject.

For reference, all of the pronoun substitutes are listed below.

Pronoun Substitutes

Singular	Plural
I	we
you	you
he	they
she	
he or she	
it	

NOTE: You may wish to review the material on finding subjects in Chapter 1 before doing these exercises.

Exercise 11

Pronoun Substitutes

Write the **pronoun substitute** for each of the following items on the line.

example	____*it*____ highway

1. _____ night

2. _____ lawyer

3. _____ fraud

4. _____ eyes

5. _____ chair

6. _____ the family

7. _____ the Browns

8. _____ everyone

9. _____ people

10. _____ each

11. _____ animals

12. _____ class

13. _____ paintings and photographs

14. _____ pens

15. _____ the car

16. _____ plants

17. _____ many

18. _____ buttons

19. _____ Mario and Silvie

20. _____ she

21. _____ doctor

22. _____ Mr. Hernandez

23. _____ Buick

24. _____ Secretary Stevenson

289 Verbs that add *-s*

25. _____ wheels

26. _____ the dean and her assistants

27. _____ piano

28. _____ cabinets

29. _____ the television and the radio

30. _____ dentists

Exercise 12

Pronoun Substitutes in Sentences

For each of the sentences in this exercise, do the following.

a. Mark the **verb** and **subject.**

b. Write the **pronoun substitute** above the subject.

Be careful — some of these sentences have more than one subject.

example

he or she
A <u>dentist</u> (has) a house in the neighborhood.

1. The plane landed on level ground.

2. Each of the museums refused the painting.

3. Mr. Dickey never witnessed the flight.

4. Each of them voiced another complaint.

5. Her birthday and her anniversary come close together.

6. An eagle or a hawk was spotted in the canyon.

7. Several windows were broken in the storm.

8. Mr. Brown's stories are often published.

9. Many of the runways were icy.

10. Mike and Martin looked for the lost calf.

11. Half of the profits went back into the business.

12. Her jewels were never found.

13. Her jewelry was never found.

14. Eva and her mother will take the trip together.

15. Neither the potatoes nor the wine was poisoned.

16. Not a grocery store, but a drugstore is being built on the corner.

17. You must arrive by eight o'clock, however.

18. Most of the statues are made of marble.

19. Only one of the bank accounts is closed.

20. The news or a drama will be telecast at ten this evening.

Sentences with Noun Subjects

Now let's look at sentences with nouns as subjects. The key to correct subject-verb agreement in these sentences is pronoun substitution.

To make a verb agree with a noun subject, do the following.

1. Mark the **subject**.

2. Write its **pronoun substitute**.

3. **Choose the verb** that agrees with the pronoun substitute following the Present Tense Rule.

For example:

My **mother** *she* (**speaks**) fluent German.

(Present Tense Rule: *she speaks*)

These **commuters** *they* (**work**) at the Penwicker Building.

(Present Tense Rule: *they work*)

Both his **parents** and **Frank** *they* (**watch**) football every Sunday.

(Present Tense Rule: *they watch*)

Neither his **parents** nor **Frank** *they* *he* (**watches**) football every Sunday.

(Present Tense Rule: *he watches*)

Sentences with Reversed Word Order

Sentences with reversed word order must be watched carefully for subject-verb agreement. Errors in these sentences can be difficult to notice. (You studied reversed word order in Chapter 2.)

In speech people often use the *-s* form of the verb in all sentences with reversed word order, regardless of subject. This is especially true in sentences starting with *here* and *there*.

Incorrect

Here (is) your test <u>scores</u>.

Corrected

Here **are** your test **scores**.

Present Tense Rule: *they are*

The *-s* form of the verb should be used only if the subject has *he*, *she*, or *it* as a pronoun substitute.

Here **is** your test **score**.

Present Tense Rule: *it is*

Exercise 13

Using Present Tense Verbs with Noun Subjects

Each of the sentences in this exercise contains a blank line where a present tense verb belongs.

a. Mark the **subject** of each verb.

b. Write the **pronoun substitute**.

c. Then **complete each sentence** with the correct present tense verb.

Be sure to follow the Present Tense Rule.

example

She
<u>Marylynn</u> __*wants*__ one of the vases for herself.
      (to want)

1. The new government _____ every citizen to vote.
      (to require)

2. Too much juniper extract _____ the body.
      (to poison)

3. Officer Brady and his partner _____ at the station.
      (to sleep)

4. A dollar _____ less than it did.
      (to buy)

5. Pamela sometimes _____ to leave early.
      (to ask)

6. Good plans _____ many mistakes.
      (to eliminate)

7. Joey _____ his friends every night at Dante's Pizza Inferno.
      (to meet)

8. My sisters and my girlfriend _____ to me regularly.
                              (to write)

9. Either the janitors or Mr. Chin _____ the trash every
                                   (to remove)

other day.

10. Brian _____ happy with his test results.
          (to appear)

Exercise 14

Using *To Be* and *To Have* with Noun Subjects

Each of the sentences in this exercise contains a blank line where a present tense verb or *was* or *were* belongs.

a. Mark the **subject** of each verb.

b. Write the **pronoun substitute**.

c. Then **complete each sentence** with the correct verb form.

Be sure to follow the Present Tense Rule.

example

The manager _*is*_ a friend of mine.
    he or she   (to be)

1. Roy _____ in the library tonight.
           (to be)

2. The players _____ Sandra and Michele.
              (*was* or *were*)

3. Neither the students nor the teacher _____ familiar.
                                        (to be)

4. My left eye _____ a touch of green in the iris.
              (to have)

5. Here _____ your cruise tickets.
         (to be)

6. The vegetables _____ not fresh here.
                 (to be)

7. The test _____ some surprise questions.
            (to have)

8. There _____ several people at the gas station.
          (to be)

9. Her objective _____ to become a registered nurse.
                (*was* or *were*)

10. The dockyards and harbor _____ open now.
                           (to be)

The following exercise contains all of the kinds of verbs you have been studying so far.

Correcting Present Tense Verbs with Noun Subjects

Each of the sentences in this exercise contains either a present tense verb or *was* or *were*.

a. Mark the **verb** and **subject** and write the **pronoun substitute**.

b. Then **correct** any incorrect verb forms.

c. If the sentence contains no errors, write **OK** in the margin.

1. The tickets be for sale.

2. The bank closes at seven o'clock on Fridays.

3. Alvin always call her in the afternoon.

4. Good fences make good neighbors.

5. Judy and her brother laughs at anything.

6. Jack rabbits grow wild and is common in Wyoming.

7. These ideas was once very popular.

8. Allie and Jill leads the basketball team in rebounds.

9. Here be the latest prices.

10. The dinner were excellent after all.

11. A jet or small plane take off or land every two minutes.

12. The class start at noon and end at two.

13. The teacher or his assistant, however, usually arrive five minutes late.

14. My whole family ride horses well.

15. There is two samples in his room.

16. Neither you nor Sara have fun at these gatherings.

17. Both you and Sara has fun at these gatherings.

18. The capsules is better for you and tastes like imitation orange flavor.

19. Their political plans frighten most people.

20. Either the book or your notes has an answer to that question.

USING THE PRESENT TENSE RULE IN VERB PHRASES

The present tense rule can also apply to the first helping verb in a verb phrase. These helping verbs are the ones printed in **boldface** in the helping verb list below.

Helping Verbs

1	2	3	4	5
shall	should	**do**	**have**	**am**
will	would	**does**	**has**	**is**
can	could	did	had	**are**
may	might			**was**
must				**were**
				be
				been
				being

Notice that the boldfaced words are the same words you have been working with already in this chapter.

they
Bill and Simon (**have** been receiving) mail regularly.

Present Tense Rule: *they have*

it
The university (**is** building) a new radio station.

Present Tense Rule: *it is*

Recall that the past tense forms *was* and *were* must also agree with the subject.

he
Henry (**was** decorated) for bravery in the Vietnam

War.

As before, be especially careful of sentences with reversed word order. Errors in these sentences can be difficult to notice.

Reversed word order (question)

he
(**Is**) Carlos (waiting) for a ride?

Present Tense Rule: *he is waiting*

The Present Tense Rule applies only to the first word in a verb phrase and not to verb phrases like *would see* or *could take*.

Exercise 16

Correcting Verbs in Verb Phrases

For each sentence in this exercise

a. Mark the **verb** and **subject** and write the **pronoun substitute**.

b. Then **correct** any incorrect verb forms.

c. If the sentence contains no errors, write **OK** in the margin.

NOTE: Some of the verbs that need correction are one-word verbs.

example

She   was
Susan (were standing) near the wreckage and (have taken)   *has*

notes.

1. The horse have escaped through the break in the fence and are running away.

2. The singer were asked about concert tickets.

3. Do the evening performance usually start on time?

4. Mario and Vito be looking for Ben Garetski.

5. The two faculty members has responded to the complaints.

6. Is the films being shot in Brooklyn?

7. Neither the shirt nor the shoes are made in Taiwan.

8. The chicken is cooking on the outdoor grill and will be done shortly.

9. Jim and Annette is not attending the concert this evening.

10. Here is more examples of Jim's careful work.

BONUS: The restaurants on this block has supported the radio station in the past and is buying tickets to the benefit again this year.

RELATED SKILL   SUBJECT-VERB AGREEMENT IN PROBLEM SENTENCES

If you have worked in Units 2 and 3 of this book, you know that sentences can have more than one clause and can contain complex verbal phrases and appositives.

Verb errors in these sentences can be more difficult to correct for a number of reasons.

For one thing, there are usually more subject-verb pairs to notice.

For another, many of these sentences contain verbs that are widely separated from their subjects.

Finally, the subject itself can be a clause or a phrase.

More Than One Subject-Verb Pair

You have seen that when two or more subjects are connected by *and*, the pronoun substitute must be *they*. On the other hand, if the connecting word is *but*, *or*, or *nor*, the verb agrees with the one subject nearest to it.

Subjects joined with *and*

they
Ms. Williams and **Mr. Hanson** (have) night classes.

Present Tense Rule: *they have*

Subjects joined with *nor*

they   *he*
Neither the **students** nor **Mr. Hanson** (works) on Tuesday night.

Present Tense Rule: *he works*

When one sentence contains more than one clause, each verb must agree with its subject. (Recall that each clause, by definition, contains a subject-verb pair.)

Two clauses

it   *they*
The **theater** (looks) full, but **tickets** (are) still available.

Present Tense Rule: *it looks*
                                    they are

Be thorough in correcting sentences for subject-verb agreement. It's easy to overlook the second or third verb in a sentence.

Widely Separated Subjects and Verbs

Many sentences have phrases or clauses between the subject and its verb. These phrases or clauses can contain words that are mistaken for the real subject of the verb.

In the following sentence, for example, the verbal phrase *running on that train* comes between the subject and verb. *Train* might appear to be the subject of the sentence. Nevertheless, the verb must agree with *cars*, not *train*, since *cars* is the real subject of the sentence.

Phrase between subject and verb

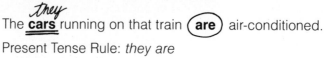

The **cars** running on that train (**are**) air-conditioned.

Present Tense Rule: *they are*

Notice that if you mistake *train* for the subject, you will choose *is* as the verb.

The problem becomes more difficult if a whole clause is placed between the subject and the verb.

Clause between subject and verb

Her aunt, who leaves at ten in the morning, is taking the train.

Notice that in this sentence there are two subject-verb pairs to check — *aunt is taking* and *who leaves*. The first pair is widely separated by the clause.

she
Her **aunt,** who leaves at ten in the morning, (**is taking**) the train.

Present Tense Rule: *she is*

The second pair contains the tip-off word *who*, which has the same meaning as the word it describes — in this case, *aunt*.

She
Her aunt, **who leaves** at ten, is taking the train.

Present Tense Rule: *she leaves*

Clauses and Phrases as Subjects

You know that verbal phrases and noun clauses can be subjects.

Keep in mind that if the subject is a phrase or clause, like *running down the beach* or *what she found in the closet,* **the pronoun substitute is always** *it*.

Verbal phrase as subject

it

[Running down the beach] (is) fun.

Present Tense Rule: *it is*

Noun clause as subject

it

| What you see| (is) what you get.

Present Tense Rule: *it is*

Skill Exercise

Correcting Problem Sentences

For each of the following sentences
a. Mark each **verb** and **subject** and write each **pronoun substitute**.

b. Then **correct** any incorrect verb forms.

c. If the sentence contains no errors, write **OK** in the margin.

example

he   *goes*   *I*

The man in the blue suit (go) to the store after I (leave) school.

1. The ladies in the laundry room is running a football pool.

2. Mr. Vanagan, one of my sister's neighbors, like to tell war stories.

3. Here is the prizes that you have ordered.

4. The water in these glasses, which has been standing for three

   days, are stale and smelly.

5. The film look good, but the sound be terrible.

6. It seem like the whole week were wasted.

7. Are this your lab examination book?

8. Neither Mr. Brandt nor his students is coming back on the bus;

   they be taking Jim's car instead.

9. Whatever you find in his pockets are yours to keep.

10. Mr. Brandt and Mr. Dowd, whom the dean have hired, is teaching

    here in the fall.

Chapter Review

In this chapter you learned

1. **Present tense verbs** have two forms.
   a. The Basic Form (like *see*)
   b. The *-s* Form (like *sees*)

2. **Subject-Verb Agreement:** Present tense verbs must agree with their subjects according to the Present Tense Rule.

3. **Present Tense Rule:** For one-word present tense verbs and those that start a verb phrase
   a. Use the *-s* form when the subject is *he*, *she*, or *it*.
   b. Use the basic form in all other cases.

   This rule also applies to the past tense forms *was* and *were*.

4. The verb *to be* has the following forms:

   ### Present Tense Forms of *To Be*

Singular	Plural
I am	we are
you are	you are
he **is**	
she **is**	they are
it **is**	

   ### Past Tense Forms of *To Be*

Singular	Plural
I **was**	we were
you were	you were
he **was**	
she **was**	they were
it **was**	

5. The verb *to have* has the following forms.

   ### Present Tense Forms of *To Have*

Singular	Plural
I have	we have
you have	you have
he **has**	
she **has**	they have
it **has**	

In the RELATED SKILL section you learned to **be especially careful** of present tense verbs in sentences with

1. **Reversed word order**

2. **Widely separated subject and verb**

3. **More than one clause**

4. **Phrases and clauses as subjects**

Review Exercise 1

This paragraph contains only sentences similar to those discussed in Unit 1.

Correct all errors in subject-verb agreement. Then **rewrite** the paragraph on the lines provided.

The morning breaks clear and hot. It be a scorcher. By ten o'clock, the temperature reach 92°. The city pavement are probably worse. Windows opens in hopes of a breeze. The hopes go unfulfilled, however. Nothing move, not even the air. Who called Chicago the Windy City? According to my sister, an egg would fries on the sidewalk. I be always interested in science. I grabs an egg and heads for the door.

_____

_____

_____

_____

_____

_____

_____

_____

_____

_____

_____

_____

Review Exercise 2

This paragraph contains sentences like those discussed in Units 2 and 3 — sentences with verbal phrases, appositives, and more than one clause.

Correct all errors in subject-verb agreement. Then **rewrite** the paragraph on the lines provided.

The idea that there exist a basic building block of nature called the "atom" go back to the early Greeks. Atoms are the basic unit of all elements, but they is not the most basic units of matter. All atoms has parts, and no matter what atom they comes from, these basic parts all looks alike. Of course, no one know yet what these parts be, but we knows they exists because we can finds them with very sophisticated experiments. There is several examples of science "finding" something before it know for sure what it have found. This be one of them.

_____

_____

_____

_____

_____

_____

_____

_____

_____

_____

_____

Review Exercise 3

Most of the sentences in these paragraphs are simple sentences. The story is written as though it happened in the past. **Change the story to the present time** by doing the following.

1. **Mark** each subject and verb.

2. **Change each verb** to a present tense form similar to one of the following.

> Sees
> Is seeing
> Can see
> May see

3. **Recopy** your new paragraph on the lines provided.

Make sure all of your subjects and verbs agree.

His name was Mr. Torres. He was my friend. He told me about a baseball game in town, a pre-season game with no admission charge. He always seemed so wise and gentle. He shared everything with me.

We went to the game together. Mr. Torres bought hot dogs and peanuts for us both. We ate and cheered every play. I didn't care about the winner. I cared about being with this man.

Mr. Torres taught me about life, about kindness, about love. He was my friend. He was my father.

_____

_____

_____

_____

_____

_____

_____

_____

_____

_____

_____

Chapter 11 Writing Assignment

Write a paragraph that defines, or tells what *you mean* by, "loyalty." Include two short examples of loyalty shown by well-known people. Then tell a longer story that shows loyalty shown by someone you know.

When you have made your final copy

1. Mark each **verb and subject**.

2. Make sure that
   a. All **verbs and subjects agree**.
   b. All **clauses and phrases** are correctly punctuated.
   c. Your paragraph contains **no fragments**.

Hints for Definition Paragraphs

This paragraph has a slightly different structure than the others you have done, but it should be a very effective paper if you follow the hints below.

For this paragraph we will make three lists to write from. These lists will help make the writing go smoothly and result in the best paragraph possible.

Before the rough draft:

1. Make a preliminary list of qualities of loyalty — ways that you think loyal people act. Try to include at least one quality that most people would not expect to see in your list.

2. Edit this list (by adding things in and taking things out) until you are sure it shows your own thinking — not just what "everyone" thinks loyalty is.

3. Now make a list of five or six well-known people who have done something you think shows real loyalty.

4. Edit this list until it includes two examples — the best and most interesting you can imagine.

5. Now make your last list — of people you know who have really shown what you mean by loyalty.

6. Now edit this list down to one name — the person you most want to write about.

Writing the rough draft:

1. Start your rough draft by writing a short group of sentences that tells
   a. What word you are going to explain (in this case, "loyalty") and
   b. Why you want to explain it.

2. Using your list of qualities, write a few sentences that explain what you think loyalty is.

3. Next write two (or more) sentences that mention the well-known people as examples. (Be sure to tell what they do or did.)

4. Now tell your story about the person you know.

5. Write a closing sentence or two that sums up what you think these examples show about loyalty.

After the rough draft:

1. Do your best to correct any errors on this first copy. Be especially careful to correct all errors in
   a. Subject-verb agreement
   b. Punctuation

2. Make any other changes you think will make your paragraph more interesting and readable.

3. Recopy your corrected paragraph on a clean sheet of paper and turn in all of your work.

12
Verbs that add -*ed*

**Chapter
Preview**

This chapter will show you how to find and correct **errors with verbs that add** -*ed*, like *looked* and *had worked*.

In addition, a RELATED SKILL section will help you find and correct errors in past participles that add -*ed* used as **verbals and in verbal phrases**.

NOTE: The chapters in this Unit can be worked by any student who has completed Unit 1.
   For students who have also completed Units 2 and 3, the RELATED SKILL section contains exercises that rely on knowledge of that material as well.

In Chapter 11 you learned to write and correct verbs that add the endings -s and -es. In this chapter you will learn about verbs that add the endings -d and -ed.

PAST TENSE AND PAST PARTICIPLE

Unlike the ending -s, which shows changes in the subject, the endings -d and -ed show changes in the verb — usually from the present time to some kind of past or completed action.

One way to show past time action is with a simple one-word form called the **past tense**. Another way is with verb phrases that combine *have-* and *be-* group helping verbs with a verb form called the **past participle**. Verb phrases with past participles also show completed actions.

NOTE: Any student can do this chapter before completing Units 2 and 3 in this book.

If you have done those units, however, you will recognize that the past participle is one of the verbals you studied in Chapter 8. (The RELATED SKILL section of this chapter contains exercises that rely on your knowledge of verbals.)

The Three Principal Parts of Verbs

Let's look at the past tense and past participle more closely and see which verbs add -d and -ed to make them.

As a group these two forms, along with the basic present tense form, have a special name. They are called the **three principal parts** of a verb. The three principal parts of a verb are simply its three main forms.

The **present tense** shows present time actions. (You studied the present tense in the last chapter.)

The **past tense** shows past time action. It is never used with helping verbs.

The **past participle** shows past and completed actions by combining with helping verbs to make verb phrases.

Regular and Irregular Verbs

Some verbs, called **regular verbs**, form the past tense and past participle by adding either -d or -ed to the present tense form with no major change in pronunciation.

The past tense and past participle of regular verbs are always spelled the same. The verb *play* is a regular verb (past tense: *played*; past participle: *played*).

Other verbs, called **irregular verbs**, are spelled in a number of different ways. For most irregular verbs, the past tense and past participle are NOT spelled the same. The verb *see* is an irregular verb (past tense: *saw*; past participle: *seen*).

Following are the three principal parts of some common regular verbs.

Three Principal Parts of Regular Verbs

Present Tense	Past Tense	Past Participle
add	added	(have) added
allow	allowed	(have) allowed
apply	applied	(have) applied
close	closed	(have) closed
die	died	(have) died
occur	occurred	(have) occurred
plan	planned	(have) planned
postpone	postponed	(have) postponed
study	studied	(have) studied
work	worked	(have) worked

Notice that some verbs add -*d*,

close	closed
die	died

some add -*ed*,

add	added
work	worked

some double the final letter before adding -*ed*,

plan	planned
occur	occurred

and some that end in *y* change the *y* to *i* before adding -*ed*.

apply	applied

See Chapter 18, Spelling, to learn more about spelling the past tense and past participle of regular verbs.

USING THE PAST TENSE AND PAST PARTICIPLE OF REGULAR VERBS

The most common error students make with regular verbs is to drop the -*d* or -*ed* ending. Because the -*ed* sound is sometimes hard to hear in speech, students sometimes fail to write it.

To correct this error, you must know when the *-ed* ending is needed. For regular verbs, add *-ed* or *-d*.

1. One-word past tense verbs
   Example: *I prepared.*

2. Past participles in verb phrases
   Example: *I have prepared.*

3. Past participles used in other ways (for example, as subjects, objects, or adjectives)
   Example: A *prepared* answer

   The first two situations listed above will be studied in the regular material of this chapter. Any student who has completed Unit 1 of this book can do these sections successfully.

   The third situation, past participles used in other ways, will be discussed in the RELATED SKILL section. Do this section only if you have completed Units 2 and 3.

Adding *-ed* to Make Past Tense Verbs

The following sentence contains a one-word past tense verb. Note that there are no helping verbs.

Regular past tense verb

The author (**visited**) the scene of the crime.

The following sentence contains a past tense verb with the *-ed* ending left off.

Incorrect

The messenger (return) the package last Friday.

The verb *return* is clearly wrong in this sentence. For one thing, the meaning of the sentence is past time, since the action happened *last Friday*.

And secondly, as you learned in the last chapter, the correct present tense form for this sentence is *returns*. (Messenger = he or she. Present tense rule: *he or she returns.*)

The correct past tense verb for this sentence is *returned*.

Corrected

returned

The messenger (return) the package last Friday.

Exercise 1

Using Past Tense Verbs

Mark the **subject** of the following sentences. Then **complete each sentence** with the correct **past tense verb**.

Sheila *received* their latest offer yesterday.
(to receive)

1. Yesterday he _____ first trombone in the band concert.
   (to play)

2. He _____ to go to college last fall.
   (to want)

3. The registrar _____ the spring catalogue already.
   (to publish)

4. She _____ herself well for her new career.
   (to prepare)

5. Jerry _____ every question he could think of.
   (to ask)

6. The dean _____ making the error.
   (to admit)

7. The big man _____ , and tears filled his eyes.
   (to frown)

8. Michael's Buick _____ away from the stop sign.
   (to roar)

9. They _____ in the afternoon and studied at night.
   (to play)

10. Mr. Wagner _____ his students to compete in the national
    (to urge)

science competition.

The next exercise asks you to decide between present and past tense forms in sentences. Before doing it, you may wish to review the Present Tense Rule (pages 273–274) and pronoun substitution (pages 287–288) in the last chapter.

Exercise 2

Choosing Between the Past Tense and Present Tense

Each of the following sentences contains a regular one-word verb. Some of the verb forms are correct, and some are not.

a. Use the meaning of the sentence and your common sense to tell you whether the present tense or past tense is needed. Then write **present** or **past** on the line.

b. **Mark** each verb and subject.

c. **Correct** any incorrect verbs or write **OK** over any correct verb.

examples

past Alice then (pick) *picked* a card from the deck.

present Dr. Herrera and Mr. James often (lecture) *OK* here in

the past.

_____ 1. Susan play records all yesterday afternoon.

_____ 2. Last weekend he want to drive to the farm.

_____ **3.** Jennifer learn too late about the deadline.

_____ **4.** Robert Fulton invented the steamboat in the 1800s.

_____ **5.** People at the time call the steamboat

"Fulton's Folly."

_____ **6.** Now they offer either soup or salad before dinner.

_____ **7.** Mr. Simms replace the picture tube for $150.00.

_____ **8.** The Founding Fathers of our country never want

one branch of government to become too strong.

_____ **9.** Their son always asks for ice cream after a meal.

_____ **10.** Sandro repair the broken antenna before the

last storm.

Exercise 3	Correcting Past Tense Verbs

Mark each **verb** and **subject** of the following sentences. **Correct** any incorrect verbs. If the verb is already correct, write **OK** in the margin.

Use the meaning of the sentence and your common sense to tell you whether the present tense or past tense is needed.

moved

example	Barry's <u>boss</u> (move) into the corner office.

1. Last year's vacation never follow our plans.

2. The gentlemen like the restaurant from the start.

3. Yesterday the Harrises invite us skiing with them.

4. He promise another article for the school newspaper.

5. She wait for a better time.

6. Then she ask the question.

7. After much discussion, the judges eventually declare Another Horse's

Color the winner.

8. The finish line pictures show a foul by the original winner, Southern

Cal Comfort.

311 Verbs that add *-ed*

9. The band receive an invitation for a return engagement.

10. Her boss also hire her for the final evaluation.

11. Careless campers often cause forest fires.

12. The play receive good reviews from all three critics.

13. Last night the president appear on television.

14. This man seems ready for tomorrow's test.

15. Brenda correct the error in the computer yesterday.

16. The librarians discuss the growing problem with fines at their last week's meeting.

17. Last time the local politicians allow the company's engineers to draft their own policy.

18. Then, surprisingly, they reject the proposal without even a discussion.

19. The cat remain in his box all night.

20. Descartes almost single-handedly turn the course of philosophy in a new direction.

Adding *-ed* to Make Past Participles in Verb Phrases

When a verb phrase contains a *have-* or *be*-group helping verb, the action word must be either an *-ing* word or a past participle.

Past participles of regular verbs always end in *-d* or *-ed*. If this ending is dropped, the sentence seems to contain an incorrect present tense form. Present tense verbs cannot be used with *have-* or *be*-group helping verbs.

The following sentences contain regular past participles in verb phrases. Notice the *-d* or *-ed* endings.

Past participles in verb phrases

Wilma <u>(has fulfilled)</u> her fondest ambition.

The faculty (is housed) in Lambert Hall.

Both action words end in *-d* or *-ed* because

1. They are regular verbs, and
2. The verb phrases contain a *have-* or *be*-group helping verb.

Past participles

has fulfill**ed**

is hous**ed**

Exercise 4

Using Past Participles

Place an **X** over each *have-* or *be-*group helping verb. Then complete each verb phrase with a correct **present tense or past participle** form.

Use the list of regular verbs on page 309 as examples for your work in this exercise. (You can also consult the dictionary.) Do not use any verb twice. If a sentence is already correct, write **OK** in the margin.

examples

should be X *received*

could *work*

1. could have been _____

2. could _____

3. did _____

4. should be _____

5. was _____

6. will be _____

7. might have been _____

8. had _____

9. will _____

10. is _____

11. do _____

12. shall _____

13. are _____

14. were _____

15. has _____

16. can _____

17. can be _____

18. might have _____

19. does _____

20. have _____

Exercise 5

Correcting Past Participles in Verb Phrases

Mark each **verb phrase** in the following sentences, and place an **X** over any *have-* or *be-*group helping verb.

Then **correct** any incorrect verb phrase. If a sentence is already correct, write **OK** in the margin

example

Sean's image (was reflect) in the mirror.
X *reflected*

1. Several pieces of wood were place on the worktable.

2. The last bell has already sound.

3. This game should be play by more than three players.

4. That question was never ask.

5. The infected organs will be remove Wednesday.

6. Three men were arrest yesterday for the Lucky's Liquor Barn holdup.

7. We could serve them fried eggs and ham for breakfast.

8. The arbitrator's ruling was appeal to the governing board.

9. Michael was stop in the restricted zone.

10. We are not prepare for an indoor picnic.

11. Calbert was interest in my car.

12. The missing books were return yesterday.

13. Despite the blizzard, the mail was deliver all week.

14. A new benefit program was announce by the board of directors.

15. Each of the senators has benefit from the passage of the pension bill.

16. The request for noncompressive widgets will be process by the accounting clerks as soon as possible.

17. She has organize the refreshments for Glenda's retirement party.

18. The mechanic's accident was probably cause by a worn gasket.

19. Your film will not be develop until the day after Tuesday.

20. Professor Nudelbaum will probably cancel next week's class.

Used To and Supposed To

The regular verbs *to use* and *to suppose* deserve special attention. When either of these verbs is followed by an infinitive — a word like *to go* or *to study* — they present a special spelling problem.

Every time these words are followed by *to*, they must end in -*d*. There is no other way to spell these phrases.

use**d** to

suppose**d** to

Notice the -*d* on the end of *used* and *supposed* in these sentences.

Jerry **used to** love reading mysteries.

Jerline was **supposed to** wake us at dawn.

Even the best students sometimes misspell these phrases. Because of the *t*-sound in *to*, no one hears the -*d*. To spell these words correctly, learn to see the -*d*.

Exercise 6

Using *Used To* and *Supposed To*

Complete each of the following sentences with a form of *to use* or *to suppose*. The present tense form, the past tense form, or the past participle might be needed.

example

Franklin was ___*supposed*___ to arrive by eight.
         (to suppose)

1. I _____ to raise our puppies on dry food.
   (to use)

2. They were _____ to help us when they finished work.
       (to suppose)

3. The past tense is _____ as a one-word verb form.
       (to use)

4. His mother was _____ to meet us downtown later
      (to suppose)

this afternoon.

5. I _____ you want to stay longer.
   (to suppose)

6. Do you _____ that brand of after-shave?
     (to use)

7. Have you _____ that brand of lotion?
   (to use)

8. The lawn mower _____ to work.
   (to use)

9. Brandy is sometimes _____ to treat cold symptoms.
   (to use)

10. He _____ to be an altar boy at our local church.
    (to use)

11. Jason was _____ to bring the mailing list; I hope
    (to suppose)

    he remembered.

12. Marylou _____ several notebooks last year to keep her
    (to use)

    schoolwork organized.

13. I wanted to _____ a word processor to complete my
    (to use)

    term paper.

14. Michael was _____ to shovel snow this afternoon.
    (to suppose)

15. Now that we have moved south, we _____ the winter
    (to use)

    months for activities like going to the beach.

Exercise 7

Correcting *Used to* and *Supposed to*

Correct any errors in the verbs *use* or *suppose* in the following sentences. If a sentence is already correct, write **OK** in the margin.

NOTE: Look for errors only in these two verbs. All other verbs or verb forms in these sentences are correct.

example

Juan is ~~suppose~~ *Supposed* to call us soon.

1. I use to like writing.

2. Do you use basil in your spaghetti sauce?

3. Brenda is suppose to solve the last three problems by herself.

4. Did you suppose the instructor would be ill two days in a row?

5. This medicine was suppose to help, but it didn't.

6. The game did not end as it was suppose to.

7. The dollar is not worth as much as it use to be.

8. Yesterday Mr. Jeffries use the elevator to reach his second floor office.

9. I prefer to use the stairs.

10. Walking is suppose to be good exercise.

11. Sammy's teammates use a lighter bat; I suppose that's why he gets more hits than they do.

12. Is Simon use to the cold weather here?

13. This store use to be a bakery.

14. Now it is use as the Sampson campaign headquarters.

15. You are suppose to have the article ready for the January edition of the magazine.

The following exercise brings together everything you have learned about correcting regular verbs.

Exercise 8

Correcting Errors with Regular Verbs

Mark each **verb and subject**. Then **correct any errors** in regular verbs or past participles. If a sentence contains no errors, write **OK** in the margin.

Be careful — some of these sentences have more than one verb joined with *and*, *or*, *but*, or *nor*.

1. The fence was finish before the garden.

2. We could have work a little longer and answer the rest of the mail.

3. The mall close at noon yesterday.

4. Barry enter the room and start an argument with his brother.

5. Several of the checks were discover in this envelope.

6. The grass is water in the morning and mow in the afternoon.

7. According to Caroline, she has suffer enough.

8. She will ask Professor Herrera for a raise in her history grade to a C+.

9. According to Brad, Formalda was use to more intelligent company.

10. According to Formalda, Brad use too many big words on last night's date.

11. Bruce mention his high school track trophy several times.

12. His fraternity brothers were not impress.

13. The party was unplan and underattended.

14. The sergeant listen carefully to Ben's story of the assault.

15. Then he ask several questions and note the answers carefully.

16. Carlos cook his first dinner for Petrova last night.

17. The food tasted good, but need lots of chewing.

18. Even the four fruit bars had been somehow overcook.

19. The emperor was suppose to raise taxes for his war in Silesia.

20. Unfortunately the prisoner's last meal was scorch.

RELATED SKILL   ADDING *-ED* TO MAKE OTHER PAST PARTICIPLES

Do this section if you have completed Units 2 and 3.

In Chapter 8 you saw that past participles are not used just in verb phrases. They can be used in other ways as well. The following sentences show some of these other uses.

Past participle as adjective

The **wrecked** car (sat)(by the freeway.)

Past participle as subject

The **deceased** (was) a friend (of Ms. Jefferson.)

Past participle in adjective verbal phrase

The film, **edited** for television, was shown on Sunday.

Even though these words are not used in verb phrases, they are past participles and need -*d* or -*ed* ending. (*Wrecked* is the past participle of *to wreck*. *Deceased* is the past participle of *to decease*, meaning *to die*. *Edited* is the past participle of the verb *to edit*.)

Past participles like these are often spelled incorrectly, even by some professional writers.

If you doubt that, ask yourself how many times you have seen the word *old-fashioned* spelled *old-fashion*. (The verb *to fashion* means *to make*. *Old-fashioned* means *fashioned*, or *made*, in the "old" way.)

When you are correcting sentences for -*d* and -*ed* endings, watch carefully for past participles used in all of these ways.

Skill Exercise 1

Using Other Past Participles

Mark each **verb and subject**. Then write the **correct past participle** on the line.

example

The senator, *reached* for comment, would say nothing.
(to reach)

1. The soldiers gave a _____ account.
   (to muddle)

2. The _____ organs will be removed Wednesday.
   (to infect)

3. _____ foods don't sit well in my stomach.
   (to fry)

4. The highway to the left is marked as a _____ area.
   (to restrict)

5. That sounds like the opinion of a _____ person.
   (to prejudice)

6. The greatly _____ highway building program goes into ef-
   (to reduce)

   fect next January.

7. Sheila suffers from a slightly _____ spine.
   (to compress)

8. My younger brother wants to enter the field of _____
   (to apply)

   electronics.

9. For most people, washing dishes is a _____ chore.
   (to hate)

10. _____ boots are coming back into style.
    (to lace)

Skill Exercise 2 — Correcting Other Past Participles in Sentences

Most of the following sentences contain a regular past participle used in some way *other* than as part of a verb phrase.

Mark each **verb and subject**. Then **correct any errors** in past participles NOT used in a verb phrase.

If a sentence contains no errors, write **OK** in the margin.

example

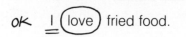

Unanswered
Unanswer <u>letters</u> (sit) on my desk.

OK   <u>I</u> (love) fried food.

1. Their act is performed with specially treat clothing.

2. The police looked for signs of force entry.

3. The Meyers asked about our special price on recently repair vehicles.

4. The fluid flowed faster through previously heat pipes.

5. The paint statues must be ready by noon Saturday, or the production will be delayed.

6. The search party rode north for twenty-five miles.

7. Workmen will have to remove the stain carpet in the living room also.

8. Please place all previously check baggage on the floor in front of you.

9. She reminded him about the unanswer question.

10. The varnish, apply in layers, produces a nice surface shine.

11. Angelica learned about his alter plans only yesterday.

12. A confuse mayor spoke to the town council last night.

13. Mrs. Forbush's best flowers were displayed at the Sunset Garden Show.

14. The cleaners returned a wrinkle pair of pants.

15. Wreck autos litter Highway 409.

16. Old-fashion blueberry ice cream is my favorite.

17. My parents changed their Easter vacation plans at the last minute.

18. Her well-plan trip was ruined by the railroad strike.

19. An edit version of the film was seen on television last evening.

20. The open door revealed a surprise young boy.

Chapter Review

In this chapter you learned that

1. The three **principal parts** of a verb are its
  a. Present tense
  b. Past tense
  c. Past participle

2. **Regular verbs** form the past tense and past participle by adding -d and -ed.

3. The -ed ending is sometimes dropped in writing.

4. You can **correct errors** with the -ed ending by looking at
  a. One-word past tense verbs
  b. Verb phrases that use the past participle

5. The phrases used to and supposed to are always spelled with a -d.

In the RELATED SKILL section you also learned how to correct errors in **past participles used as verbals and in verbal phrases.**

Review Exercise 1

This paragraph contains only sentences similar to those discussed in Unit 1.
  Correct all errors in -ed verbs. Then **rewrite** the paragraph on the lines provided.

    Eduardo jammed hard on the brakes. The car swerve. The windshield

shatter. Inside, we were push to the corner. Terror was plastered on our faces. We pray quickly. Outside, our car collide with another, twisted around and around, and finally stop.

God answered our prayers. None of us was badly injure. We look at the other car. It was flipped over onto its top. A thin, pale leg was push out from an open window.

Berna pry open a door and helped each of us out. Then he cross the street to the other car.

_____

_____

_____

_____

_____

_____

_____

_____

_____

_____

_____

_____

Review Exercise 2

This paragraph contains sentences like those discussed in Units 2 and 3. It includes past participles used as verbals and sentences with verbal phrases, appositives, and more than one clause.

Correct all errors in the *-ed* forms of verbs in the following paragraphs. Then **rewrite** the paragraph on the lines provided.

Mr. Mendez call Brad Palmer this morning and ask him to come over and look at his refrigerator. He want Brad's opinion about whether to repair it or replace it. He knew that Brad use to work on refrigerators and air conditioners all through high school. The refrigerator just stop working sometime during the night. There was an electrical storm at two in the morning, and he was concern that there might have been an electrical overload that damage the refrigerator.

Mr. Mendez did not wanted to buy a new one if he did not need to, since his daughter was suppose to go to college in the fall and he could not afford the add expense of another new appliance. Brad look at the refrigerator carefully, but could not find any real damage — just a switch that had become burn. He replace it easily and charge nothing.

_____

_____

_____

_____

_____

_____

_____

_____

_____

_____

_____

_____

_____

_____

_____

_____

_____

_____

_____

_____

_____

Chapter 12 Writing Assignment

Everyone is creative in some things he or she does. Write a paragraph that discusses the ways in which *you* are creative.

Notice that this paragraph must define the term "creative." Therefore, include a few sentences that tell what "creative" means to you, and then give at least one example of your creativity.

When you have made your final copy

1. Mark each **verb and subject**.

2. Make sure that
   a. All **present tense verbs** and *-ed* **verbs** are correct.
   b. All **clauses and phrases** are correctly punctuated.
   c. Your paragraph contains **no fragments**.

Hints for Definition Paragraphs

This paragraph is really another definition paragraph, similar to the one you did for Chapter 11. For this paragraph we will make two lists to write from.

Before the rough draft:

1. Make a list of qualities you think make up "creativity" — ways that you think creative people act. Try to include at least one quality that most people would not expect to see in your list.

2. Edit this list (by adding things in and taking things out) until you are sure it shows your own thinking — not just what everyone else thinks creativity is.

3. Now make a list of five or six things you have *done* or *made* that show your creativity.

4. Edit this list as you did your first one, until it includes only one or two examples — the best and most interesting you can think of.

Writing the rough draft:

1. Start your rough draft by writing a short group of sentences that tells
   a. What word you are going to explain (*creativity*), and
   b. Why you want to explain it.

2. Using your list of qualities, write a few sentences that explain what you think creativity is.

3. Now write five or six (or more) sentences that either
   a. Describe what you have made, or
   b. Tell what you have done to show your creative side.

4. Write a closing that tells how important this side of your life is to you.

After the rough draft:

1. Do your best to correct any errors on this first copy. Be especially careful to correct all errors in
   a. Present tense verbs
   b. *-ed* verbs
   c. Punctuation

2. Make any other changes you think will make your paragraph more interesting and readable.

3. Recopy your corrected paragraph on a clean sheet of paper and turn in all of your work.

13
More about verb phrases

Chapter
Preview

This chapter will show you how to **choose correctly between verb forms** like *saw* and *had seen*.

In addition, a RELATED SKILL section will help you find and correct these errors in sentences with **more than one clause and verbal phrases**.

NOTE: The chapters in this Unit can be worked by any student who has completed Unit 1.
 For students who have also completed Units 2 and 3, the RELATED SKILL section contains exercises that rely on knowledge of that material as well.

CORRECTING IRREGULAR VERBS

This chapter will help you correct verb phrases by showing you how to choose between the forms of **irregular verbs** — forms like *saw* and *seen*, for example. (You learned about regular verbs in Chapter 12.)

There are two ways to correct errors with irregular verbs. One way involves memorizing the names of all verb forms and the rules for constructing them. (There are twenty-four verb forms, not counting the variations for singular and plural.)

A second way involves recognizing verb phrases that contain *have-* and *be-*group helping verbs. Many students find that this way is easier.

To correct verb phrases using the second method is a three-step process. You must

1. **Find verbs and verb phrases** accurately, identifying *have-* and *be-*group helping verbs.

2. **Learn the three basic forms** (present tense, past tense, and past participle) of the verbs you are using.

3. **Choose the correct verb form** for each verb or verb phrase based on the above information.

In this chapter we will practice this second method, starting with the first step — finding verbs and verb phrases.

FINDING VERBS

To correct verbs and verb phrases, it is necessary to find them. In addition, you need to notice which verb phrases contain *have-* and *be-*group helping verbs, since these words tell whether a form like *saw* or *seen* should be used.

This section contains exercises to help you practice these skills. If you wish, review the information on verbs and verb phrases in Chapters 1 and 2 (pages 4–10 and 34–46). The exercises that follow will reinforce what you learned in those chapters.

For your reference, the list of helping verbs is printed below.

Helping Verbs

Group 1	Group 2	Group 3	Group 4	Group 5
shall	should	do	have	am
will	would	does	has	is
can	could	did	had	are
may	might			was
must				were
				be
				been
				being

Exercise 1

Finding Verbs

Mark all **verbs** and **subjects** in the following sentences. Then place an **X** over all *have-* and *be-*group helping verbs.

NOTE: Some of these sentences contain more than one subject or verb joined by *and, or, but,* or *nor.*

> **example**
>
>   X X
>
> The <u>Ford</u> (is being repaired) at New Castle Auto.

1. Next week's game is played at Shaughnessy Stadium.

2. Jim's parties usually last until morning.

3. Ten thousand dollars is usually awarded to the winner.

4. Those loud noises from the new factory have been frightening the children and are the subject of many complaints.

5. These essays had been received in January, but were not graded until now.

6. Has the Separatist Party voted for the new prime minister?

7. Neither Malcolm nor Jeremy could find the missing samples.

8. Nevertheless, new cars have not been shipped to the dealers in several western states and will not be shipped for several more months.

9. Rain has been falling for weeks now.

10. All of the ceilings and walls have been checked for asbestos.

11. The chair was thrown away last winter.

12. The dog swam several hundred feet to the boat and climbed in.

13. Medical supplies have already been flown into the stricken area and will be distributed by the hospital there.

14. I have never worn that tie.

15. The Princess Award was given to Mrs. Ettard for outstanding telephone sales.

16. Colonel Stroud has been busy for several hours.

17. This will take just a minute.

18. Doctor Parkinson spoke to the medical affairs committee in a closed-door session.

19. I wanted an answer to the disposal question.

20. The birthday cake could have been made this morning, but will not be started until tomorrow.

Being able to find verbs and verb phrases in separately printed sentences is important. But being able to find them in paragraphs is more important, since your own writing consists of paragraphs.

Do the following exercise as carefully as you can. It will help you practice this important skill.

Exercise 2

Finding Verbs in Paragraphs

Mark all **verbs** and **subjects** in the following paragraphs. Then place an **X** over all *have-* and *be-*group helping verbs.

NOTE: Some of these sentences contain more than one subject or verb joined by *and*, *or*, *but*, or *nor*. Nevertheless, all sentences have only one subject-verb pair.

Malcolm has been wondering about his younger brother. Jeremy has just turned eighteen and will join the Navy in September. According to Malcolm, this is a wise decision. But Malcolm is concerned about Jeremy's high school diploma. Jeremy needs one more class. Otherwise, he cannot graduate.

It is already June. Jeremy has not yet registered for summer school, but instead has been spending the last two weeks on a trip with his friends. Jeremy's friends are good people. Nevertheless, they cannot help him with his class. According to Malcolm, Jeremy should spend his final summer in school, not on vacation, and should earn his diploma before the start of his Navy career. According to Jeremy, Malcolm should give no more free advice.

Malcolm and Jeremy have always loved each other and have been even closer since their father's death. But this disagreement may cause a chill in the relationship. Malcolm considers this matter important. His advice may not be welcome. But for the next few weeks, it will be offered strongly.

RELATED SKILL   FINDING VERBS IN SENTENCES WITH MORE THAN ONE CLAUSE

If you have worked in Units 2 and 3, you know that many sentences contain more than one clause. In addition, many sentences contain complex verbal phrases and appositives.

The following exercise contains these kinds of sentences. If you wish, review your work in Units 2 and 3 before continuing. Then work as carefully as you can.

NOTE: If you have NOT done Units 2 and 3, you can still benefit from this exercise. Just watch carefully for sentences with more than one subject-verb pair.

Skill Exercise

Finding Verbs in Paragraphs

Mark all **verbs** and **subjects** in the following sentences. Then place an **X** over all *have-* and *be-*group helping verbs.

NOTE: Many of these sentences have more than one subject and/or verb.

Can Jose get Lisa out of his mind? He doesn't think so, and the members of his basketball team would have to agree. They have seen him acting distracted lately. They have watched him taking shots in practice that touch nothing but air before falling to the floor. They have noticed that he listens to the coach with his eyes on the place where Lisa once sat during the one game that she attended. They have been very unhappy with the way he has been playing.

What are they going to do? Lisa doesn't even know that Jose goes to the same college that she does.

One of Jose's friends, a man named Johnny who had lived in the same neighborhood as Jose, has come up with a suggestion. Johnny thinks that Lisa should be told that Jose is interested in her. She should be told that Jose is the best player on the team and that he conducts himself as a fine young man. She should be told that the team will win next month's tournament if Jose is playing well. Then she should be told that the team may not win another game if Jose never again sees her in the stands.

The choice will then be hers. She can be admired for four weeks by the best shooting guard in the conference, or she can live forever knowing that she has killed the hopes of ten worthy young men and one overdue coach. Johnny thinks that this argument cannot fail. He has used it many times on his parents. He believes that Lisa is at least as smart as they are.

LEARNING THE THREE PRINCIPAL PARTS

The second step in correcting irregular verb phrases is to learn their main forms. As you saw in Chapter 12, these forms are called the "three principal parts." Let's review some of the things you know about these forms.

The three principal parts of a verb are the

> Present tense
>
> Past tense
>
> Past participle

For example, the three principal parts of *to see* are

Present	Past	Past participle
see	saw	(have) seen

Regular and Irregular Verbs

Verbs differ in how the three principal parts are created.

Some verbs, called **regular verbs**, spell the past tense and past participle by adding *-d* or *-ed* to the present tense form without any other change in pronunciation.

This means that for regular verbs, the past tense and past participle are always spelled alike. The principal parts of the regular verb *to walk*, for example, are

Present	**Past**	**Past participle**
walk	walked	(have) walked

You studied regular verbs in Chapter 12.

Other verbs, called **irregular verbs**, have past tense and past participle forms that are created and spelled in a variety of ways. *To go* is an example of an irregular verb. Its principal parts are

Present	**Past**	**Past participle**
go	went	(have) gone

The three principal parts of some common irregular verbs are listed below.

Three Principal Parts of Some Common Irregular Verbs

Present Tense	**Past Tense**	**Past Participle**
become	became	(have) become
bring	brought	(have) brought
buy	bought	(have) bought
go	went	(have) gone
grow	grew	(have) grown
hear	heard	(have) heard
see	saw	(have) seen
teach	taught	(have) taught

Learning the three principal parts of all verbs is important. But learning the principal parts of irregular verbs is especially important, since these forms cannot always be spelled by guessing.

Exercise 3

Three Principal Parts

Following is a list of thirty common irregular verbs. Using the lists of irregular verbs on pages 342–43, 344, and 346–47, write the past tense and past participle forms next to the present tense form.

	Present Tense	Past Tense	Past Participle
example	become	*became*	(have) *become*
	1. bid	_____	(have) _____
	2. teach	_____	(have) _____
	3. fight	_____	(have) _____
	4. mean	_____	(have) _____
	5. grow	_____	(have) _____
	6. see	_____	(have) _____
	7. choose	_____	(have) _____
	8. get	_____	(have) _____
	9. bring	_____	(have) _____
	10. hit	_____	(have) _____
	11. drive	_____	(have) _____
	12. know	_____	(have) _____
	13. wear	_____	(have) _____
	14. give	_____	(have) _____
	15. rise	_____	(have) _____
	16. speak	_____	(have) _____
	17. let	_____	(have) _____
	18. dig	_____	(have) _____
	19. drink	_____	(have) _____
	20. read	_____	(have) _____
	21. meet	_____	(have) _____
	22. hold	_____	(have) _____
	23. shut	_____	(have) _____

333 More about verb phrases

24.	run	_____	(have) _____
25.	go	_____	(have) _____
26.	do	_____	(have) _____
27.	begin	_____	(have) _____
28.	lead	_____	(have) _____
29.	come	_____	(have) _____
30.	keep	_____	(have) _____

CHOOSING CORRECT VERB FORMS

The greatest confusion for students in using irregular verbs is between the past tense and past participle.

The **past tense** includes words like *saw*. It is always used by itself to express an action that has already occurred.

Past tense used alone

<u>Lisa</u> (**saw**) him at the game.

The **past participle** includes words like *seen*. It is always used with *have-* and *be*-helping verbs to form verb phrases (like *has seen* and *will be seen*).

Past participle in verb phrase

<u>She</u> (**has seen**) him on campus as well.

Keep in mind that there are other kinds of verbs which use neither the past tense nor the past participle (such as *will be seeing* and *would see*). Our concern here is just with verbs and verb phrases that use the past tense and past participle.

Using the Past Tense Alone

The past tense must be used by itself. It is never used with helping verbs. The following sentence contains the past tense form of *to go* (principal parts: *go, went, gone*).

<u>We</u> (**went**) to Texas on our vacation.

Notice that *went* is a one-word verb, and since it is the past tense form of *to go*, it is used correctly.

Unlike present tense verbs, past tense verbs have only one form. The form *went* is used with all subjects.

Exercise 4

Choosing Past Tense Verbs

Each of these sentences can be completed with either the past tense or a present tense form.

a. To the left of each sentence, write the **three principal parts** of the verb in parentheses.

b. Then write the **correct verb form** on the line within the sentence.

c. Finally, mark the **verb** and **subject** in each sentence.

Use the lists on pages 342–43, 344, and 346–47 to help you. If necessary, review subject-verb agreement in Chapter 11 before doing this exercise.

NOTE: Assume the past tense is intended unless the sentence clearly needs a present tense verb.

example

write, wrote, written They (*wrote*) _____ to Mr. Willis for his advice.
(to write)

1. _____ No snake can _____ through a tire.
   (to bite)

2. _____ What _____ of Mr. Henderson?
   (to become)

3. _____ The horse _____ yesterday afternoon.
   (to win)

4. _____ Her first album _____ in the millions.
   (to sell)

5. _____ Dr. Farnsworth _____ February 29 as the
   (to choose)
   date for his retirement party.

6. _____ Simon _____ his hand during the second
   (to hurt)
   quarter of the game.

7. _____ She will always _____ her best.
   (to do)

8. _____ She _____ her best in the past.
   (to do)

9. _____ She usually _____ before noon.
   (to eat)

10. _____ How much farther must we _____ ?
    (to go)

11. _____ The alarm finally _____ us up.
    (to wake)

12. _____ The old tree _____ during the storm.
    (to fall)

13. _____ The train _____ several hours ago.
    (to come)

14. _____ Selma _____ the brunt of his anger.
    (to bear)

335 More about verb phrases

15. _____ The rebels _____ outside the gate to
   (to stand)

   the palace.

16. _____ She _____ a large diamond in her hands.
   (to hold)

17. _____ The equipment director _____ us about the
   (to tell)

   inventory on Tuesday.

18. _____ Our library staff _____ a record of visitors
   (to keep)

   during open house.

19. _____ Italian troops _____ warnings to Major
   (to send)

   Murabi's staff.

20. _____ They always _____ advice from Fred in
   (to get)

   the past.

Exercise 5

Correcting Past Tense Verbs

Mark each **verb** and **subject** in the following sentences. Write its **three
principal parts** on the line. Then **correct** any incorrect past tense forms.
   NOTE: Some of these sentences contain more than one verb connected
with *and, or, but,* or *nor.*

example

see, saw, seen
speak, spoke, spoken | (saw) James and (spoken) *spoke* about you.

_____ **1.** The opening of the pier drawn a large crowd.

_____ **2.** Bits of the ceiling fallen onto the office floor.

_____ **3.** The customers spent most of their money at the

   kissing booth and leaved disappointed.

_____ **4.** Misha lost several of his best poems during

   the move.

_____ **5.** Steve took a grade of "incomplete" in the course.

_____ **6.** Dr. Ali spoken to him on May 24 about his

   final essay.

_____ 7. We seen another soldier and heard three tanks.

_____ 8. They can bought the dishes at any hardware store.

_____ 9. The weatherman went to a meteorological convention and learnt a lot.

_____ 10. He make too many mistakes in his predictions last year.

_____ 11. The phone rang three times before breakfast.

_____ 12. Melissa bought a new printer at the Computerworld sale and setted it up herself.

_____ 13. Whatever become of Mary Jane?

_____ 14. Michael never stoled the book.

_____ 15. They eaten between meals this morning.

_____ 16. A casting director made the decision to hire Louisa.

_____ 17. Phil meeted every challenge during last semester and risen to the occasion each time.

_____ 18. He losted fifteen pounds during the illness.

_____ 19. She teached herself to enjoy oysters.

_____ 20. The manager drived to the warehouse and tooken the inventory himself.

Using the Past Participle with Helping Verbs

The past participle can be used only in verb phrases with _have-_ and _be-_group helping verbs. The following sentences use the past participle correctly.

<u>Michael</u> (could **have broken**) the program's access code.

The <u>story</u> (**was written**) in 1897.

The past participle is needed because these verb phrases contain at least one *have-* or *be-*group helping verb. The past tense (*broke* and *wrote*) would have been incorrect here.

Notice that other kinds of verb phrases also use *have-* and *be-*group helping verbs (for example, *will be seeing*). We are concerned only with those that use the past participle.

Exercise 6

Choosing Past Participles

Each of these sentences can be completed with either the past tense or the past participle.

a. To the left of each sentence, write the **three principal parts** of the verb in parentheses.

b. Draw an **X** over any *have-* or *be-*group helping verb.

c. Then write the **correct verb form** on the line within the sentence.

d. Finally, mark each **verb** and **subject**.

Use the lists on pages 342–43, 344, and 346–47 to help you.

example

choose, chose, chosen The coach (will have *chosen*) his assistants
(to choose)
by now.

_____ **1.** I had _____ that story.
(to forget)

_____ **2.** The children were _____ to safety by the
(to lead)   police sergeant.

_____ **3.** Several students have _____ to the dean
(to speak)   about his proposed grading changes.

_____ **4.** She has already _____ her work on scripts.
(to begin)

_____ **5.** Three dresses like this were _____ at
(to wear)   the ball.

_____ **6.** We could have _____ to Texas for the
(to drive)   weekend celebration.

_____ **7.** I have _____ evidence of his
(to see)   abilities already.

_____ **8.** Several thousand dollars were _____ for
(to spend)

the redecoration of his office.

_____ **9.** The cabinets could have _____ twice
(to cost)

as much.

_____ **10.** Three senators have _____ full responsibil-
(to take)

ity for the disclosure.

_____ **11.** The dog was _____ by the morning sun.
(to awaken)

_____ **12.** We were not _____ about the change
(to tell)

in classroom.

_____ **13.** The mailroom has already _____ the pack-
(to send)

age to her office.

_____ **14.** Traffic has _____ to a halt.
(to grind)

_____ **15.** Raymond might have _____ us
(to give)

more warning

_____ **16.** Our house was _____ by the real
(to find)

estate agent.

_____ **17.** Their trust in the government has been
(to break)

_____ .

_____ **18.** The Essenes had _____ their home in
(to make)

this valley.

_____ **19.** The men had _____ the scrolls and hidden
(to write)

them in those caves.

_____ **20.** We were never _____ about cleaning
(to teach)

test tubes.

Exercise 7

Correcting Past Participles

Do the following for each sentence in this exercise.

a. Mark each **verb** and **subject**.

b. Place an **X** over all *have-* or *be-*group helping verbs.

c. Write the **three principal parts** of each verb on the line.

d. Finally, **correct** any incorrect verb forms.

Use the lists on pages 342–43, 344, and 346–47 to help you.

NOTE: Some of these sentences contain more than one verb connected with *and*, *or*, *but*, or *nor*.

example

run, ran, run <u>Mr. Hicks</u> (has) often (~~ran~~) for county treasurer.

_____ **1.** She has spoke of her love of Michael.

_____ **2.** We seen several examples of Indian art.

_____ **3.** Three quail had sat every day on the log.

_____ **4.** Three hundred sixty dollars were spent on the awards banquet.

_____ **5.** The knee was rebuilt in a two-hour operation.

_____ **6.** She swam several yards to the dock and rise out of the water.

_____ **7.** None of the villagers could be founded.

_____ **8.** The statue was broke in shipping.

_____ **9.** My instructor has wrote his own textbook.

_____ **10.** The native chief had wore his new badges with pride.

_____ **11.** Was anyone chose to play goalie?

_____ **12.** Martin's elbow was tore in the auto accident.

_____ **13.** Birds stole the remaining bread and eaten it in front of us.

_____ **14.** The remaining bread was stole by birds and was ate
in front of us.

_____ **15.** New evidence was founded near the campsite.

_____ **16.** Who has ever did a research paper before?

_____ **17.** My father has grew roses for the last fifteen years.

_____ **18.** Alexander has hitted a single in each of his last seventeen games.

_____ **19.** She had known his secret for a few months and had
told no one.

_____ **20.** The skin was cutted in two places.

PRACTICE WITH PAST TENSE AND PAST PARTICIPLE FORMS

Irregular verbs are not really that irregular. They fall into a small number of easily learned groups.

Irregular verbs can create their past tense and past participle forms by one or more of the following.

1. Adding an -*n* sound to the past participle

2. Changing the sound of the main vowel

3. Changing the last sound to -*d* or -*t*

4. Not changing at all

In the following sections these possibilities are organized for you with a simple descriptive code printed above each group.

In this code, the letters *X*, *Y*, and *Z* stand for the sound of the main vowel inside the verb. The letters *N*, *D*, and *T* stand for sound of the added endings. For example, an irregular verb like "to eat" whose three principle parts follow the pattern X, Y, XN has the same vowel sound for the present tense and the past participle (X-XN), but a different sound for the past tense (Y). In addition, the past participle adds an "n" sound (XN). A common verb that follows this pattern is the verb "to eat." Its three principle parts are

X	**Y**	**XN**
eat	ate	eaten

Notice that the main vowel sound in the present tense (eat) is the same vowel sound in the past tense (eaten).

341 More about verb phrases

The code is there to help you learn the three principle parts of these verbs by helping you to learn the groups into which these verbs fall. Learning the three principle parts of the most common verbs is necessary if they are to be used correctly in your writing.

Verbs That Add -*N*

Three groups of verbs add an -*n* sound to the past participle.
Group 1 changes only the sound of the past tense.

(Pattern: X Y XN)

Group 2 changes the past tense and past participle in the same way.

(Pattern: X Y YN)

Group 3 changes the past tense and past participle in different ways.

(Pattern: X Y ZN)

Common verbs in these three groups are listed below. Refer to these lists when doing the exercises that follow, and try to develop an "ear" for which verbs are in which group.

Verbs That Add -*n*

Verb	Present Tense	Past Tense	Past Participle
Group 1	**X**	**Y**	**XN**
to bid	bid	bade	(have) bidden
to eat	eat	ate	(have) eaten
to fall	fall	fell	(have) fallen
to give	give	gave	(have) given
to grow	grow	grew	(have) grown
to know	know	knew	(have) known
to see	see	saw	(have) seen
Group 2	**X**	**Y**	**YN**
to bear	bear	bore	(have) borne
to bite	bite	bit	(have) bitten
to break	break	broke	(have) broken
to choose	choose	chose	(have) chosen
to get	get	got	(have) gotten
to speak	speak	spoke	(have) spoken
to wake	wake	woke	(have) woken
to wear	wear	wore	(have) worn

Group 3	X	Y	ZN
to arise	arise	arose	(have) arisen
to do	do	did	(have) done
to drive	drive	drove	(have) driven
to ride	ride	rode	(have) ridden
to rise	rise	rose	(have) risen
to write	write	wrote	(have) written

Exercise 8

Correcting Verbs That Add -*n*

Mark each **verb** and **subject** in the following sentences. Place an **X** over any *have-* or *be*-group helping verb. Then **correct** any incorrect verb. If a sentence is already correct, write **OK** in the margin.

NOTE: Some of these sentences contain more than one verb connected with *and*, *or*, *but*, or *nor*.

example

Mr. Hicks (has) often (ran) for county prosecutor as well.

1. The ice in the bucket was froze before morning.

2. Angelica thought that she seen a UFO.

3. The doll's clothes have wore out long ago.

4. Sandy wrote to her sister but has not got a reply.

5. Professor Thomas should never have gave his keys away.

6. Our pilot has flown many hours in worse weather than this.

7. Three speakers were chose by the faculty and spoken to the graduates.

8. All of the leaves have fell into the river.

9. The cart was drew by several large horses.

10. Herman already threw the ball to second base.

11. The cloth of this shirt tore in the laundry.

12. Many of us had already knew the date of the test.

13. Caterpillars eaten holes in all the leaves.

14. He woken to the sound of bees.

15. He born the bulk of her problems himself.

16. The newspaper was got by one of the children.

17. Grass has never been grown behind the oak trees.

18. The Dutch ambassador spoken to one of the waiters.

19. The letter was wrote in a hurry.

20. Have you ever rode horses bareback?

Verbs That Change to *-d* or *-t*

The next two groups imitate regular verbs by changing the last sound to *-d* or *-t*.

Group 4 verbs keep the same main vowel sound.

(Pattern: X   XT   XT)

Group 5 verbs change the main vowel sound.

(Pattern: X   YT   YT)

For all of these verbs, the past tense is the same as the past participle. Common verbs in these two groups are listed below.

Verbs That Change to *-d* or *-t*

Verb	Present Tense	Past Tense	Past Participle
Group 4	**X**	**XT**	**XT**
to build	build	built	(have) built
to have	have	had	(have) had
to make	make	made	(have) made
to spend	spend	spent	(have) spent
Group 5	**X**	**YT**	**YT**
to bring	bring	brought	(have) brought
to buy	buy	bought	(have) bought
to hear	hear	heard	(have) heard
to keep	keep	kept	(have) kept
to leave	leave	left	(have) left
to lose	lose	lost	(have) lost
to mean	mean	meant	(have) meant
to say	say	said	(have) said
to teach	teach	taught	(have) taught
to tell	tell	told	(have) told
to think	think	thought	(have) thought

Exercise 9

Correcting Verbs That Change to *-d* or *-t*

Mark each **verb** and **subject** in the following sentences. Place an **X** over any *have-* or *be-*group helping verb. Then **correct** any incorrect verb. If a sentence is already correct, write **OK** in the margin.

NOTE: Some of these sentences contain more than one verb connected with *and*, *or*, *but*, or *nor*.

1. I had thought of you often.

2. The prospector told Mrs. Andersen about the ghost of the mine.

3. Michael had kept the information from his father for a long time.

4. They were lost somewhere in the dormitory.

5. The exercise equipment can be buyed on credit.

6. The archbishop had never said anything about the tax issue.

7. Kenny sayed everything yesterday.

8. Has anyone brought mayonnaise?

9. Alexander soon made plans for the invasion of Greece.

10. Buddy never meant that remark.

11. I too have felt like that.

12. Had you heared about John's scholarship?

13. He spended his last dollar on that beer.

14. I thinked of another way and buyed the computer myself.

15. I heard them in the back room.

16. The boys had told her about the fight.

17. Nick and Valerie bought a small condo in the hills.

18. The sisters found another reason for their trip to Aunt Mattie's.

19. Will could sent the letter for you.

20. The groceries were brung into the house by the neighbor's son and were payed for by my mother.

Verbs That Do Not Add Endings

The next four groups of verbs either show no changes at all or change vowel sounds without adding endings.

Verbs That Do Not Add Endings

Verb	Present Tense	Past Tense	Past Participle
Group 6	**X**	**X**	**X**
to cost	cost	cost	(have) cost
to cut	cut	cut	(have) cut
to hit	hit	hit	(have) hit
to hurt	hurt	hurt	(have) hurt
to let	let	let	(have) let
to shut	shut	shut	(have) shut
Group 7	**X**	**Y**	**X**
to become	become	became	(have) become
to come	come	came	(have) come
to run	run	ran	(have) run
Group 8	**X**	**Y**	**Y**
to bind	bind	bound	(have) bound
to dig	dig	dug	(have) dug
to feed	feed	fed	(have) fed
to fight	fight	fought	(have) fought
to find	find	found	(have) found
to hang*	hang	hung	(have) hung
to hold	hold	held	(have) held
to lead	lead	led	(have) led
to meet	meet	met	(have) met
to read	read	read	(have) read
to sit	sit	sat	(have) sat
to stand	stand	stood	(have) stood
Group 9	**X**	**Y**	**Z**
to begin	begin	began	(have) begun
to drink	drink	drank	(have) drunk
to ring	ring	rang	(have) run
to swim	swim	swam	(have) swum

To hang has the forms *hang, hanged, hanged* when it refers to a form of execution. All other meanings have the forms listed here.

Very Irregular Verbs

Finally, two important verbs have very irregular forms.

Three Principal Parts of Very Irregular Verbs

Verb	Present Tense	Past Tense	Past Participle
Group 10			
to be	am, is, are	was, were	(have) been
to go	go	went	(have) gone

Exercise 10

Correcting Verbs That Do Not Add Endings

Mark each **verb** and **subject** in the following sentences. Place an **X** over any *have-* or *be-*group helping verb. Then **correct** any incorrect verb. If a sentence is already correct, write **OK** in the margin.

NOTE: Some of these sentences contain more than one verb connected with *and, or, but,* or *nor.*

1. Joey swung through the branches of the tree and comed lightly to the ground.

2. Judy has ran into the house.

3. The remarks of the newspapers had stung her deeply.

4. Several of the scarves were torn and cutted.

5. The package from Ohio State had came in the afternoon mail.

6. Milos swum the river at its widest point.

7. He drunk the last of the wine with dinner.

8. The most aristocratic senators won every vote.

9. Kenny's son become a Cub Scout last month.

10. Mr. Springfield digged several mysterious holes in the garden recently.

11. We had came to see the cardinal.

12. Mrs. Jennings has ran the store by herself for years.

13. Mike readed the test and begun it immediately.

14. They leaded him by the hand to the side of the well.

15. The statue has been let down safely.

16. The entire regiment had came down with influenza.

17. The chimpanzee hung upside down for over an hour.

18. Their meals had cost less than fifteen dollars.

19. The Wranglers beated the Redmen by four points.

20. Polee had fought well, but had losted anyway.

Chapter Review

In this chapter you learned that

1. The **three principal parts** of a verb are its
   a. Present tense
   b. Past tense
   c. Past participle

2. **Regular verbs** form the past tense and past participle by adding -d and -ed.

3. **Irregular verbs** form the past tense and past participle in a variety of ways.

4. The **past tense** is never used with helping verbs.

5. The **past participle** is used only with *have*- and *be*-group helping verbs.

6. You can **correct errors** in verb phrases by
   a. Finding verb phrases accurately, including *have*- and *be*-group helping verbs
   b. Learning the past tense and past participle forms of common verbs
   c. Choosing the correct verb form for each verb or verb phrase

In the RELATED SKILL section you also learned how to find verbs in **sentences with more than one clause**.

Review Exercise 1

Most of the sentences in this paragraph are like those discussed in Unit 1.
Correct all verb errors in the following paragraphs. Then **recopy** the corrected paragraphs on the lines provided.

Alberta had came to school for the first time last spring. She had been a mother, a nurse, and the manager of a small office, in that order. Now she standed in the corner of the cafeteria and holded her plastic tray like all of the other students. A young man in front of her buyed a sandwich wrapped in plastic. Alberta seen the label. It sayed "tuna on white." The line moved slightly. Alberta's turn come. She chosen "egg on rye."

Once Alberta would have ran screaming from such food. She would not have gave it to her children or her patients. Only students live like this. Then she broken out in a big smile. She holded her sandwich close to her mouth and bitted into it eagerly. It has took her forty years. But she has become a student at last. And she meaned to enjoy every minute of it.

_____

_____

_____

_____

_____

_____

_____

_____

_____

_____

Review Exercise 2

These paragraphs contain sentences like those discussed in Units 2 and 3 — sentences with verbal phrases, appositives, and more than one clause. **Correct all verb errors** in the following paragraphs. Then **recopy** the corrected paragraphs on the lines provided.

When we arrived at the other end of the valley, we seen that the British were already camped on the other side of the river. Captain Wainwright had receive orders from General Latrobe not to surrender the valley, so he sended me and Will Jennings to scout their position. He also told us to find out how many of them there were. Night had just fell, and we left immediately. Neither Will nor I had ate any supper.

We gone by foot to the river's edge and had no trouble until we tried to cross. We thought that there might be several small boats by the water's edge, but the Redcoats had sank them. If we wanted to cross, it would have to be by swimming. I turned to Will, and I seen a strange look in his eyes. Then I remembered. Will had growed up in the back country and never learned to swim. I looked at the water. It had rose almost to its yearly high, thanks to the melting spring snow from the mountains. I looked again at Will. He say he wanted to try, and without looking at me, he bended down to remove his boots. I prayed briefly and setted to work on mine.

_____

_____

_____

_____

_____

_____

_____

_____

_____

_____

_____

_____

_____

_____

_____

_____

_____

_____

_____

_____

Chapter 13 Writing Assignment

Write a paragraph that discusses, in your life, the single most important **effect of your success in this course.**

When you have made your final copy

1. Mark each **verb and subject**.

2. Make sure that
   a. All **verbs** are correct
   b. All **clauses and phrases** are correctly punctuated
   c. Your paragraph contains **no fragments**

Hints for Cause and Effect Paragraphs

This paragraph will be most effective if you pay attention to the steps listed under "Before the rough draft." Doing these steps carefully will make your paragraph as convincing as possible.

Before the rough draft:

1. Make a list of _all_ of the possible effects of your success in this course that you can think of.

   Be realistic with this list. There are certainly some effects that may be true for others, but are not true for you. There are also some effects that will be true only for you.

2. Now edit this list (by adding things in and taking things out) until it includes only the most important effect.

3. Finally, make a second list of ways to prove that what you say is true for you.

   Your goal is to convince a friendly, but disbelieving, reader that what you are saying is not just "talk." How can you convince someone that if you succeed in this course, the good effect will definitely happen to you?

Writing the rough draft:

1. Start your rough draft by writing a short group of sentences that
   a. Tells why you entered this course, and
   b. Explains that you foresee the effect you kept on your first list. (Be sure to tell what that effect is!)

2. Using your second list, write several sentences that will prove that this effect really will be true for you.

3. Finally, write a closing that feels like an ending.

After the rough draft:

1. Do your best to correct any errors on this first copy. Be especially careful to correct all errors in
   a. Verbs
   b. Punctuation

2. Make any other changes you think will make your paragraph more interesting and readable.

3. Recopy your corrected paragraph on a clean sheet of paper and turn in all of your work.

Nouns and pronouns

In this Unit you will learn to correct errors in nouns ("name" words) and pronouns (words that stand for nouns).

14
Nouns

Chapter Preview

This chapter will show you

1. How to find **nouns** in sentences and paragraphs

2. How to spell the **plural forms** of nouns

3. How to **use singular and plural nouns correctly** in sentences

In addition the RELATED SKILL section will help you learn to find and correct noun errors in sentences with **verbal phrases, appositives, and more than one clause**.

NOUNS

Nouns are name words. They name persons, places, things, and ideas.

There are many kinds of nouns. Some, called **common nouns**, name general things, like *car* and *house*. Others, called **proper nouns**, name specific things, like *Buick* or *White House*. Notice that proper nouns are capitalized.

Nouns can be used in many ways in a sentence. In Chapter 1 you saw how nouns are used as subjects, objects, and complements. In Chapter 4 you saw how nouns are used as objects of prepositions.

Unit 2 shows how nouns act in sentences with more than one clause — that is, sentences with more than one subject-verb pair. And Unit 3 shows how nouns can be appositives and objects of verbals.

In this chapter you will learn to find and solve the most common noun problems — how and when to make them singular or plural.

NOTE: This chapter can be worked by any student who has completed Unit 1. Students who have also completed Units 2 and 3 should do the RELATED SKILL sections as well. These sections contain additional exercises that rely on knowledge of that material.

FINDING NOUNS

There are several ways to find nouns in a sentence or paragraph.

One way is to look for sentence clues — words or phrases that point to nouns. Another way is to use your knowledge of sentence structure.

Noun Pointers — Words That Point to Nouns

The adjectives *a*, *an*, and *the* often point to nouns. (*A*, *an*, and *the* are often called **articles**.)

> **the** candidate
>
> **an** offer
>
> **a** salesman

In the above examples, *candidate, offer,* and *salesman* are all nouns.

In many cases, the noun is not the first word after *a*, *an*, or *the*. In English, adjectives that describe nouns come before the noun and after the noun pointer.

For example, in the following sentence, the word *the* points to a noun. Can you find the noun?

> **The** last presidential candidate came from Arizona.

The points to the noun *candidate*, used as the subject of *came*.

> **The** last presidential **candidate** (came)(from Arizona.)

The words *last* and *presidential* describe *candidate*. As you know from Chapter 3, words that describe nouns are called **adjectives**, not nouns, and do not have singular and plural forms.

Let's look at a few more examples. In each of the following sentences, the word *a* points to a noun. Can you find the noun in each sentence?

A new book has been returned.

A new book salesman called for you.

In the first sentence, *a* points to the noun *book*, here used as the subject.

A new **book** (has been returned) .

In the second, *a* points to *salesman*, also the subject.

A new book **salesman** (called)(for you.)

We know that *book* is an adjective in the second example because it answers the adjective question "What kind of salesman?" Notice also that in both sentences, the noun comes after all one-word adjectives.

Other noun signals like *a*, *an*, and *the* are listed below.

Noun Signals (Adjectives That Point to Nouns)

a	this	my	one
an	that	your	two
the	these	his	three
	those	her	(etc.)
		its	
		our	
		their	

When you look for nouns, look for these words. A noun will almost certainly follow. Just remember that the noun is the word that follows all adjectives.

Exercise 1

Words That Point to Nouns

In the following groups of words, place an **X** over all words that point to nouns.

Then draw an **arrow** from all adjectives to the nouns they describe.

X
The harbor police

X
In a broken doll house

1. His latest report form

2. An ideal solution to the problem

3. Between two of my best friends

4. Those old, worn-out clothes

5. This meal

6. The first sensible suggestion

7. These beautiful stuffed chairs

8. A colorful maze

9. Answering her classified ad

10. One approach

11. Their new dress design

12. After hearing a long, old story

13. Spending the rest of the night reminiscing

14. One of his high school teachers

15. Her only good raincoat

16. Our English essays

17. Its twelve o'clock message

18. This speech of yours

19. A company with a better reputation

20. One of the nicer ladies in the office

RELATED SKILL   USING SENTENCE STRUCTURE TO FIND NOUNS

Do this section if you have completed Units 2 and 3.

Not all nouns have noun signals in front of them. For this reason, we also rely on our knowledge of sentence structure to find nouns.

Nouns can be used as

Subjects

Objects of verbs
        prepositions
        verbals

Complements following linking verbs

Appositives

Let's practice by finding all nouns in the following long sentence.

> Byron, one of Mrs. Black's younger boys, plays tennis when his work schedule will let him.

We start by marking the sentence.

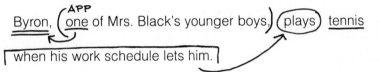

It has a main clause with a prepositional phrase, an appositive, and an adverb clause. In the main clause, the subject **Byron** and the object **tennis** are both nouns.

Byron, one of Mrs. Black's younger boys, (plays) **tennis**

when his work schedule will let him.

In the appositive phrase, *boys* is the object of the preposition *of*. Notice that *Mrs. Black's* is not a noun, but an adjective describing *boys*. (*Whose* boys? *Mrs. Black's*.)

Appositive phrase

one (of Mrs. Black's younger **boys**)

The adverb clause, *when his work schedule will let him*, has a noun subject, *schedule*. Notice that *work* is not a noun, but an adjective describing *schedule*. (*What kind of* schedule? *Work* schedule.)

Adverb clause

when his work **schedule** (will let) him

The sentence has four nouns in it.

Byron, one of Mrs. Black's younger **boys**, plays **tennis** when his work **schedule** will let him.

Analyzing sentences like this may seem like a lot of work, especially when confronted with a paragraph or two of writing. But consider:

1. If you truly wish to correct noun errors, you must be able to find nouns reliably.

2. In the first three units, you learned everything you need to know to find every noun in every sentence.

3. As you have no doubt learned already, understanding sentence structure becomes easier with practice.

Use the good tools you have been given, and you may be surprised at how quickly you can eliminate noun errors from your writing.

Skill Exercise 1

Identifying Nouns

In these sentences, each noun is printed in **boldface** type. Do the following.

a. Mark each sentence completely.

b. Then tell what **each noun does**.

example

The police **inspector** noticed **footprints** in the rose **garden**.

inspector - subject of noticed

footprints - object of noticed

garden - object of preposition in

1. The harbor **police** are investigating a recent **theft**.

_____

_____

2. **Scotty** now has full **control** of the **project**.

_____

_____

3. She starts in the **morning**.

_____

_____

4. The **game** has not been going well.

_____

_____

5. One of the university's **trustees** asked for a full **report**.

_____

_____

6. I am meeting **Joanne** at the **restaurant** instead.

_____

_____

7. His **cousin** got the **job** at the **Henley Tower**.

_____

_____

8. He is never hungry for **breakfast**.

_____

_____

9. The **van** needs a new **motor**.

_____

_____

10. **Ace's Body Barn** is offering a **discount** on exercise **equipment**.

_____

_____

Skill Exercise 2

Finding Nouns

In these sentences, the nouns are NOT printed in boldface type. Do the following.

a. **Mark** each sentence completely.

b. Then place an **X** over **all nouns**.

c. Finally, tell what **each noun does**.

example

An old bicycle wheel (lay) (in the water) (of the pond.)

wheel - subject of lay   *water - object of in*

pond - object of of

1. The sausage pizza didn't taste right.

   _____

   _____

2. Maybe those gray mushrooms had something to do with it.

   _____

   _____

3. Michael's boss sent him back to the clerk's room for another copy

   of the Brill contract.

   _____

   _____

4. The old television in the garage could be repaired instead.

   _____

   _____

5. Nel could take it back to school with her.

   _____

   _____

6. The highway took a sharp turn to the right.

   _____

   _____

7. Most of the stores in this area honor that credit card.

   _____

   _____

8. The salesman said that these colors come alive.

_____

_____

9. Maybe it happens when everyone is sleeping.

_____

_____

10. The long comet's tail blazed dramatically across the face of

the sky.

_____

_____

Finding Nouns in Paragraphs

Unfortunately it is easier to find nouns in sentences when the sentences are printed separately than when they are printed in paragraphs. But finding nouns in paragraphs is more like what you face when correcting your own writing.

The exercises that follow are designed to help you find nouns in paragraphs. Exercise 2 asks you to find nouns in a paragraph. In the first two paragraphs, the sentences are printed separately. Then they are printed in normal paragraph form.

Exercise 3 contains two practice paragraphs, both from published writing. Do this exercise if you have completed Units 2 and 3.

Work carefully and do the best you can. You will work faster later if you work more slowly and accurately here.

Exercise 2

Finding Nouns in Paragraphs

Place an **X** over all nouns in the following sentences.

example

$$\overset{\text{X}}{}\qquad\overset{\text{X}}{}$$
Her recent dancing class was held at noon.

Paragraph 1

1. Every good piece of writing has a structure.

2. Everything with structure has a beginning, a middle, and an end.

3. In a paragraph or essay, these parts have special names.

4. The beginning is called "the introduction."

5. The middle is called "the body."

6. And the end is called "the closing."

Paragraph 2

1. Logical relationships between the parts of a paragraph give meaning to the paragraph.

2. Without this relationship, the sentences of a paragraph or essay are like mindless rambling.

3. Sections of a paragraph or essay must be related to each other in the following way.

Paragraph 3

The introduction names the subject of the writing. One piece of writing might be about space research. Another might discuss Paris fashions. Still another might have crime in Los Angeles as a subject. By the end of the introduction, the reader should be very clear about the subject.

Paragraph 4

For most writing, the introduction does one other job. It states the "main idea." The main idea is sometimes called the "topic sentence." It is the writer's main point about that subject. For instance, the following is a main idea about space research. *Space research should get more support from our government.* Every good piece of writing makes a point about a subject. Most of the time, that point is stated in the introduction.

Paragraph 5

The body has a different and important job. The sentences of the body must support and prove the main idea. This proof can take many forms. It can include logical arguments, examples, stories, comparisons, and statistics.

Main ideas can be supported in all of these ways and more. By the end of the body, the reader should be convinced of the truth of the main idea.

Paragraph 6

The closing has a simple task. The closing must feel like an ending. It can do this in a variety of ways. The closing can restate the main idea. It can mention a key word from the introduction. It can include a large summary of the author's main points. Or it can be simply the last detail of the body. Any satisfying ending is a good closing.

Paragraph 7

A good piece of writing has a clear structure. Use the above structure in your writing. Both you and your readers will be pleased with the results.

Exercise 3

Finding Nouns in Paragraphs

Do this exercise if you have completed Units 2 and 3. Place an **X** over all nouns in the following sentences.

A. This paragraph is from a book called *How to Write Romance Novels,* by Marilyn M. Lowery.[1]

I first became interested in writing romance novels when I was teaching English literature to high school honors students. I was encouraging them not to waste their time on paperback romances. Over the months, no one paid attention to me. I observed, especially, one girl who read at least three of these novels every day. As I watched her slim down and become more graceful, more stylish, and less shy, it appeared that she was identifying with these heroines and that they were making a genuine contribution to her happiness. The school library was having a sale, so

[1]Marilyn M. Lowery, adapted excerpt from the introduction of *How to Write Romance Novels.* Copyright © 1983 Marilyn M. Lowery. Reprinted with the permission of Charles Scribner's Sons, an imprint of Macmillan Publishing Company.

I bought most of the popular romances, read them, and decided to contribute to this form myself as Philippa Castle.

B. This longer, beautiful paragraph is from *The Summer Game,* a wonderful book on baseball by Roger Angell.[2]

The last dimension is time. Within the ballpark, time moves differently, marked by no clock except the events of the game. This is the unique, unchangeable feature of baseball, and perhaps explains why this sport, for all the enormous changes it has undergone in the past decade or two, remains somehow rustic, unviolent, and introspective. Baseball's time is seamless and invisible, a bubble within which players move at exactly the same pace and rhythms as all their predecessors. This is the way the game was played in our youth and in our fathers' youth, and even back then — back in the country days — there must have been the same feeling that time could be stopped. Since baseball time is measured only in outs, all you have to do is succeed utterly; keep hitting, keep the rally alive, and you have defeated time. You remain forever young. Sitting in the stands, we sense this, if only dimly. The players below us — Mays, DiMaggio, Ruth, Snodgrass — swim and blur in memory, the ball floats over to Terry Turner, and the end of this game may never come.

CORRECTING NOUN ERRORS

Errors using nouns are usually of two types.

1. A plural noun is misspelled, or
2. A noun is singular when it should be plural, or vice versa, usually because the *-s* ending has been dropped or added incorrectly.

[2]Roger Angell, "The Interior Stadium," in *The Summer Game* (New York: Viking), 1972.

Let's first see how to spell common plural nouns. Then we will look at how to choose between singular and plural nouns in sentences.

Spelling Singular and Plural Nouns

Most nouns do more than name a person, place, or thing. They also tell how many persons, places, or things they are referring to.

Singular nouns, like *car* and *book*, show that only one person, place, or thing is referred to. **Plural nouns**, like *cars* and *books*, refer to more than one.

Most singular nouns become plural by adding endings. Sometimes these endings are not pronounced, but they must still be present in writing. This section will show you how to make nouns plural.

Making Nouns Plural with *-s* or *-es*

Most English nouns add *-s* or *es* to the singular to make the plural form. Other ways of making plural nouns will be discussed later.

Most nouns simply add *-s,*

Singular	Plural
actor	actors
idea	ideas
fortune	fortunes
Pontiac	Pontiacs
sidewalk	sidewalks
Wilson	Wilsons

Some add *-es,*

	Singular	Plural
s:	boss	bosses
x:	ax	axes
z:	Perez	Perezes
sh:	ash	ashes
ch:	church	churches
o:	potato	potatoes

and some that end in *-y* change the *y* to *i* before adding *-es.*

	Singular	Plural
y:	ally	allies
	library	libraries
	story	stories
ey:	alley	alleys
	key	keys

These rules are covered in detail in Chapter 18, Spelling. In addition, any dictionary can help you spell plural nouns.

369 Nouns

Exercise 4

Spelling Plural Nouns

Write the correct **singular or plural form** for each noun. Be sure the words you write are spelled correctly.

examples

Singular	Plural
chart	*charts*
feeling	feelings

Singular	Plural
1. writer	_____
2. saying	_____
3. kiss	_____
4. box	_____
5. Benedict	_____
6. fear	_____
7. dentist	_____
8. desk	_____
9. test	_____
10. apple	_____
11. video	_____
12. story	_____
13. friendship	_____
14. push	_____
15. marble	_____
16. alley	_____
17. pillow	_____
18. radio	_____
19. Johnson	_____

20. father   _____

21. _____   boats

22. _____   dresses

23. _____   spellings

24. _____   essays

25. _____   libraries

26. _____   rodeos

27. _____   tapes

28. _____   potatoes

29. _____   drivers

30. _____   fairies

Exercise 5

Spelling Plural Nouns in Sentences

Correct any incorrectly spelled **plural noun** in the following sentences.

Do not change any noun from singular to plural. Just make sure that all plurals are spelled correctly. If a sentence contains no errors, write **OK** in the margin.

example

loans
Her three government ~~loanes~~ were approved last week.

1. He saw several watchs in the store window.

2. Roger owned three Buickes before the Chevrolet.

3. Albert's Market is selling potatos for $2.00 a bag.

4. Three ash trees fell in the storm and damaged several oakes.

5. Mike and LeRon quickly became allyes against the Sno Kings and

   other street ganges.

6. Rhonda includes lots of action in her storys.

7. Here are your lost keyes.

8. Six of the kids in camp have Perry as a last name.

371 Nouns

9. Each of the six boyes has cards for three local librarys.

10. Each of the three librarys has two doors.

11. Each of the two doors has one handle.

12. Each of the handls is broken.

13. Many radio stations run those commerciales.

14. My brother collects radioes as a hobby.

15. Ina owns two hatchets and several broad-blade axes.

16. Sheila spent a fortune just on makeup cases.

BONUS (contains Unit 2 and 3 material):

1. The West Coast writers are opposed to the deal, since television and film scripts are excluded from the bonus plan.

2. The fireplace is filled with ashs, and the wood pile is stacked high with fresh logs and kindling.

3. Your ideaes are good, but your plans for achieving them need some work.

4. The local churchs have offered to help by collecting toyes and other useful items.

Using Singular and Plural Nouns in Sentences

In most sentences, when a singular noun is needed, a plural noun will be incorrect, and vice versa. In order to correct mistakes using nouns, you will need to know when to use a singular noun and when to use a plural.

This section will show you how to use sentence signals like adjectives and phrases to help you choose between singular and plural nouns.

Signal Words — Adjectives That Tell How Many

The first group of sentence signals are adjectives that tell how many. As you learned in Chapter 3, adjectives are words that describe nouns. The following adjectives will always tell you whether a noun should be singular or plural.

Adjectives That Signal Noun Forms

Singular	Plural
this	these
that	those
one	two, three (and so on)
a, an	all
	both
another	many
each	several
every	few
much	

Many sentences contain these adjectives.

Singular noun signal

Another church was just constructed on Second Street.

Plural noun signal

We watched **several drummers** audition for the band concert.

Note that many adjectives similar to those on the list can be used with either singular or plural nouns. *Some* and *the* are examples of these adjectives.

Singular noun

Some evening we will go to State Beach.

Plural noun

Some evenings we go to State Beach.

Refer carefully to the list above when doing the exercises that follow.

Exercise 6

Signal Words — Adjectives

Place an **X** over the signal words in the following phrases. Then **write the correct noun** form on the line.
Be sure your plurals are correctly spelled.

1. Those telephone _____ (bill)

2. A farewell _____ (dinner)

3. These small _____ (inconvenience)

4. Scott's many wonderful _____ (quality)

5. Three fine _____ (linebacker)

6. A right _____ (answer)

7. Another blue _____ (carpet)

8. An unopened _____ (envelope)

9. Those _____ (mannequin)

10. Four unfortunate _____ (trade) in a _____ (row)

11. Three great _____ (week)

12. Several front-row _____ (desk)

13. A better _____ (microprocessor)

14. Every small single-family _____ (home)

15. A _____ (radio) in the store

16. Two _____ (radio) from that store

17. A _____ (hat) from the closet shelf

18. Few _____ (student) in the class

19. A remarkable new _____ (antidote)

20. These _____ (artist)

Exercise 7

Correcting Nouns

Place an **X** over the signal words in the following phrases. Draw an **arrow** to the noun it describes. Then **correct any incorrect nouns**.

X   drapes
These green drape

1. Many cousin

2. Five new pen

3. A few used carburetor

4. Several neighborhood friend

5. Barry's last twelve game

6. A foreign student

7. This chair

8. Two unusual place

9. Each painting

10. A shirt

11. A large stone librarys

12. Several unused classroom

13. Those wicker basket

14. A bright colors

15. Every box

16. A well-formed apple

17. Several printing press

18. One of a few letter

19. A blind, darkened alley

20. Many different telephone

Exercise 8

Correcting Nouns in Sentences

Place an **X** over any signal words in the following sentences. Draw an **arrow** to the noun it describes. Then **correct any incorrect noun**.

Do not change a noun that does not need to be changed.

She has borrowed three ~~book~~ *books* from Brad.

1. Correct all incorrect noun in the following sentences.

2. Both of my sweaters are at the cleaners.

3. We were there from the beginning.

4. Two door stood slightly open.

5. A sudden fear overwhelmed Franklin.

6. A cool fire burns in the laser ovens.

7. Three boxed book sat on the operations table.

8. A tie stains marred his perfect appearance.

9. The Rose Building stood against a bright sunset skyline.

10. Those fire were set by the lightning.

11. A man in a green plaid suits walked behind us.

12. Another local network systems was introduced last week at an engi-
    neering seminar.

13. Several shot were fired.

14. This nouns should not have been used.

15. We ordered three more chair for the dining room.

16. Her two living uncle are from Greece.

17. The police "battering ram" was outlawed by a local judge recently.

18. The first five president of the young republic supported a tax
    reform bill.

BONUS (contains Unit 2 and 3 material):

1. Many client like to do business over lunch.

2. The newspaper made several mistake in reporting the Loyola game.

376 Nouns and pronouns

Signal Words — Phrases That Tell How Many

The next group of noun signals includes phrases like the following.

> **One** of his **answers**
>
> **Two** of my mother's good **sandwiches**
>
> **Several** of the best railroad **stocks**
>
> A **pair** of **socks**
>
> A **bunch** of **grapes**

It makes no difference whether the phrase begins "*one* of . . ." or *two* of . . ." Each of these signals points to a group and therefore points to a plural noun.

Note the following.

1. Each signal phrase contains the word *of*.

2. Each signal phrase starts with a number, not an amount.

Let's look at these points one at a time.

1. **Each signal phrase contains the word *of*.**

If of is not present, the signal may require a different kind of noun.

> **Singular noun signal**
>
> **One** sweater

> **Plural noun signal**
>
> **One of** my sweaters

One of my sweaters points to a plural noun. *One sweater* points to a singular noun.

2. **Each signal phrase starts with a number, not an amount.**

The signal starts with words like *one*, *two*, and *several*. Each of these words implies a number and points to things that are counted.

> **Several** of her hairpins

Words like *some*, *none*, and *all* can point either to a number or to an amount. Compare the following phrases.

> **Several** of her hairpins
>
> **Some** of her time
>
> **Some** of her hairpins

Hairpins are counted. Time is measured in amounts. Words like *several* point only to things that are counted. Words like *some* can point either to things that are counted or measured.

Be careful with words like *some*, *none*, and *all*.

Exercise 9

Phrase Signals

Write the correct noun form on the line.

example

Each of the _answers_ (answer)

1. A pair of _____ (pant)

2. None of the _____ (guy) from the neighborhood

3. Two of these _____ (desk)

4. Several of the _____ (teenager)

5. One _____ (motor)

6. One of the _____ (motor)

7. Each of the _____ (phrase)

8. Each _____ (box)

9. Two of Martin's _____ (friend)

10. A few of those _____ (glass)

11. Three _____ (sock)

12. Three of my _____ (sock)

13. A man with one brown _____ (shoe)

14. Two _____ for each _____ (manager/hotel)

15. A few of those sugar _____ (cube)

16. One dry _____ (potato)

17. Each of her test _____ (score)

18. Twelve of those _____ (phone)

19. One _____ (event)

20. One of Michael's _____ (story)

Exercise 10

Place an **X** next to all phrase signals in the following items. Then **correct any incorrect nouns**.
Don't change any phrase that is correct.

examples		*friends*
	X	Few of her ~~friend~~
	OK	A man with a book

1. One of the test paper

2. Some of his mustard

3. Three of the government officer

4. One blank check

5. One of the blank check

6. No blank checks

7. A ride to the station

8. Part of the stage crew

9. Some of the butter

10. Each of the stagehand

11. The president of the club

12. A pair of avocado

13. Two of their couch

14. The mark of the unicorn

15. The challenge of the century

16. Several of his answer

17. A bunch of grape

18. Few of the candidate

19. One of my television set

20. Two pianos

Correcting Nouns in Sentences

Correct all incorrect nouns in the following sentences.

example

charts
Two of the ~~chart~~ were missing from the shelf.

1. Fifteen of those dollar came from the poker game.

2. The doctor found two possible sources of the infection.

3. Two of my friend will be waiting for us.

4. The book has several of its page missing.

5. We bought a few inexpensive picture frame.

6. Steve Sutton founded the university on three principle.

7. Two of the recipe were better than the others.

8. We wrote to both of the college on the list.

9. He replaced a window with a sheet of plywood.

10. The Italian Renaissance displayed all of these characteristic.

11. Some of this coffee comes from Turkey.

12. She received one telegram in the morning.

13. A message for the dean was also received.

14. Each of the member of the orchestra was asked for a contribution.

15. Sammy scored two of his touchdown on long runs.

16. Her tap shoes were once worn by one of the Melody sister.

17. They starred with my mother in one of the local talent show.

18. A piano was delivered to his apartment.

BONUS (contains Unit 2 and 3 material):

1. Each member of the orchestra was asked to contribute one of his or

   her bonus check.

2. I have already read some of his paper; he chose a good subject and developed his idea well.

Nouns with Unusual Plurals

Some nouns have unusual plural forms. These include

Nouns that end in *-f* or *-fe*
Nouns that change the main vowel sound
Nouns that don't change
Letters and numbers

The plurals of these words are often sources of writing errors.

Nouns Ending in *-f* or *-fe*

Most nouns that end in an *f*-sound make their plural by changing the *f* or *fe* to *v* and adding *-es* to make their plural forms.

Singular	Plural
knife	knives
self	selves
wife	wives

Nouns That Change Vowel Sounds

Some nouns make their plural forms by changing the way they are pronounced and spelled. Many of these words also add *-n*, *-en*, or *-ren* to the plural.

	Singular	Plural
No *n*:	die	dice
	foot	feet
	goose	geese
	mouse	mice
	tooth	teeth
	woman	women
	man	men
Added *n*:	child	children
	ox	oxen

Nouns That Do Not Change

A few nouns have the same singular and plural form.

Singular	Plural
deer	deer
fish	fish
sheep	sheep

Plurals of Letters and Numbers

Numbers and letters can form plurals either with or without an **apostrophe** — that is, by adding either *s* or *'s*.

Many people prefer the form without the apostrophe, since the apostrophe usually shows possession. We recommend that you use this form in your own work.

Plural

We have several **IBM PCs** in the office.

Possessive

There is something wrong with the **PC's** power supply.

Exercise 12

| example |

Nouns with Unusual Plurals in Sentences

Correct any incorrect nouns in the following sentences.

knives

Hilda keeps all of her ~~knife~~ on the kitchen shelf.

1. Several goose have started using the pond at my father's farm.

2. He keeps goats and sheeps most of the year and raises a few cash crop.

3. The woman in this company are all eligible for raise.

4. I spoke to the childs yesterday about their behavior.

5. The office was visited by several salesmans.

6. Barry bought three new fishes for his home aquarium — all guppy.

7. Janet received several A's on her physiology exams.

8. Rita received three 87 on her recent quizzes.

9. The members of the commission decided the issue for themselfs.

10. She broke two of her tooth in the fall.

Chapter Review

In this chapter you learned that

1. Adjectives like *a*, *the*, *this*, and *my* can help you find nouns in sentences.

2. You can also find nouns in sentences by looking at **sentence structure**.

3. Most nouns make their **plural form** by adding *-s* or *-es*.

4. Some nouns have **unusual plurals**.

5. You can choose the correct noun form in sentences by looking at
   a. Adjective signals like *one* and *few*
   b. Phrase signals like *one of the . . .*

In the SKILL section you learned how to find nouns in sentences with **verbal phrases, appositives, and more than one clause**.

Review Exercise 1

Correct all errors in singular and plural nouns in the following sentences. If a sentence contains no errors, write **OK** in the margin.

1. The many bright light shine across the highway.

2. One of Brad's best friend is looking for an apartments.

3. The science writer's convention has been scheduled for June

   in Atlanta.

4. One of the new delegate wants to hold the meeting here.

5. Essays were assigned to each of the student yesterday.

6. Each of his cars carried a parking tickets on the windshield.

7. Their storys always sound interesting.

8. This colleges will need several new librarys soon.

9. The neighborhood's newest store has a sales going on right now.

10. These donut taste fresher this times.

11. The sandwich has too much mustards.

12. A victorys by any local football team makes news in this towns.

13. Many of the knife in his collection are valuable collector's item.

14. All maple tree shed their leaves at this times.

15. Most of the representative from the union spoke on Tuesday.

16. Another dozen baseball jersey have been ordered by one of the team manager.

17. Some player have trouble fielding the ball in this winds.

18. These drama production cost very little money to attend.

BONUS (contains Unit 2 and 3 material):

1. Most of the leafs have already fallen, and the garbage mens have removed them from the street.

2. All of Brad's essay have earned A and B, and several will be published in *Rising Tide*, one of the better college literary magazine in the country.

Review Exercise 2

Do this exercise if you have completed Units 2 and 3. **Correct all errors** in singular and plural nouns in the following paragraphs.

At bedtime Jenny asked her parent about Santa Claus. She said that she had some question that she had never thought about before. For example, why did Santa live at the North Pole? And where did his many elf come from? Jenny told her mother and father that she was now five. She was not a little kids like her two younger brothers anymore. She deserved to know these thing.

Her parent agreed with her. Big girl like Jenny needed to know more than little kids. So they told her the truth about how Santa's many allergy forced him to move north, and about how he found the elf on one of his camping trip.

It was one of the best bedtime story they ever told. Jenny was asleep before it ended.

Chapter 14 Writing Assignment

Write a paragraph that discusses the main "causes" or **reasons you entered this school**.
   When you have made your final copy

1. Place an **X** over each **noun** in each of your sentences.

2. Make sure that
   a. All **verbs** and **nouns** are correct.
   b. All **clauses and phrases** are correctly punctuated.
   c. Your paragraph contains **no fragments**.

Hints for Cause and Effect Paragraphs

This paragraph will be most effective if you pay attention to the steps listed under "Before the rough draft." Doing these steps carefully will make your paragraph as convincing as possible.

Before the rough draft:
1. First, make a list of *all* of the reasons you entered this school, not just the ones you think you are going to write about. Take enough time to make this list complete.

2. Edit your list (by adding things in and taking things out) until it includes the main reasons.

3. Starting with the **least** important reason and ending with the most important, copy the edited list onto a clean sheet of paper.

4. Next to each reason on your recopied list, note one or two things you will say when discussing that reason.

Writing the rough draft:

1. Start your rough draft by writing a short group of sentences that
    a. Tells why other people have entered this school, and
    b. Explains that you entered it for several other reasons.

2. Using your list of reasons, write a sentence that mentions your first reason. Then write a few sentences that explain that reason.

3. Do the same for each reason on your list.

4. Write a closing sentence or two that feels like an ending.

After the rough draft:

1. Do your best to correct any errors on this first copy. Be especially careful to correct all errors in
    a. Nouns
    b. Verbs
    c. Punctuation

2. Make any other changes you think will make your paragraph more interesting and readable.

3. Recopy your corrected paragraph on a clean sheet of paper and turn in all of your work.

PRONOUNS AND INTENSE NOUNS

c h a p t e r

15
Pronouns

Chapter
Preview

This chapter will show you

1. How to recognize the kinds of **pronouns**

2. How pronouns are used in **sentences**

3. How to use the **subject and object forms** of pronouns correctly

4. How to make pronouns **agree in number and gender**

5. How to avoid **offensive use of pronouns** when referring to people in occupations.

NOTE: In order to work in this chapter, you must have completed Units 1, 2, and 3.

PRONOUNS AND REFERENCE WORDS

You have learned that nouns are words that name persons, places, things, and ideas. **Pronouns** are words that take the place of nouns. They usually get their meaning from a noun that has been mentioned or will be mentioned soon. (You first studied pronouns in Chapter 1.)

In the following sentence, for example, the pronoun *he* means *President Eisenhower.*

President Eisenhower, in a speech **he** made before

leaving office, warned the nation against the growing

"military-industrial complex."

Notice that this sentence could have been written:

In a speech **he** made before leaving office,

President Eisenhower \ warned the nation against the

growing "military-industrial complex."

The sharing of meaning between a noun and a pronoun is called **pronoun reference**. The pronoun takes its meaning from a noun called the **antecedent**, or **reference word**. In the above example, the pronoun is *he* and the antecedent or reference word is *President Eisenhower.*

In this chapter you will learn how to choose the correct pronoun forms and how to make pronoun references clear and correct.

KINDS OF PRONOUNS

There are several kinds of pronouns. They are described and listed below.

Personal Pronouns

Personal pronouns, like *I* and *you*, refer to people (and sometimes things).

Personal pronouns change form, depending on whether they refer to the speaker (*I*), the person spoken to (*you*), or the person spoken about (*they*).

Personal pronouns also change form depending on whether the reference word is

Singular or **plural** in number (for example, *I* and *we*)
Masculine, feminine, or **neuter** in gender (for example, *he, she,* and *it*)
A **subject,** an **object,** or shows **possession** (for example, *I, me,* and *mine*)

Personal pronouns will be discussed in greater detail later in this chapter.

Demonstrative Pronouns

Demonstrative pronouns, like *this* and *that*, point things out ("demonstrate"). They change form depending on whether the reference word is near (*this* and *these*), or far (*that* and *those*), or singular or plural.

Interrogative Pronouns

Interrogative pronouns, like *who* and *what*, are used to ask questions. Of these pronouns, only *who* changes form, depending on whether it is used as a subject or object.

    Who and *whom* will be discussed more completely in the next section. (You studied interrogative pronouns in Chapter 2.)

"Relative" Pronouns

"Relative" pronouns, like *who* and *which*, are really **tip-off word** pronouns for adjective and noun clauses. (You may recall that adjective clauses are sometimes called "relative" clauses. You studied adjective clauses in Chapter 7.)

    Of these pronouns, only *who* changes form. You studied *who* and *whom* in RELATED SKILL sections in Chapters 5 and 7. *Who* and *whom* will also be discussed in the next section.

Indefinite and Universal Pronouns

Indefinite pronouns, like *some* and *few*, refer to a small and often indefinite part of a group.

    Universal pronouns, like *every* and *all*, refer to every member of a group.

    Though some of these pronouns are singular and some are plural, they never change form.

Numerical Pronouns

Numerical pronouns are the counting words, *one*, *two*, *three*, and so on. Like *some* and *every*, they never change form.

List of Pronouns

A list of these common pronouns appears below.

Pronouns

Personal Pronouns and *Who*

	Subject Form	Object Form	Possessive
Singular:	I	me	mine
	you	you	yours
	he	his	his
	she	her	hers
	it	it	its
Plural:	we	us	ours
	you	you	yours
	they	them	theirs
Singular or plural:	who	whom	whose

Demonstrative Pronouns

Singular	Plural
this	these
that	those

Interrogative Pronouns

Singular or Plural
who (whom, whose)
which
what

"Relative" Pronouns

Singular or Plural
who (whom, whose)
whoever (whomever, whosoever)

which
what
that

Indefinite Pronouns

Singular	Plural
one (a person)	both
none	some
	many
	several

another

either
neither
somebody
nobody

Singular or Plural
any
other

Universal Pronouns

Singular	**Plural**
each	all
everyone	
everybody	

Numerical Pronouns

one
two
three
and so on

USES OF PRONOUNS

As you have seen many times, pronouns can be used as subjects, as objects of verbs, prepositions, or verbals, as complements, and as appositives. The following sentences contain some of these uses of the pronoun *someone*.

Someone **as subject**

Someone (borrowed) my golf jacket.

Someone **as object of verb**

I (saw) someone (with your golf jacket.)

Someone **as object of preposition**

Sheila (lent) (your golf jacket) (to someone.)

Someone **as object of verbal**

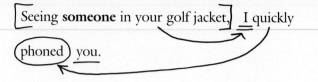

Seeing **someone** in your golf jacket, I quickly phoned you.

Someone **as complement**

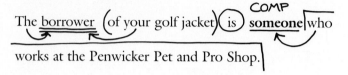

The borrower (of your golf jacket) is **someone** who works at the Penwicker Pet and Pro Shop.

Many pronouns, like *some*, *many*, and *one* can also be used as adjectives. Be careful, therefore, in marking sentences that contain them. Compare the following. Notice that in both sentences, *one* means "student."

One as pronoun

Several students looked for the answer.

Only one found it.

One as adjective

Several students looked for the answer.

Only one student found it.

Exercise 1

Using Pronouns in Sentences

Draw a **box** around each pronoun in the following sentences. Then **tell what each pronoun does.**

Do not box any word used as an adjective.

example

Rick bought several for her on the way to work.

several - object of bought

her - object of preposition for

1. LaWalter brought his from home.

_____

_____

2. Her boat sailed slowly toward him.

_____

_____

3. They found it in his yard.

_____

_____

4. Each of her brothers sold three.

_____

_____

5. Each of the dolphins ate all of his food.

_____

_____

6. Every lady in the room counted to ten and cheered.

_____

_____

7. These are yours, but three will not last long.

_____

_____

8. Several people who claim to be his son are waiting for their

inheritance.

_____

_____

9. Nine points was all that either team would allow.

_____

_____

393 Pronouns

10. Who wrote this poem? Was it you?

_____

_____

11. I visited Stratford this year, a town that depends on tourists for most of its income.

_____

_____

12. Could this be yours?

_____

_____

13. The jets have landed there.

_____

_____

14. Zelda wanted to finish this before sunset.

_____

_____

15. Clayton and his wife bought their house in the neighborhood, close to her school and his work.

_____

_____

16. We thought that neither was good enough to eat.

_____

_____

17. One was made, but another could not be assembled in time.

_____

_____

18. These novels that you like were made into films.

_____

_____

19. Another unsigned letter from him was discovered at her door.

_____

_____

20. No one knew this as well as he did.

_____

_____

FORMS OF PRONOUNS

In several RELATED SKILL sections, you saw how some pronouns change forms depending on how they are used. In this section we will summarize and add to that information.

Let's start by looking at the forms of pronouns. All pronouns have three forms.

Subject form

Object form

Possessive form

The **subject form** (also called the **subjective case**) is used for

1. Subjects
2. Complements following linking verbs
3. Appositives following subjects or complements

The **object form** (also called the **objective case**) is used for

1. Objects of action verbs
2. Objects of prepositions
3. Objects of verbals
4. Appositives following objects

The **possessive form** or the **possessive case** is a pronoun (like _mine, ours,_ and _someone's_) that shows that something is possessed or owned.

Pronouns with Only One Form

Most pronouns (and all nouns) have the same spelling for both their subject and object forms. The pronoun *each*, for example, has only one form for both subjects and objects — *each*.

Each as subject

Each (of the brothers) (agreed) (with Sam.)

Each as object

Wendy (marked) **each** (of her books.)

Pronouns with More Than One Form

As you have seen, many personal pronouns and the pronoun *who* have different subject and object forms.

When the pronoun *she* is used as a subject, for example, the correct form is *she*, but when it is an object, *her* is correct.

She as subject

She (spoke) (to the dean) (for me.)

Her as object

Brad (saw) **her** (at the administration center.)

The following list shows the subject and object forms of possessive pronouns and *who*.

Forms of Personal Pronouns and *Who*

Subject Form	Object Form
I	me
you	you
he	his
she	her
it	it
we	us
they	them
who	whom

Forms of Possessive Pronouns

The possessive form of all pronouns can be used like either the subject or object form with no change in spelling.

Possessive forms as subjects

COMP

Where is your book? **Mine** (is) the one (on the left.)

Where is your book? **Someone's** (is sitting) (on the

ledge.)

Possessive forms as objects

Where is your book? I (have) **mine** (in my locker.)

Where is your book? I (see) **someone's** (on the ledge.)

Using the Subject Form

Sometimes it is not easy to choose between the subject and object forms of personal pronouns and *who*.

Recall that the subject form is required for

1. Subjects
2. Complements following linking verbs
3. Appositives following subjects

The following sentences show these uses. Notice that the subject form is used in each.

Who as subject

Who (came) (to the door) (last night?)

He as complement

COMP

The department secretary (was) **he**.

She as appositive following subject

APP

The best candidate, **she** (was) not (in the race.)

Watch especially for

Pronouns used as complements

Pronouns joined to other words with *and*

These sentences are sometimes harder to correct than others.

Pronoun as complement

The last fraternity secretary (was) I.   COMP

Pronoun with *and*

Joey and I (went) (to the ballet) for the first time (last night.)

Using the Object Form

The object form of personal pronouns and *who* is required for

1. Objects of action verbs
2. Objects of prepositions
3. Objects of verbals
4. Appositives following objects

The following sentences show these uses. Notice that the object form is used in each.

***Them* as object of verb**

Martina (saw) **them** (at the kissing booth.)

***Us* as object of preposition**

Mr. Jimbabwe (spoke)(to **us**) about his trip.

***Him* as object of verbal**

Shelly (wanted) | to see **him** | one more time.

***Her* as appositive following object**

Mr. Winters (asked) to see the waitress, **her.**   APP

Who and Whom

The pronouns *who* (subject form) and *whom* (object form) deserve special attention.

Whom is almost never heard in speech. But in writing, *whom* must be used whenever the object form is required.

The following sentences show *who* and *whom* in questions and as tip-off words in adjective clauses.

Who as subject of question

<u>**Who**</u> (found) the <u>test</u> difficult?

Who as subject in adjective clause

COMP
<u>It</u> (was) <u>Nicolette</u> |who recorded that song.|

Adjective clause: <u>who</u> (recorded) that <u>song</u>

Whom as object in question

<u>**Whom**</u> (did) <u>she</u> (find) there?

Whom as object of adjective clause

COMP
<u>It</u> (was) <u>Nicolette</u> | for **whom** he recorded that song. |

Adjective clause: (for **whom**) <u>he</u> (recorded) that <u>song</u>

Exercise 2

Correcting Pronouns in Sentences

Correct all pronoun errors in these sentences. If a sentence contains no errors, write **OK** in the margin.

example

The president of the yacht club was ~~him~~ *he*.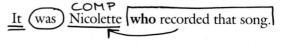

1. The war was explained to Marion and she by Dr. Flemming.

2. Whom is the most eligible candidate?

3. Both students, Mrs. Brown and her, wanted to retake the test.

4. Which is the designer in who you have the most confidence?

5. Who found this piece of evidence?

6. The office is being run by Alicia and she.

7. Both of us wanted to speak to her about the recipe.

8. Whom are you?

9. She had more success calling Dr. French and he on the phone.

10. Those ornaments were bought for who?

11. Dr. Riesman was enthusiastic, and she wanted we to do well.

12. When will the car be ready, and whom will be the first driver to race it?

13. We haven't seen Sam and they in weeks.

14. This has never happened to her.

15. The former owners, Dr. Mandeville and he, regretted their decision to sell to her.

16. She is a person who we all admire.

17. The house was furnished by a couple who we knew from church.

18. It entered the bar and spoke to the first human who looked at it.

19. It waited two hours, drank three beers, and met a friend who it knew from another galaxy.

20. I worked last summer for they and their friends.

PRONOUN REFERENCE

Most pronouns get their meaning by referring to another word. This **reference word** or **antecedent** is usually a noun, pronoun, or short phrase that appears nearby in the same or the previous sentence.

The relationship between the pronoun and its reference word must have two important qualities.

1. It must be clear which word the pronoun refers to, and
2. The pronoun and its reference word must "agree" (match in gender and number).

Let's look more closely at these qualities.

Clear Pronoun Reference

The first rule of pronoun reference is clarity. There must be no doubt which word a pronoun refers to.

A reader will become confused if

Several references are possible for the same pronoun.

A pronoun has no reference word when it should.

A pronoun refers to a general group of statements instead of a specific word or phrase.

The following sentences contain examples of both clear and unclear pronoun references.

Clear

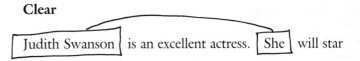

in the next community theater production.

(*She* = Judith Swanson)

Unclear

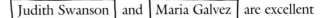

actresses. | She | will star in the next community theater

production.

(*She* = Judith Swanson? Maria Galvez?)

Clear

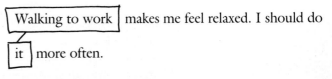

(*It* = Walking to work)

Unclear

The French re-colonized Vietnam after World War II, when Ho Chi Minh fought on the side of the Allies against the Japanese. | That | created a complicated situation.

(*That* = French colonizing Vietnam? Ho Chi Minh fighting for the Allies? World War II? All of these?)

All words that have antecedents, not just pronouns, must have clear references. This includes adjectives made from pronouns like

my	this	whose
our	that	which
his	these	
her	those	
its		
their		

Agreement of Pronouns and Reference Words

A pronoun and its reference word (antecedent) must have exactly the same meaning. When they do, the two are "in agreement." The two ways that a pronoun and its reference word agree are

Agreement in number

Agreement in gender

If the reference word is plural (like *cars*), the pronoun must also be plural (like *them*). If the reference word is singular (like *fun*), the pronoun must also be singular (like *it*). A word like *we* cannot refer to *Mr. Winston*. This is called **agreement in number**.

In the same way, if the reference word has a masculine meaning (like *man*), the pronoun must also be masculine (like *he*). The pronoun *she* cannot refer to *Bill Rafferty*. This is called **agreement in gender**.

Of course, not all pronouns have separate singular and plural forms, and most do not have separate masculine, feminine, and neuter (neither masculine nor feminine) forms. But when you use those that do, you must use the correct form.

Notice that the rules of agreement also apply to possessive adjectives related to pronouns, like *his* and *their*. The following sentence, for example, contains an error in agreement. Can you find it?

Incorrect

Every passenger carried their own luggage.

Did you notice that *passenger* is singular and *their* is plural?

Incorrect

Every ⌐passenger⌐ carried ⌐their⌐ own luggage.

This error could be corrected as follows.

Corrected

his or her

Every passenger carried ~~their~~ own luggage.

Errors in agreement are common in speech, so they are sometimes hard to pick out. Nevertheless, they should be eliminated from professional writing.

Avoiding Offensive Pronoun References

Be careful when referring to members of groups — especially members of occupations or professions — with words like *he*, *she*, *his*, or *her*. Using these words may reveal assumptions that aren't correct.

A sentence like the following, for example,

Look for a dentist who does his own lab work.

assumes that all dentists are male.

Incorrect

Look for a ⌐dentist⌐ who does ⌐his⌐ own lab work.

All dentists are not male, so the use of *his* is inaccurate.

Many people are offended by pronoun errors like the one above. Correct it in either of the following ways.

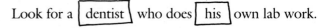

Look for a ⌐dentist⌐ who does ⌐his or her⌐ own lab work.

OR

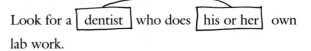

Look for ⌐dentists⌐ who do ⌐their⌐ own lab work.

You can also correct errors like these by rewriting the sentence entirely.

Exercise 3

Pronoun Reference

Many of the items in the following exercise contain pronoun references that are unclear or not in agreement.

Correct all incorrect pronoun references by rewriting the sentences that contain them.

If the item is already correct, write **OK** on the lines.

example

Janice and Gloria were both invited to the audition. I hope she gets the part.

Janice and Gloria were both invited to the audition. I hope Janice gets the part.

1. We asked for the dean's opinion. She gave a surprising answer.

   _____

   _____

2. Let's spend a day at the beach. They always relax me.

   _____

   _____

3. Place an X over every pronoun and correct them if they are wrong.

   _____

   _____

4. Every car dealer in the country has his own way of providing service.

   _____

   _____

5. Solitary stars and solar systems make up our galaxy. There certainly are a lot of them.

   _____

   _____

6. Fred saw the ad in the newspaper. It was the first thing he looked at every morning.

_____

_____

7. Everyone should carry their own equipment.

_____

_____

8. A good secretary knows how to keep her boss organized.

_____

_____

9. Cleaning windows and ironing shirts are my least favorite jobs. I never want to do it again.

_____

_____

10. Did you enjoy attending the workshop on journalism and the new obscenity law? I'm looking forward to reading about it.

_____

_____

_____

Chapter Review

In this chapter you learned that

1. **Pronouns** take the place of nouns.

2. **Pronouns can be used** as subjects, objects of all kinds, complements, or appositives.

3. The **personal pronouns** and the **pronoun** *who* have different subject and object forms.

4. The **subject form** is used for
   a. Subjects
   b. Complements
   c. Appositives following subjects or complements

5. The **object form** is used for
   a. Objects of verbs, prepositions, or verbals
   b. Appositives following objects

6. Most pronouns and many adjectives take their meaning from a **reference word** or **antecedent**.

7. Pronouns and reference words must **agree in gender and number**.

8. Avoid using pronouns and adjectives that refer incorrectly to members of a group.

Review Exercise 1

Correct all errors in pronoun form or reference in the following paragraph.

Roweena has been working with small computers and computer systems for years. For her it started as a hobby. In her junior year at Joliet State College she entered the local science fair. All of them showed interesting projects. Roweena's project about computer codes won first prize, and she received a fellowship for graduate school. This meant a lot, both to her mother and she. Their adviser, Ms. Christiansen, was proud of them all. But most of all he was proud of Roweena.

Review Exercise 2

Rewrite the paragraph above, changing "Roweena" to "Roweena and Bill." Be sure to make all necessary changes in pronoun and adjective reference.

_____

_____

_____

_____

_____

_____

_____

_____

_____

_____

_____

Chapter 15 Writing Assignment

Write a paragraph that discusses the main effects of an important present or previous relationship with another person.

Hints for Cause and Effect Paragraphs

This paragraph will be most effective if you pay attention to the steps listed under "Before the rough draft." Doing these steps carefully will make your paragraph as convincing as possible.

Before the rough draft:

1. First, make a list of *all* of the effects of this relationship, not just the effects that come into your mind immediately. Take enough time to make this list complete.

2. Edit your list (by adding effects and taking them out) until it includes all of the main effects.

3. Starting with the **least** important effect and ending with the most important, copy the edited list onto a clean sheet of paper.

4. Next to each effect on your recopied list, note three stories that would support each effect.

5. Finally, check the one story that will best support each effect.

Writing the rough draft:

1. Start your rough draft by writing a short group of sentences that tells why you liked the person that you've chosen to write about.

2. Using your edited list of effects as a reference, write a sentence that mentions the first effect. Then tell the story that supports that effect.

3. Do the same for each effect on your list.

4. Write a closing sentence or two that feels like an ending.

After the rough draft:

1. Draw a box around each pronoun.

2. Do your best to correct any errors on this first copy. Be especially careful to correct all errors in
   a. Verbs
   b. Nouns
   c. Pronouns
   d. Punctuation

3. Make sure your paragraph contains no fragments.

4. Make any other changes you think will make your paragraph more interesting and readable.

5. Recopy your corrected paragraph on a clean sheet of paper and turn in all of your work.

U N I T
VI

Punctuation and spelling

When you studied phrases and clauses earlier in this book, you learned how to punctuate them. The next two chapters will tell you more about how to punctuate the various parts of a sentence and will help you review all that you have learned about punctuation so far. The last chapter in this Unit will show you ways to avoid spelling errors.

NOTE: Any student who has completed Units 1 through 3 — Chapters 1 through 10 — in this book may study the chapters in this Unit.

16
Other punctuation skills

**Chapter
Preview**

This chapter will show you how to punctuate

1. Simple sentence **interrupters**

2. Direct and indirect **quotations**

3. Sentences with **colons, dashes, and hyphens**

4. Contractions

PUNCTUATION

Punctuation helps your readers. Good punctuation makes the ideas in your sentences easier to understand because good punctuation identifies the main structures of the sentences that contain them.

In this way, readers can therefore spend more time thinking about your ideas and less time thinking about your sentences. Readers who can move smoothly from sentence to sentence are happier than those who have to pause often because the punctuation is not helpful.

The result, of course, is obvious. Happy readers continue reading, while readers who have to struggle with poorly punctuated sentences eventually stop reading those sentences entirely.

As you can see, clear punctuation is an important aspect of good writing, and the ability to punctuate well is an important skill.

In this book you have already learned many punctuation principles — principles that are already improving your writing.

In Chapter 1 you learned how to use **commas with more than one subject or verb**. Of course, what you learned there applies to all of the other structures you have learned about — objects, complements, phrases of various types, and clauses.

In Chapter 5 you learned

> How to **separate main clauses with end punctuation** (periods, question marks, and exclamation points)
>
> How to **join main clauses** by using a semicolon or a comma + conjunction like *and*

In Chapter 6 you learned how to avoid several common **errors in punctuating main clauses**.

> Run-on sentences
>
> Comma splices
>
> Errors using commas with conjunctions like *and*
>
> Semicolon errors
>
> Fragments

In Chapters 7, 9, and 10 you learned how to **punctuate adjective and adverb clauses, descriptive verbal phrases, and appositives** that

> Are out of normal position
>
> Contain "extra" information

In this chapter and the next, you will conclude your study of punctuation. Here you will add to what you already know by studying

> Commas with simple interrupters (words and phrases like *however* and *of course*)
>
> Direct and indirect quotations

Colons, dashes, and hyphens

Apostrophes

The next chapter will help you review all of the punctuation rules and principles you have studied in this book.

Let's begin by looking at commas with simple interrupters.

USING COMMAS WITH SIMPLE INTERRUPTERS

There are several small words and phrases that seem to interrupt the clauses they are in. These **simple interrupters** almost always require special punctuation.

Simple interrupters

The law, **however,** was on her side.

The lab work could, **of course,** be postponed.

In these sentences, *however* and *of course* are simple interrupters. If you read these sentences aloud, you can almost hear the pauses before and after the interrupting words.

Marking Interrupters

Interrupters can be marked with a **long bracket** and the letter **I.**

The law, **however,** was on her side.

The lab work could, **of course,** be postponed.

Punctuating Interrupters

Except in a very few cases, simple interrupters are punctuated according to the Interrupter Rule.

The Interrupter Rule

Punctuate any sentence interrupter by separating it from the rest of the sentence with commas.

Interrupter, *******************************.
*************** , **interrupter,** ***************.
****************************** , **interrupter.**

You first saw the Interrupter Rule in Chapter 7, where you used it to punctuate adjective and adverb clauses. In Chapters 9 and 10, you applied it to certain verbal phrases and appositives as well.

In those chapters, you learned when the Interrupter Rule applies and when it doesn't. Simple interrupters, however, *must* be punctuated with commas. (Those few simple interrupters that do not require punctuation are discussed in the next section and in the next chapter.)

Let's look at some examples. As you have already learned, interrupters can appear in three places in a clause — in the middle, at the beginning, or at the end.

The following sentence contains the interrupter *for example*.

Interrupter in the middle of clause

One of the actors, **for example,** was educated in England.

Here the interrupter comes between the subject and its adjectives, and the verb.

Interrupter in the middle of clause

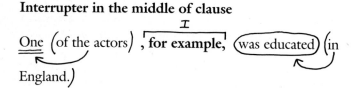

One (of the actors) , **for example,** (was educated) (in England.)

Notice that *for example* is separated from the rest of the sentence with commas.

Interrupter within sentence

**************** , **interrupter,** ************** .

One of the actors, **for example,** was educated in England.
        ↑   ↑
       COMMAS NEEDED

This sentence could also have been written with the interrupter at the beginning or at the end of the clause.

"Interrupter" at beginning of clause

Interrupter, ****************************** .

For example, one of the actors was educated in England. ↑
    COMMA NEEDED

"Interrupter" at end of clause

*********************************** , interrupter.

One of the actors was educated in England, **for example.**

↑
COMMA NEEDED

Notice that in all three cases, commas are used to separate the interrupter from the sentence.

List of Interrupters

Simple interrupters fall into three groups, as the following chart shows.

Common Simple Interrupters

Group 1:

besides	therefore	by the way
consequently	as a result	of course
furthermore	yes	for example
however	no	on the one hand
moreover	well	on the other hand
nevertheless	oh	
meanwhile		

Names and
  titles of people
  spoken to

Group 2:

I believe	I think
I suppose	it seems to me

Group 3:

not . . .	according to . . .
such as . . .	but . . .

This list is not complete, but it does contain many of the most common interrupters. Use it as a reference for your work in this chapter.

Let's look at each group more closely.

Group 1. Most of the words and phrases in this group are familiar, and many like them are in common use. Note that this group also contains names of people spoken to.

The following sentences contain interrupters from Group 1. In the first example, the phrase *on the other hand*, though it provides a transition from the sentence before, seems to break the flow of the sentence it is in.

> The Church of Saint Teresa, **on the other hand**, is more than 200 years old.

In this next example, *Mr. McCormack* is the name of a person spoken to.

> **Mr. McCormack**, would you restate your question?

Group 2. The interrupters in this group are clauses. Each contains a subject and a verb. Yet when they are used *within another clause*, they act (and "feel") like interrupters.

> *I believe* **as interrupter within a clause**
>
> The water, **I believe**, should be tested.

Notice that clause interrupters don't act like interrupters when placed before a clause.

> *I believe* **before a clause**
>
> **I believe** <that> the water should be tested.

When clauses like *I believe* begin a sentence, they become the main clause of the sentence. The rest of the sentence is a noun clause introduced with the hidden tip-off word *that*. (See Chapter 7, pages 175–180, for a discussion of noun clauses in sentences.)

Group 3. Interrupters in this group contain phrases that occur frequently in college and business writing.

> History, **according to some writers**, is merely the record of the lives of great men.
>
> We spoke to Dr. Granger, **not Mrs. Atchison**, about the illness.

There are more phrases in Group 3 than are listed in the chart on page 415.

Exercise 1

Punctuating Simple Interrupters

Apply the Interrupter Rule by **adding commas** to the following sentences. The interrupters are printed in **boldface** type.

example

Jonathan **,** **nevertheless** **,** found the tripe undercooked.

1. The Jacksons **on the other hand** loved every minute of it.

2. The blue velvet rose **however** won first prize.

3. **Nevertheless** her investments never deserted their obligations to her.

4. Several spinach leaves graced the salad plates **according to Mrs. Gracia's report**.

5. The clock **he said** struck the hour.

6. **For example** three new Chernobyl pansies were introduced at the garden exposition.

7. The book **for your information** cited several cases from the local police archives.

8. **Moreover** the Consequential Insurance Company banquet and awards supper will be held at the Penwicker Auditorium.

9. Several international athletes will gather **therefore** at a special service in her honor.

10. Kirk responded **she said** with his usual macho unintelligibility.

Exercise 2

Punctuating Simple Interrupters

Mark and punctuate all interrupters in the following sentences. If the sentence is correctly punctuated, write **OK** in the margin.

example

The news will be followed, therefore, by a special sports presentation.

1. In the first place tonight is our fifth anniversary.

2. Miss Simmons furthermore will not be present this evening.

3. The Navy it seems to me offers greater opportunities to women in those professions.

417 Other punctuation skills

4. It seems to me that the Navy offers greater opportunities to women in those professions.

5. Each credit card charges 20 percent interest however.

6. According to Dr. Homan the test results are correct.

7. On the one hand his grades are very good.

8. Chemical oven cleaners do a very good job however.

9. The cause of his anger moreover has yet to be discovered.

10. The *Saturday Evening Post* for example went out of business for a while.

11. As a result the truck was already full of baby clothes.

12. They discovered gold and copper for example in the ore that they tested.

13. They discovered gold and copper in the sample that they tested.

14. The belt can be worn of course with the tan pants.

15. They nominated Judith and Bradley moreover for the negotiating team.

16. New York not New Jersey is actually my uncle's childhood home.

17. It is not the books but the magazines that are important.

18. Nevertheless I didn't do what they say I did.

19. The lucky winner is out of the country it seems.

20. The lucky winner it seems is out of the country.

Interrupters Used with Semicolons

Certain interrupters are sometimes used with semicolons to join main clauses. In Chapter 5, for example, you saw the following sentence.

Main clauses joined with ; *however*,

Last year I played intramural football; **however,** this year I might try soccer.

This punctuation pattern

; however,

is really two punctuation rules combined. The semicolon is used to join main clauses,

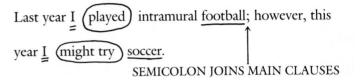

Last year I (played) intramural football; however, this year I (might try) soccer.

SEMICOLON JOINS MAIN CLAUSES

and the comma punctuates an interrupter at the beginning of a clause.

Last year I played intramural football; **however,** this

year I might try soccer.

Interrupter, ****************************** .

Notice that this sentence could have been punctuated as follows.

Last year I played intramural football. However, this year I might try soccer.

PERIOD BETWEEN MAIN CLAUSES

Notice also that if a comma is used before the interrupter, a comma splice results.

Comma splice (incorrect)

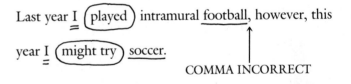

Last year I (played) intramural football, however, this year I (might try) soccer.

COMMA INCORRECT

Words that are used in this way are called **conjunctive adverbs**. For your reference a list is printed below. Note that all of these words are simple interrupters from Group 1.

Conjunctive Adverbs

Similarity	Opposition
besides	however
consequently	nevertheless
furthermore	
moreover	
therefore	

Watch carefully for sentences with more than one main clause when using interrupters like *however*.

<table>
<tr><td>

Exercise 3

</td><td>

Simple Interrupters in Sentences with More than One Main Clause

Many of these sentences contain more than one main clause.

1. Mark the **verb** and **subject** of each main clause.
2. Mark each **simple interrupter**.
3. Using **commas** and **semicolons**, punctuate each sentence correctly.

</td></tr>
</table>

<table>
<tr><td>

example

</td><td>

The Tricorder 7000 (is) a tape player COMP for the upwardly mobile**;** therefore**,** it (sells) at an astronomic price.

</td></tr>
</table>

1. Brandee had trouble gathering all of her research nevertheless she got the paper done.

2. Gregory decided to risk everything therefore he asked Amantha that evening for her hand.

3. He didn't know however that she had other ambitions.

4. Brian Poulson watched carefully nevertheless he failed to see the pickpocket with the wallet.

5. Castle Dracula is a hit nevertheless among the teenage date crowd.

6. Castle Dracula is a hit among the teenage date crowd nevertheless the amusement park will close the popular ride for the summer.

7. Castle Dracula is a hit among the teenage date crowd nevertheless.

8. The burgers are cooked rare moreover they are reasonably priced.

9. Brad assumed that his test scores were high consequently he applied to several prominent graduate schools.

10. Several turned him down however because of his disinterest in hard work.

PUNCTUATING QUOTATIONS

Quotations are references to another speaker or writer's exact words. Quotations often contain a *he said/she said* statement that often acts like an interrupter and introduces the quotation by naming its speaker or writer.

There are two kinds of quotations, **direct quotations** and **indirect quotations**. Let's start with the easiest to punctuate — the indirect quotation.

Punctuating Indirect Quotations

Indirect quotations are usually sentences with noun clauses as objects. (See Chapter 7 for a discussion of noun clauses in sentences.)

The following sentence contains an indirect quotation.

Indirect quotation

The manager said **that she was tired**.

(Speaker's exact words: *I am tired.*)

Notice that the speaker's exact words were changed slightly to fit the writer's point of view. (This is what makes the quotation *indirect.*)

Notice also that the noun clause containing the speaker's words acts as the object of the verb.

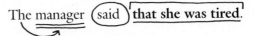

The manager (said) that she was tired.

Because they are simple subject – verb – object sentences, indirect quotations like the one above receive no special punctuation.

A variation of this pattern places a *he said/she said* statement in the middle of the quotation. There it acts like an interrupter. Compare the following.

"He said" at beginning

A company spokesman said today that no more workers would be laid off this year.

"He said" as interrupter

No more workers, **a company spokesman said today,** would be laid off this year.

(Speaker's exact words: *No more workers will be laid off this year.*)

Note that the speaker said "**will** be laid off" while the writer wrote "**would** be laid off."

Notice also that commas are required when the "he said" part of the sentence is used as an interrupter.

Punctuating Indirect Quotations

Rewrite each of the following into an indirect quotation. Use the "he said" part as an interrupter where requested.

| example |

Speaker: Professor Thorsen

Statement: *Class will be dismissed early.*

Professor Thorsen said that the class would be dismissed early.

1. Speaker: Thomas

   Statement: *The strike will soon be over.*

   _____

   _____

2. Speaker: An industry spokesman

   Statement: *A new product will be released before June 15.*

   (Use "he said" as interrupter.)

   _____

   _____

3. Speaker: Dr. Velikovsky

   Statement: *Your editing skills improve with practice.*

   _____

   _____

4. Speaker: The ship's captain

   Statement: *The damage to the ship was extensive, but no one was injured.*

   (Use "he said" as interrupter.)

   _____

   _____

5. Speaker: My brother

Statement: *Will you be ready by eight o'clock?*

_____

_____

Punctuating Direct Quotations

All direct quotations receive some kind of special punctuation. At the very least, the exact words of the quoted speaker (or writer) are surrounded by **quotation marks (" ")**.

Punctuating Direct Quotations without "He said/She said" Statements

The following sentence contains one word quoted from another person. Notice that there is no *he said/she said* statement in the following sentence. Instead the speaker is referred to.

Marilyn called the test "unusual."

Unusual was Marilyn's exact word, and the writer wants us to know that. Therefore, *unusual* is placed in quotation marks.

Sometimes an entire sentence is quoted, again without a "he said/she said" introduction, as in the following example.

Note that the first letter of the sentence is still capitalized, and that the period at the end of the sentence comes *before* the quotation mark.

Entire sentence as direct quotation

The dean's words were clear. **"Everyone who has donated to the college will receive an invitation."**
↑
PERIOD BEFORE QUOTATION MARK

| Exercise 5 | Direct Quotations without "He said/She said" Introductions |

Rewrite each of the following sentences so that the direct quotation is properly punctuated.

| example | Dawn asked if Hank was really a student.

Quoted words: *really a student*

Dawn asked if Hank was
"really a student."

1. Don questioned the effectiveness of her exercise program.

   Quoted words: *exercise program*

   _____

   _____

2. This four-page letter is much more than the thank-you note I expected.

   Quoted words: *thank-you note*

   _____

   _____

3. I was asked to explain my conclusion. Dr. Beaumont did not, as he put it, understand my logic.

   Quoted words: *understand my logic*

   _____

   _____

4. Their resistance was clearly stated. We will never alter the conclusions of this committee.

   Quoted words: *We will never alter the conclusions of this committee.*

   _____

   _____

5. Actually, our anniversary is on Tuesday, though I still don't understand why you want to celebrate a water fight that happened in third grade.

   Quoted word: *anniversary*

   _____

   _____

Punctuating Direct Quotations with "He said/She said" Statements

Direct quotations with "he said/she said" statements are not difficult to punctuate. Placing the quotation marks, commas, and capital letters follows a simple and logical pattern.

The four steps printed below will allow you to punctuate any direct quotation quickly and accurately. Practice this process until it becomes automatic.

Punctuating Direct Quotations with *He said/She said* Interrupters

1. Place **quotation marks** around the speaker's exact words.
2. Use **commas** to punctuate the *he said/she said* statement, if any, as an interrupter.
3. **Capitalize** the first letter of the speaker's sentence, no matter where it appears.
4. Use a **question mark** instead of a comma or period to show a question by the speaker or the writer.

Study the following unpunctuated examples. In all three sentences, the speaker's exact words are *the test will be postponed.*

"She said" at the beginning

Dr. Hellman said the test will be postponed.

"She said" in the middle

The test said Dr. Hellman will be postponed.

"She said" at the end

The test will be postponed said Dr. Hellman.

Now let's apply the punctuation rules to these examples.

Step 1. Place quotation marks around the speaker's exact words.

Dr. Hellman said "the test will be postponed."

"The test" said Dr. Hellman "will be postponed."

"The test will be postponed" said Dr. Hellman.

Notice once again that the period at the end of the sentence is printed *before* the quotation mark.

Step 2. Use commas to punctuate the "he said/she said" statement, if any, as an interrupter.

Dr. Hellman said **,** "the test will be postponed."

"The test **,** " said Dr. Hellman **,** "will be postponed."

"The test will be postponed **,** " said Dr. Hellman.

Here again, the commas are placed *before* the quotation marks.

Step 3. Capitalize the first letter of the speaker's sentence, no matter where it appears.

Dr. Hellman said, "~~the~~ *The* test will be postponed."

"The test," said Dr. Hellman, "will be postponed."

"The test will be postponed," said Dr. Hellman.

In the first sentence, the speaker's words begin in the middle of the sentence. Nevertheless, because the quotation is introduced with a *he said/she said* interrupter, the quotation starts with a capital letter.

   That's all there is to it. Since neither the quotation nor the sentence itself is a question, the punctuation is finished. The printed version of these sentences looks like this.

"She said" at the beginning

Dr. Hellman said, "The test will be postponed."

"She said" in the middle

"The test," said Dr. Hellman, "will be postponed."

"She said" at the end

"The test will be postponed," said Dr. Hellman.

   Now let's look at sentences that show how to use question marks with quotations. We'll start by doing the first three steps, just as you have seen already. Then we'll do the following.

Step 4. Use a question mark instead of a comma or period to show a question by the speaker or the writer.

Speaker asking question

Dr. Hellman asked, "Has the test been postponed?"

"Has the test," asked Dr. Hellman, "been postponed?"

"Has the test been postponed?" asked Dr. Hellman.

Because the speaker asks the question, the question marks come where you would expect, *before* the quotation mark.

If the writer, and not the speaker, asks a question, the question mark comes *after* the quotation mark.

Only writer asking question

Did Dr. Hellman say, "The test has been postponed"?

↑

QUESTION MARK OUTSIDE QUOTATION

This principle is less complicated than it seems. Just remember that the question mark goes after the quotation mark only when the writer alone asks the question. In all other cases, the question mark goes where you would expect — before the quotation mark.

The rule about question marks also applies to exclamation points.

Speaker's exclamation

"Stop that man!" shouted the lady.

The lady shouted, "Stop that man!"

Writer's exclamation

Don't keep saying, "I'm sorry"!

↑

EXCLAMATION POINT OUTSIDE QUOTATION

Finally, never use double punctuation, such as a period and a question mark, at the same place in the sentence.

INCORRECT (double punctuation)

He kept saying, "I'm sorry!".

↑

PERIOD INCORRECT

Punctuating Direct Quotations

Punctuate and capitalize each of the following direct quotations correctly.

| example |

"Marcie likes this club," answered Barbara.

1. He escaped in the horse cart said Colonel Vallejo angrily

2. The manager responded yes

3. In the afternoon said Mr. Marciano we need only two waiters

4. This is an equal opportunity employer

5. Where did you find the coat asked Janet

6. Did Walter just say I'm ready

7. The singer asked would you like to hear a new song or an old one

8. Please type this for me said Miss Foreman

9. The ticket seller replied we have only balcony seats available

10. Labor Day said Bill is the earliest that I can get away

11. The young man said I think this is my bus

12. This class she said is too long

13. Let's change the program said her husband

14. The first step will be the hardest

15. This medicine said the pharmacist is as good as any of these others

16. The waiter suggested maybe you should try the roast chicken

17. These gas prices are way too high Mrs. Hanson complained

18. The driver got out of her car and yelled watch where you're going

19. The Church moves said Cardinal Donovan from a position of certainty to a position of certainty

20. Would you please help me with my groceries

PUNCTUATING LONG QUOTATIONS AND CHANGING SPEAKERS

Students who can punctuate short quotations correctly sometimes have difficulty with longer ones.

Punctuate quotations of more than one sentence according to the samke principles as one-sentence quotations. Keep in mind that

1. A new sentence does NOT require a new set of quotation marks.
2. New quotation marks show a *new* speaker's words.

Compare the following examples. The first shows one speaker saying four sentences. The first sentence is introduced by a *he said/she said* statement. The rest are simply quoted. (The speaker's exact words are printed in boldface type.)

One speaker

Professor Penwicker said, **"The war continued for several years more. Neither side wanted to admit defeat. Both sides, however, had suffered greatly. The Athenians had lost all of their territory, and Sparta had lost most of its young men."**

This same quotation could be printed with the *he said/she said* statement elsewhere in the paragraph.

One speaker

"The war continued for several years more," Professor Penwicker said. **"Neither side wanted to admit defeat. Both sides, however, had suffered greatly. The Athenians had lost all of their territory, and Sparta had lost most of its young men."**

In both examples the quotation marks do exactly what the boldface type does: they mark the speaker's exact words.

Now let's see what happens if these remarks are made by two speakers. (The first speaker's words are printed in boldface type. The second speaker's words are printed in italics.)

Two speakers

Professor Penwicker said, **"The war continued for several years more."** *"Neither side wanted to admit defeat,"* added Ms. Marshall. *"Both sides, however, had suffered greatly. The Athenians had lost all of their territory, and Sparta had lost most of its young men."*

The quotation marks between *more* and *Neither* show that a new speaker is being quoted.

Often, but not always, a new paragraph is also used to show that a new speaker is talking.

Two speakers

Professor Penwicker said, **"The war continued for several years more."**

"Neither side wanted to admit defeat," added Ms. Marshall. *"Both sides, however, had suffered greatly. The Athenians had lost all of their territory, and Sparta had lost most of its young men."*

Skill Exercise

Punctuating Long Quotations

Correct any punctuation errors in the following paragraphs. NOTE: In each item, there are only two speakers, and the only errors in this exercise involve the punctuation of quotations.

A.

"Step aside said Rosie Carter as she pushed her way past me in the hall. I'm coming through. She gave me such a jolt, completely unexpected, that I was pushed sideways into the cold gray tiles of the science building. I stopped to watch this human torpedo complete her course down the hall and enter one of the classrooms. "Who is this woman I asked." "Doesn't she know how to behave?" "Someone should teach her some manners."

I was angry, but it soon passed. I walked to the door of Room 205 and noticed Rosie sitting in the front row. The room was full, but the chairs around Rosie were empty. What, I said quietly "makes a person act like that"? Later, as I walked the dirt path that led to my quiet dormitory room, I decided to find out.

B.

"I would love to watch our team play in the basketball finals." "But they are held in Hayward this year. How would I pay for the trip?"

asked Lisa. She was confused. One of her school's basketball players said that it was critical that she attend the basketball tournament. But so far he had not told her why.

That's easy, he answered. The team will pay for the trip. All of your expenses will be taken care of. That is, all of your *reasonable* expenses, he added. Lisa was surprised. "And what" she asked "do I have to do for the team?" "I don't know you or anyone else who plays for our school." "And I've only been to one game this year." It's because of that one game, he responded, "that you have to go. It seems that our best shooting guard has fallen in love." "And as for what you have to do — nothing. Just sit in the front row as our guest and enjoy the victory."

This was the strangest offer Lisa had ever had. Did she even like basketball enough to play along? She would have to think about this one.

USING THE COLON, DASH, AND HYPHEN

The **colon** (:), the **dash** (—), and the **hyphen** (-), are punctuation marks with special uses in essay and story writing.

Using the Colon, Dash, and Hyphen

Use a **colon or dash** to attach a list or explanation to a complete sentence.

Use a **hyphen** to form some compound words and to divide a word at the end of a line.

Let's look at these punctuation marks one at a time.

The Colon

The colon has several uses. You are probably already familiar with some of them. A colon is used, for example, to show the time.

Colon to show the time

My 8:15 class usually starts at 8:25.

In this section you will see how the colon is used to add a list or explanation to the end of an otherwise complete sentence. Study the following sentences.

Colon with a list

I am taking four classes this semester: **microbiology, computer science, intermediate statistics, and surfing.**

Colon with an explanation

I have very little sympathy for Ray: **his decisions have damaged a number of promising careers.**

The words that follow the colon are not part of the main clause of the sentence. The colon is required to attach these words to the rest of the sentence.

A colon should NOT be used to attach words to a sentence if those words are already part of the sentence. The following sentence, for example, is incorrectly punctuated.

INCORRECT

This semester I am taking: microbiology, computer science, intermediate statistics, and surfing.

CORRECTED

This semester I am taking microbiology, computer science, intermediate statistics, and surfing.

Note that in the first example above, *I am taking* is NOT a complete sentence.

The Dash

A dash can be used much like a colon — to attach a list or explanation to the end of a sentence. The dash, however, is more informal than the colon.

Dash with a list

I am taking four classes this semester — microbiology, computer science, intermediate statistics, and surfing.

Dash with an explanation

I have very little sympathy for Ray — his decisions have damaged a number of promising careers.

Dashes can also be used to insert a list or explanation into the middle of a sentence.

Dashes with a list

I am taking four classes this semester — microbiology, computer science, intermediate statistics, and surfing — and I like all of them but one.

When typing the dash, use two hyphens next to each other.

There are other ways to use colons and dashes, but these are the most important. Use colons and dashes with great care. Writing that contains too many of them (especially dashes) will appear awkward and overpunctuated.

Exercise 7

Using Colons and Dashes

A. **Use colons or dashes** to punctuate each of the following sentences correctly. If a sentence is already correct, write **OK** in the margin.

example

We will travel to three cities this summer — Nice, Brussels, and Siena.

1. Shannon needs help in two classes European History and Humanities Seminar.

2. The girls wanted to leave the party was breaking and the hostess was getting tired.

3. My favorite instructors Dr. Sarandon, Mrs. Endicott, and Mr. Lee are all out sick this week.

4. Each of the panelists had a question for us.

5. Stuart told two good stories the one about the ice cream and the one about Frank's red truck.

6. Two brands are under consideration IBM and Xerox.

7. The next months will be the most difficult.

8. The Palace opened its doors early the crowds were becoming too large.

9. The school gave a special citation to Jessie Cates and Bill Benson.

10. The school gave a special citation to two remarkable students Jessie Cates and Bill Benson.

B. **Correct any punctuation errors** in the following sentences. If a sentence is punctuated correctly, write **OK** in the margin.

1. The government helps students to attend college by offering: loans and grants.

2. The fire marshal announced that: Wembly Street would be closed all afternoon.

3. Three radio stations: WCAZ, WXZF, and WBB, are offering a free vacation.

4. We had hoped to see Tyrone and Christopher.

5. Janet contributes to all of the local charities, including: the Boy Scouts and the Junior Chamber of Commerce.

6. Hank has coffee and donuts: for breakfast every morning.

7. Everyone at the apartment was glad to see us: we were bringing the cake and ice cream.

8. Three engineers were hired today — Jackson, Carlton, and Lee.

9. We met the Flying Freeman Brothers, a circus act.

10. Several films caught my attention — *Lovers, Benedict's Problem,* and

The Answer Man were three of them.

The Hyphen

The **hyphen (-)** is used to form some compound words and to divide a word at the end of a line. (Notice the length of the hyphen. It is about half as long as a dash.)

Forming Compound Words

Many English words are made by putting two or more smaller words together. Sometimes the new word (called a **compound word**) is printed like one word, and sometimes a hyphen is used to join the smaller words. Compound words include the following.

Compound words with hyphens

mother-in-law	self-improvement
half-finished	twenty-one,
	twenty-two, etc.

Compound words without hyphens

freeway	bookmark
spellbound	seatbelt
bedroom	

If you are not sure whether a compound word is spelled with or without a hyphen, check your dictionary.

Sometimes hyphens are used with a prefix (such as *re-* or *un-*) when the last letter of the prefix is the same as the first letter of the word it is joined to.

Prefix with hyphen

re-elect

Without the hyphen, the word would look like this: *reelect.* Not all words, however, follow this rule. One example is *cooperate.* Again, if you are not sure whether a word is spelled with a hyphen, check your dictionary.

Dividing Words at the End of the Line

When you write or type a paragraph, sometimes only part of a word will fit at the end of a line, and you must carry the rest over to the next line. When you divide a word in this way, you use a hyphen at the end of the line that contains the first part of the word.

For example, in the sentence below the word *understood* is carried over from the first line to the second.

> The instructor asked if we **under-**
> **stood** the assignment.

Notice that the hyphen is placed at the end of the first line, not the beginning of the second.

When you divide words, you must follow certain principles.

1. Divide a word only between syllables. (If you do not know where to break a word into syllables, consult a dictionary.)

base- ment	NOT	bas- ement

2. Do not divide a one-syllable word.

thought	NOT	thou- ght

3. Do not separate one letter from the rest of the word.

afraid	NOT	a- fraid
mighty	NOT	might- y

4. Avoid carrying over a two-letter syllable from the end of the word.

pleas- antly	NOT	pleasant- ly

5. Always divide a hyphenated compound word at the hyphen.

self- control	NOT	self-con- trol

If you are not sure where to divide a word, use a dictionary. It will show you where you can break words. Be sure, however, not to break any of the rules above.

Exercise 8

Hyphens

Use a hyphen **to divide the following words** correctly. Write your divided word on the two lines provided.

If any word should not be divided, write the whole word on the first line.

(Use a dictionary if necessary to help you.)

| example | anxiously | _anx —_ |
| | | _iously_ |

1. sweepstakes _____

    _____

2. moreover _____

    _____

3. paper _____

    _____

4. professor _____

    _____

5. indeed _____

    _____

6. anonymously _____

    _____

7. through _____

    _____

8. pattern _____

    _____

9. punctuation _____

    _____

10. twenty-seven   _____

    _____

11. fairness   _____

    _____

12. intelligent   _____

    _____

13. green   _____

    _____

14. regular   _____

    _____

15. furtively   _____

    _____

16. rocking   _____

    _____

17. flavor   _____

    _____

18. award-winning   _____

    _____

19. evict   _____

    _____

20. Canadian   _____

    _____

APOSTROPHES

The **apostrophe** (') is used to make possessive adjectives and contractions.

Apostrophes in Possessive Adjectives

All nouns and most pronouns form possessive adjectives by using the apostrophe. The exceptions are the following:

Adjective Forms of Personal Pronouns and *Who*

my	our
your	your
his	their
her	
its	
whose	whose

Note that words like *mine*, *hers*, and *theirs* are pronouns and not adjectives. Therefore they will never be spelled with an apostrophe.

The following rule will tell you how to spell correctly possessive adjectives that use apostrophes.

▬▬ Using Apostrophes in Possessive Adjectives

To spell possessive adjectives correctly

1. Write the name of the owner or owners in the sentence.

2. Add an apostrophe to the *end* of the word.

3. Add an *s* after the apostrophe if the word is either
   a. Singular, or
   b. Plural not ending in *s*.

Apostrophes in possessive adjectives were discussed in Chapter 3. See pages 68–72 for more information and practice exercises.

Apostrophes in Contractions

Contractions are words and phrases that are shortened because letters are removed. When contractions are created, an apostrophe is used to show where the missing letters would have appeared.

The process is fairly straightforward.

do not → donot → **don't**

Common contractions include the following.

Common Contractions

Contractions with *Is* and *Has*

it is	= it's
it has	= it's
there is	= there's
there has	= there's
John is	= John's

Contractions with *Are*

we are	= we're
you are	= you're
they are	= they're

Contractions with *Would*

I would	= I'd
you would	= you'd
he would	= he'd
she would	= she'd
it would	= it'd (an awkward word)
we would	= we'd
they would	= they'd

Contractions with *Not*

does not	= doesn't
do not	= don't
is not	= isn't
was not	= wasn't
have not	= haven't
has not	= hasn't
had not	= hadn't
can not	= can't
could not	= couldn't
would not	= wouldn't
will not	= won't

Notice the last contraction especially.

will not = won't

This is the only contraction that is not spelled as you might expect.

Contractions are informal in tone, and as a result, are more common in spoken language than written language. Use them sparingly in your writing.

Exercise 9

Contractions

Correct any incorrect contractions in the following sentences. If a sentence is already correct, write **OK** in the margin.

| **example** | *Isn't*
~~Is'nt~~ this your first theater class? |

1. We didn't find further explanation necessary.

2. Theres more in the refrigerator.

3. The strike was'nt planned properly.

4. Michaels certain we're landing in a few minutes.

5. Shes' never liked another mystery film.

6. Theyre never going to understand his reasons if he won't explain them.

7. Further explorations willn't be funded for some time.

8. These are'nt stone arrowheads.

9. The're natural rock formations.

10. He wondered if they'ld ever make the first string.

Chapter Review

In this chapter you learned

1. Simple **interrupters** are punctuated according to the Interrupter Rule.

2. **The Interrupter Rule:** Punctuate any sentence interrupter by separating it from the rest of the sentence with commas.

3. **Indirect quotations** are punctuated
   a. With no additional punctuation if the "he said" part comes at the beginning of the sentence.
   b. With "he said/she said" punctuated as an interrupter if it comes anywhere else in the sentence.

4. **Direct quotations without** *he said/she said* interrupters by placing **quotation marks** around the speaker's exact words.

5. **Direct quotations with** *he said/she said* interrupters are punctuated by following these steps.
   a. Place **quotation marks** around the speaker's exact words.

441 Other punctuation skills

    b. Use **commas** to punctuate the *he said/she said* statement as an interrupter.

    c. **Capitalize** the first letter of the speaker's sentence, no matter where it appears.

    d. Use a **question mark** instead of a comma or period to show a question by the speaker or the writer.

6. Use a **colon or dash** to attach a list or explanation to a complete sentence.

7. Use a **hyphen** to form some compound words and to divide a word at the end of a line.

8. Use **apostrophes** to form possessive adjectives.

    a. Write the name of the owner or owners in the sentence.

    b. Add an apostrophe to the *end* of the word.

    c. Add an *s* after the apostrophe if the word is either singular or plural not ending in *s*.

9. Use **apostrophes** to show where letters are missing in a contraction. (Example: *do not = don't*)

A RELATED SKILL section showed you how to punctuate **long quotations** and paragraphs with **more than one speaker**.

1. A new sentence inside a quotation does NOT require a new set of quotation marks.

2. New quotation marks show a *new* speaker's words.

Review Exercise 1

Correct all punctuation errors in the following paragraph, including errors with apostrophes.

    At last Lisa decided to attend the basketball game as the players had asked. Then she and her girlfriend Mary met with the team. She asked them some questions and then told them they had to pay for Mary to go with her. Otherwise she would'nt go.

    The surprised players went into a corner and discussed her demand. "We can't turn her down" said Johnny. (Johnny knew that it was his' idea to send her in the first place.) "Why not asked Brad. This could cost us a lot of money." They argued for several minutes. Then they talked about how bad Jose's basketball playing had become since he started mooning over Lisa. Finally they realized they had: two choices — pay for two guests or lose the championship. They added up the expenses and decided: to pay. Maybe she could ride up with Brads' parents' when they drove to Hayward themselves. That would save, some money.

When Johnny gave the news to Lisa she smiled. "Thanks guys she said to them. I hope you win by a million points. By the way when does the plane take off"?

Review Exercise 2

On a separate sheet of paper, rewrite the sentences in Review Exercise 1, **changing all direct quotations into indirect quotations**.

Then **correct** any punctuation errors you might have made and **recopy** your corrected sentences on the lines below.

_____

_____

_____

_____

_____

_____

_____

_____

_____

_____

_____

_____

_____

_____

_____

_____

_____

_____

_____

_____

_____

Chapter 16 Writing Assignment

Write a paragraph that discusses **the main kinds of teachers you have had**. Briefly discuss one example of each kind.

Notice that this essay requires you to "classify," or divide into logical groups, the large group "all teachers I have had."

When you have made your final copy make sure that

a. All **verbs**, **nouns,** and **pronouns** are correct.
b. All **clauses and phrases** are correctly punctuated.
c. Your paragraph contains **no fragments**.

Hints for Classification Paragraphs

This kind of paragraph is called **classification** because it "classifies" or divides groups into smaller groups. In this case you are dividing the large group *all the teachers I have had* into several smaller groups by *kind of teacher.*

This paragraph will be most effective if you pay attention to the steps listed under "Before the rough draft." Doing these steps carefully will make your paragraph as interesting as possible.

Before the rough draft:

1. First, make a list of the teachers you have had. Make this list as complete as you can.

2. Then, on another sheet, work out at least *five* ways you could divide up this large group (for example, by effectiveness, by sense of humor). You are working to find the most interesting way to divide this group, not just the way or ways that come into your mind immediately.

3. From the list you created in step 1, select the most interesting way to classify your teachers and make a list of groups in that classification. (You might, for example, select "sense of humor" as a way to classify them, and then divide them into three groups — good sense of humor, bad sense of humor, no sense of humor.)

4. On a third sheet of paper, assign each teacher to one of your smaller groups.

5. Choose one teacher to use as an example for each group and a brief story to tell about each teacher.

6. Decide in what order to discuss your groups. Discuss the most interesting teacher last.

Writing the rough draft:

1. Start your rough draft by writing a short group of sentences that

   a. Gives a reason for classifying your teachers, and
   b. Tells how many kinds of teachers you have had.

2. Using your final list of groups and examples, write a sentence that mentions the first group. Then mention the teacher who is an example of that group and tell his or her story.

3. Do the same for each group on your list.

4. Write a closing sentence (or two) that feels like an ending.

After the rough draft:

1. Do your best to correct any errors on this first copy. Be especially careful to correct all errors in

   a. Verbs
   b. Nouns
   c. Pronouns
   d. Punctuation

2. Make any other changes you think will make your paragraph more interesting and readable.

3. Recopy your corrected paragraph on a clean sheet of paper and turn in all of your work.

17

Punctuation review

Chapter Preview

In this chapter you will

1. **Review the punctuation rules** you have seen so far.

2. Review how to use **commas with coordinating conjunctions**.

3. Learn how and when to **break punctuation rules** successfully.

PUNCTUATION RULES

This section lists all of the punctuation rules you have studied in this text. (The chapters and pages where these rules first appear are in parentheses.)

Punctuating Main Clauses

The first rule deals with the punctuation of main clauses.

Punctuation Rule 1
Punctuating Sentences

Every complete sentence begins with a capital letter and ends with one of the following punctuation marks.

1. Period   (.)
2. Question mark   (?)
3. Exclamation mark   (!)

(See Chapter 5, pages 110–114.)

Example:

Main clauses separated by periods

Several cars turned onto the expressway. Jim's was one of them.

Punctuation Rule 2
Joining Main Clauses

Join main clauses into one sentence by using one of the following methods.

1. Comma + coordinating conjunction   (, and)
2. Semicolon   (;)

(See Chapter 5, pages 117–125.)

Examples:

Main clauses joined by semicolon

Several cars turned onto the expressway; Jim's was one of them.

Main clauses joined by comma + conjunction

Several cars turned onto the expressway, **and** Jim's was one of them.

Punctuation Rule 3
Correcting Fragments

Every complete sentence must contain at least one main clause.
    Any sentence that doesn't contain at least one main clause is a **fragment** and must be corrected.

(See Chapter 6, pages 143–151.)

Examples:

Fragment (dependent clause)

Because Jim was late for work

Complete sentence (dependent clause + main clause)

Because Jim was late for work, he did not hear Mr. Water's announcement.

Punctuating Lists and Interrupters

The next rules deal with lists and interrupters.

Punctuation Rule 4
Punctuating Lists

Use commas to separate items in a list or series of three or more items.
    Do not use commas to separate items in a list of two items.

(See Chapter 1, pages 25–29.)

Examples:

List of two objects

An earthquake rocked the mountains of **Peru and Chile**.

List of three objects

An earthquake rocked the mountains of **Peru, Chile, and Bolivia**.

Punctuation Rule 5
Punctuating Interrupters

Separate interrupters from the rest of the sentence with commas.

Interrupter, ********************************* .

************** **, interrupter,** ************* .

**************************** **, interrupter.**

(See Chapter 7, pages 161–166.)

Examples:

Interrupter at beginning

According to reporters, several citizens have mysteriously disappeared from the capital.

Interrupter in middle

Several citizens, **according to reporters,** have mysteriously disappeared from the capital.

Interrupter at end

Several citizens have mysteriously disappeared from the capital, **according to reporters**.

Common Interrupters

Group 1

besides	therefore	by the way
consequently	as a result	of course
furthermore	yes	for example
however	no	on the one hand
moreover	well	on the other hand
nevertheless	oh	
meanwhile		

Names and titles
  of people
  spoken to

Group 2

I believe	I think
I suppose	it seems to me

Group 3

not . .	according to . . .
such as . . .	but . . .

NOTE: Group 2 interrupters like "I believe" are not punctuated as interrupters when they appear at the beginning of the sentence.

"I believe" as interrupter

Several citizens, **I believe,** have mysteriously disappeared from the capital.

"I believe" at beginning of sentence

I believe <that> several citizens have mysteriously disappeared from the capital.

When clauses like *I believe* begin a sentence, they become the main clause of the sentence. The rest of the sentence is a noun clause introduced with the hidden tip-off word *that*. (See Chapter 7, pages 175–180, for a discussion of noun clauses in sentences.)

Punctuating Descriptive Clauses and Phrases

The following rules apply to descriptive clauses and phrases. This includes

1. Adjective and adverb clauses

2. Adjective and adverb verbal phrases

3. Appositives

Punctuation Rule 6
Punctuating Descriptive Clauses and Phrases by Position

Any descriptive clause, verbal phrase, or appositive that is **out of normal position** should be separated from the rest of the sentence with commas.

(See Chapters 7, 9, and 10, page 162, pages 223–226 and pages 253–254.)

Normal positions of adjective phrases and clauses

Adjective – NOUN – Adjective phrases – Adjective clause

Normal positions of adverb phrases and clauses

VERB – Adverb – Adverb phrases – Adverb clause

Normal position of appositives

NOUN – Adjective phrases – Appositive

Examples:

Out-of-position adverb clauses

Because he was married before the age of twenty, Will Shakespeare faced the dual problems of family and career at an early age.

Will Shakespeare, **because he was married before the age of twenty,** faced the dual problems of family and career at an early age.

Out-of-position verbal phrase

Married before the age of twenty, Will Shakespeare faced the dual problems of family and career at an early age.

Out-of-position appositive

A married man before the age of twenty, Will Shakespeare faced the dual problems of family and career at an early age.

Punctuation Rule 7
Punctuating Descriptive Clauses and Phrases by Kind of Information

Any descriptive clause, verbal phrase, or appositive that contains **extra information** should be separated from the rest of the sentence with commas.

Do not separate adjective clauses or verbal phrases that contain "needed" information unless they are out of normal position.

(See Chapter 7, pages 163–166, Chapter 9, pages 226–230, and Chapter 10, pages 254–258.)

For adjectives, "extra" information is information that does not

1. Identify what it describes
2. Narrow down a group

For adverbs, "extra" information is usually anything introduced by tip-off words like *although*.

Examples:

"Extra" adjective clause

Mr. Stanley, **who was working in a factory at the time**, wrote several novels.

"Extra" verbal phrase

Mr. Stanley, **working in a factory at the time**, wrote several novels.

"Extra" appositive

Mr. Stanley, **a factory worker at the time**, wrote several novels.

"Extra" adverb clause

Mr. Stanley wrote several novels, **although he was working long hours in a factory at the time**.

Punctuating Direct Quotations

The next two rules deal with direct quotations.

Punctuation Rule 8
Punctuating Direct Quotations without *He said/She said* Interrupters

Place **quotation marks** around the speaker's exact words.

(See Chapter 16, pages 421–424.)

Examples:

Quotations using statement

The sales manager wanted us to take advantage of these "opportunities" while they were available.

Exact words: *opportunities*

Punctuation Rule 9
Punctuating Direct Quotations with *He said/She said* Interrupters

1. Place **quotation marks** around the speaker's exact words.

2. Use **commas** to punctuate the *he said/she said* statement as an interrupter.

3. **Capitalize** the first letter of the speaker's sentence, no matter where it appears.

4. Use a **question mark** instead of a comma or period to show a question by the speaker or the writer.

(See Chapter 16, pages 424–428.)

Examples:

Quotations using statement

The sales manager said, "We should take advantage of these opportunities."

"We should," said the sales manager, "take advantage of these opportunities."

"We should take advantage of these opportunities," said the sales manager.

Quotations asking question by speaker

The sales manager asked, "Should we take advantage of these opportunities?"

"Should we take advantage of these opportunities?" asked the sales manager.

Quotations asking question by writer

Did the sales manager say, "We should take advantage of these opportunities"?

Did the sales manager ask, "Should we take advantage of these opportunities?"

Using the Colon, Dash, and Hyphen

This rule applies to three important, but less common, punctuation marks.

Punctuation Rule 10
Using the Colon, Dash, and Hyphen

Use a **colon or dash** to attach a list or explanation to a complete sentence.
  Use a **hyphen** to form some compound words and to divide a word at the end of a line.

(See Chapter 16, pages 431–438.)

Examples:

Colon

I took this job for two reasons: money and money.

Dash

I took this job for two reasons — money and money.

Two reasons — **money and money** — made me take this job.

Hyphen in compound word

I took this job for **self-improvement** and because I needed the money.

Hyphen to divide a word

I took this job because I needed the **chal-lenge** of new responsibilities.

Using the Apostrophe

These rules show you how to use apostrophes to form possessives and contractions.

Punctuation Rule 11
Using Apostrophes in Possessive Adjectives

To spell possessive adjectives correctly:

1. Write the name of the owner or owners in the sentence.

2. Add an apostrophe to the *end* of the word.

3. Add an *s* after the apostrophe if the word is either

   a. Singular, or
   b. Plural not ending in *s*.

(See Chapter 16, pages 438–439.)

Examples:

	Sing.	Plural ending in *s*	Sing.	Plural NOT ending in *s*
OWNER	boy	boys	man	men
POSSESSIVE	boy's	boys'	man's	men's

Punctuation Rule 12
Using Apostrophes in Contractions

Use an apostrophe to show where letters are missing in a contraction.

(See Chapter 16, pages 439–441.)

Examples:

ORIGINAL	it is	we are	I **would**	does not
CONTRACTION	it's	we're	I'd	doesn't

USING COMMAS CORRECTLY

Similar situations may require different punctuation, especially situations in which conjunctions are used.

Using Commas with Coordinating Conjunctions — A Summary

The following summarizes the use of commas with coordinating conjunctions, such as *and*, *or*, but, and *nor*.

Summary — Using Commas with Coordinating Conjunctions

1. Conjunctions joining a list of two items — NO COMMAS
2. Conjunctions joining a list of three or more items — USE COMMAS
3. Conjunctions joining two or more main clauses — USE COMMAS

Coordinating conjunctions

and	for
or	yet
but	so
nor	

Examples:

Conjunction joining two verbs

Several men **returned** to the cabin after sunset **and searched** again for the old iron box.

Conjunction joining three verbs

Several men **returned** to the cabin after sunset, **turned** on their flashlights, **and searched** again for the old iron box.

Conjunctions joining two main clauses

Several **men returned** to the cabin after sunset, **and they searched** again for the old iron box.

BREAKING PUNCTUATION RULES

Under certain conditions, you may break some of the punctuation rules dealing with commas. These conditions are

1. When clauses and phrases are very short

2. When normal punctuation makes the sentence unclear

3. When simple interrupters don't seem to interrupt the flow of a clause

In addition, modern practice sometimes leaves out certain commas related to interrupters and lists.

Punctuating Short Clauses and Phrases

To avoid "overpunctuation," you can leave out commas

1. After very short introductory clauses and phrases

2. With a conjunction between very short main clauses

Examples:

Introductory phrase

To win she always fights hard.

Main clauses

We left and **she entered.**

Adding Commas for Clarity

Some sentences contain combinations of words that could be read in two ways. Usually one of the two ways does not make sense.

To keep readers from struggling with the wrong reading of a sentence, commas can be added to group phrases properly.

Examples:

Unclear phrasing

In a long sentence group ideas carefully so that they can be read easily.

Comma added for clarity

In a long sentence, group ideas carefully so that they can be read easily.

You may leave out the commas with a simple interrupter, like *nevertheless* or *therefore*, if it doesn't seem to interrupt the sentence.

Test a sentence with and without commas around the interrupters before you decide not to use them, however. Commas are required with interrupters most of the time. Example:

Commas not needed

Brenda is nevertheless a good student.

Commas needed

Brenda, nevertheless, is a good student.

Chapter Review

In this chapter you learned about

A. Punctuation rules:

1. **Punctuating Sentences:** Every complete sentence begins with a capital letter and ends with one of the following punctuation marks.

Period	(.)
Question mark	(?)
Exclamation mark	(!)

2. **Joining Main Clauses:** Join main clauses into one sentence by using one of the following methods.

   Comma + coordinating conjunction
   Semicolon

3. **Correcting Fragments:** Every complete sentence must contain at least one main clause.

   Any sentence that doesn't contain at least one main clause is a fragment and must be corrected.

4. **Punctuating Lists:** Use commas to separate items in a list or series of three or more items.

   Do not use commas to separate items in a list of two items unless the items are two main clauses.

5. **Punctuating Interrupters:** Separate interrupters from the rest of the sentence with commas.

6. **Punctuating Descriptive Clauses and Phrases by Position:** Any descriptive clause, verbal phrase, or appositive that is *out of normal position* should be separated from the rest of the sentence with commas.

7. **Punctuating Descriptive Clauses and Phrases by Kind of Information:** Any descriptive clause, verbal phrase, or appositive that contains *"extra" information* should be separated from the rest of the sentence with commas.

   Do not separate adjective clauses or verbal phrases that contain "needed" information unless they are out of normal position.

8. **Punctuating Direct Quotations without *He said/She said* Interrupters:** Place quotation marks around the speaker's exact words.

9. **Punctuating Direct Quotations with *He said/She said* Interrupters:**
   a. Place **quotation marks** around the speaker's exact words.
   b. Use **commas** to punctuate the *he said/she said* statement, if any, as an interrupter.
   c. **Capitalize** the first letter of the speaker's sentence, no matter where it appears.
   d. Use a **question mark** instead of a comma or period to show a question by the speaker or the writer.

10. **Using the Colon, Dash, and Hyphen:** Use a **colon or dash** to attach a list or explanation to a complete sentence.

    Use a **hyphen** to form some compound words and to divide a word at the end of a line.

11. **Using Apostrophes in Possessive Adjectives:** To spell possessive adjectives correctly
    a. Write the name of the owner or owners in the sentence.
    b. Add an apostrophe to the *end* of the word.
    c. Add an *s* after the apostrophe if the word is either
       1. Singular, or
       2. Plural not ending in *s*.

12. Using Apostrophes in Contractions: Use an apostrophe to show where letters are missing in a contraction.

B. Using commas with coordinating conjunctions:
1. Conjunctions joining a **list of two items** — NO COMMAS

2. Conjunctions joining a **list of three or more items** — USE COMMAS

3. Conjunctions joining two or more **main clauses** — USE COMMAS

C. Breaking punctuation rules:
1. To avoid "overpunctuation," leave out commas

   a. After very short introductory clauses and phrases
   b. With a conjunction between very short main clauses

2. Use commas to group phrases that would be unclear without them.

3. You may leave out the commas with a simple interrupter, like *nevertheless* or *therefore*, if it doesn't seem to interrupt the sentence.

Review Exercise 1

Punctuating paragraphs

These paragraphs are from the opening chapter of Dale Carnegie's book *How to Win Friends and Influence People*.

Punctuate and capitalize each of the following paragraphs correctly. They contain examples of most of the punctuation rules you have studied.

on May 7, 1931 the most sensational manhunt New York City had ever known had come to its climax after weeks of search Two Gun Crowley the killer the gunman who didn't smoke or drink was at bay trapped in his sweethearts apartment on West End Avenue

one hundred and fifty policemen and detectives laid siege to his top floor hideaway they chopped holes in the roof they tried to smoke out Crowley the cop killer with tear gas then they mounted their machine guns on surrounding buildings and for more than an hour one of New York's fine residential areas reverberated with the crack of pistol fire and the rat tat tat of machine guns Crowley crouching behind an overstuffed chair fired incessantly at the police ten thousand excited people watched the battle nothing like it had ever been seen before on the sidewalks of New York.

when Crowley was captured police commissioner E P Mulrooney declared that the two gun desperado was one of the most dangerous criminals ever encountered in the history of New York he will kill said the commissioner at the drop of a feather

but how did Two Gun Crowley regard himself we know because while the police were firing into his apartment he wrote a letter addressed to whom it may concern and as he wrote the blood flowing from his wounds left a crimson trail on the paper in his letter crowley said under my coat is a weary heart but a kind one one that would do nobody any harm

a short time before this Crowley had been having a necking party with his girl friend on a country road out on Long Island suddenly a policeman walked up to the car and said let me see your license

without saying a word Crowley drew his gun and cut the policeman down with a shower of lead as the dying officer fell Crowley leaped out of the car grabbed the officers revolver and fired another bullet into the prostrate body and that was the killer who said under my coat is a weary heart but a kind one one that would do nobody any harm

Crowley was sentenced to the electric chair when he arrived at the death house in Sing Sing did he say this is what i get for killing people no he said this is what i get for defending myself

the point of the story is this Two Gun Crowley didn't blame himself for anything[1]

Review Exercise 2

Correcting punctuation

This essay is from *Journeys Out of the Body,* a fascinating book written by a professional scientist. During mental relaxation exercises, he started having experiences in which he seemed to be out of his physical body.

In this chapter of the book, the writer describes his father's death and his own out-of-body attempts to reach the deceased man.

Correct any incorrect punctuation in the following paragraphs.

A. Describing his father's death:

1. In 1964 my father died at the age of eighty two. Although I had been rebellious in early years I felt quite close to my father in later years, I'm sure he felt close to me.

2. He had suffered a stroke several months before which had left him almost paralyzed and incapable of speech, the latter was evidently most vexing, as it would naturally be to a man, whose life had been devoted to the study and teaching of languages.

3. During this period when I visited him he made desperate heart-rending attempts to tell me something, his eyes pleaded that I understand. Only slight moans came from his lips. I tried to comfort him I talked to

[1]From "If You Want To Gather Honey, Don't Kick Over the Beehive," in *How to Win Friends and Influence People* by Dale Carnegie. Copyright © 1936 by Dale Carnegie, renewed © 1964 by Donna Dale Carnegie and Dorothy Carnegie. Reprinted by permission of Simon & Schuster, Inc.

him. He tried his best to answer. I couldn't tell if he even understood my words.

4.   My father died quietly in his sleep one afternoon. He had lived a full successful life and his death brought mingled sadness, and a sense of release.

B. *Describing his attempt to reach his father through an "out-of-body" experience:*

1.   The only reason, that I waited several months was one of convenience. Other pressing matters in my personal, and business life seemed to prevent the ability to relax. However I woke up at about 3 A.M. on a weeknight, and felt that I could try to visit my father.

2.   I went through my ritual and the vibrations came easily and swiftly, in moments I disengaged from my body without effort and was up and free in the darkneess. This time I didn't use the mental yell technique instead I concentrated on the personality of my father and reached to be where he was.

3.   I began to move rapidly through the darkness, I could see nothing but there was a tremendous sense of motion coupled with the pull of thick liquid-like air rushing past my body. Suddenly I stopped, I do not recall anyone stopping me this time nor could I feel the hand on my elbow. I was in a dim room, of large proportions.

4.   I seemed to know, that this was a hospital or convalescent home but no treatment, as we know it was practiced here. I started to look around for my father. I didn't know what to expect, but at least I looked forward to a joyful reunion.

5.   There were several small rooms off the main room, where I stood. The

third room was no larger than a monks cell. A man leaned against the wall near the window looking out. As I entered, I saw only his back.

6.   Then he turned and saw me, his face registered utter astonishment. My father spoke to me.

7.   "What are you doing here he said, in exactly the manner of someone who had traveled halfway around the world, and then met someone to whom he had just said goodbye back home.

8.   I was too excited to speak, I just stood there hoping for the joyful reunion I had expected. It came immediately my father reached forward grabbed me under the armpits and happily swung me high over his head just as I remembered as a small child.

9.   He put me on my feet and I asked him how he was feeling. "Much better now he said. The pain is gone." It was almost as if I had reminded him of something, he wanted to forget.[2]

[2]Excerpt from *Journeys Out of the Body* by Robert Monroe. Copyright © 1971 by Robert A. Monroe. Reprinted by permission of Doubleday, a division of Bantam, Doubleday, Dell Publishing Group, Inc.

18
Spelling skills

Chapter Preview

This chapter will help you improve your spelling by showing you how to spell

1. Verbs and nouns with added endings

2. Words that sound alike

3. Commonly misspelled words ("spelling demons")

ADDING ENDINGS TO VERBS AND NOUNS

The most common endings are

-ing

-ed and *-d*

-s and *-es*

Adding *-ing*

The *-ing* form of a verb is a verbal. It is used in a variety of ways. (See Chapter 8, pages 197–198 for the uses of *-ing* words.) *-Ing* forms are spelled as follows.

Spelling *-ing* Words

Most *-ing* words are spelled by adding *-ing* to the present tense verb.

Verb	***-ing* Word**
play	playing
read	reading
sing	singing

For some verbs, however, the last letter is dropped, while for others it is doubled, before the *-ing* is added. The following rules explain these exceptions.

Exception 1. Dropping the final *-e*
Drop a final silent *e* before adding *-ing*.

Verb	***-ing* Word**
love	loving
write	writing
invite	inviting

BUT

e not silent:	see		seeing

Exception 2. Doubling final consonants
If the last syllable is accented (stressed), double a *single* final consonant preceded by a *single* vowel before adding *-ing*.

(The **vowels** are *a*, *e*, *i*, *o*, *u*, and sometimes *y*. The **consonants** are all the remaining letters.)

Verb	-*ing* Word
prefer (pre-FER)	preferring
control (con-TROL)	controlling

BUT

	Verb	-*ing* Word
Two vowels:	repair	repairing
	prevail	prevailing
Not accented:	corner (COR-ner)	cornering
	travel (TRA-vel)	traveling

All one-syllable words are governed by this rule since the one syllable is always stressed.

Verb	-*ing* Word
hit	hitting
run	running

BUT

	Verb	-*ing* Word
Two vowels:	cheer	cheering
	swear	swearing

Consonants like *w* and *y* are never doubled, however.

Verb	-*ing* Word
grow	growing
say	saying
reply	replying

Knowing these rules can help you distinguish between words whose -*ing* forms are similar.

Verb	-*ing* Word
bare	baring
bar	barring

Exercise 1

Adding -*ing*

Write the correct -*ing* form of the following verbs.

example

                        -*ing* Form

foretell   *foretelling*

1. reply   _____

2. remove   _____

467 Spelling skills

3. bear   _____

4. swear   _____

5. bore   _____

6. forget   _____

7. proceed   _____

8. precede   _____

9. pan   _____

10. disband   _____

11. repel   _____

12. unmake   _____

13. offer   _____

14. characterize   _____

15. program   _____

16. order   _____

17. incite   _____

18. rain   _____

19. run   _____

20. concur   _____

Adding *-ed* and *-d*

The endings *-ed* and *-d* are added to regular verbs to create the past tense and past participle. These forms are spelled as follows.

Spelling *-ed* Verbs

Most regular past tense and past participles are spelled by adding *-ed* to the present tense verb.

Present Tense	Past Tense	Past Participle
add	added	added
allow	allowed	allowed
ask	asked	asked

As usual, there are exceptions to this rule.

Exception 1. Verbs ending in *e*
If the last letter is an *e*, simply add *-d*.

Present Tense	Past Tense	Past Participle
close	closed	closed
die	died	died
free	freed	freed

Exception 2. Verbs ending in *y*
Verbs that end in *-y* preceded by a consonant change the *-y* to *-i* before adding *-ed*.

Present Tense	Past Tense	Past Participle
apply	applied	(have) applied
study	studied	(have) studied

BUT

Preceded by vowel: play	played	(have) played

Three irregular verbs, *say*, *pay*, and *lay*, do not follow this rule.

Present Tense	Past Tense	Past Participle
say	said	(have) said
pay	paid	(have) paid
lay	laid	(have) laid

Exception 3. Doubling final consonants
If the last syllable is accented (stressed), double a single consonant preceded by a single vowel before adding *-ed*.

Present Tense	Past Tense	Past Participle
prefer (pre-FER)	preferred	(have) preferred
control (con-TROL)	controlled	(have) controlled

BUT

Two vowels:	repair	repaired	(have) repaired
	prevail	prevailed	(have) prevailed
Not accented:	corner (COR-ner)	cornered	(have) cornered
	travel (TRA-vel)	traveled	(have) traveled

Again, this rule always applies to one-syllable words.

Present Tense	Past Tense	Past Participle
plan	planned	(have) planned

BUT

Two vowels:	clean	cleaned	(have) cleaned

And as before, consonants like *w* and *y* are never doubled.

Present Tense	Past Tense	Past Participle
sew	sewed	(have) sewed
play	played	(have) played

Exercise 2

Adding *-ed* and *-d*

Write the correct *-ed* form of the following verbs.

example

-ed Form

ally *allied*

1. relay _____

2. reply _____

3. introduce _____

4. finish _____

5. cook _____

6. imagine _____

7. walk _____

8. like   _____

9. arrive   _____

10. start   _____

11. pass   _____

12. quiet   _____

13. attend   _____

14. close   _____

15. add   _____

16. pet   _____

17. regret   _____

18. infect   _____

19. disclose   _____

20. track   _____

Adding -*s* and -*es*

Adding -*s* (or -*es*) to a noun makes the noun plural (for example, *book — books*).

Adding -*s* (or -*es*) to a verb, however, means that the subject is third person singular — either *he, she,* or *it* or a word with the same meaning as *he, she,* or *it* (for example, *I sing — she sings*).

From the standpoint of spelling, however, adding -*s* to verbs is like adding -*s* to nouns. The same rules apply to both.

Spelling -*s* Words

Most verbs and nouns spell the *s*-form by adding -*s* to the root word.

Verb	*s*-Form
see	sees
play	plays
find	finds
understand	understands
compare	compares
separate	separates

Noun	Plural
actor	actors
idea	ideas
fortune	fortunes
Pontiac	Pontiacs
sidewalk	sidewalks
Wilson	Wilsons

Exception 1. Words that add -es

Words that end in *s, x, z, sh,* or *ch* add *-es* instead of *-s.*

	Verb/Noun	*s*-Form
S:	dress	dresses
	boss	bosses
X:	fix	fixes
	ax	axes
Z:	fizz	fizzes
	Perez	Perezes
SH:	flash	flashes
	ash	ashes
CH:	lurch	lurches
	church	churches

Exception 2. Words that end in -o

Words that end in *o* often add *-es* instead of *-s,* especially when preceded by a consonant.

Verb/Noun	*s*-Form
go	goes
potato	potatoes

BUT

Preceded by vowel	radio	radios

Check a dictionary for the proper spelling of words that end in *-o,* however.

Exception 3. Words ending in y

Words that end in *-y* preceded by a consonant change the *-y* to *-i* and add *-es.*

Verb/Noun	*s*-Form
apply	applies
study	studies
ferry	ferries
ally	allies
library	libraries
story	stories

Preceded by vowel:	play	plays
	delay	delays
	alley	alleys
	key	keys
Proper name:	Henry	Henrys

(Proper names should not be respelled before adding endings.)

Exercise 3

example

Adding -*s* to Verbs and Nouns

Write the correct -*s* form of the following words.

	s-Form
project	*projects*
1. hush	_____
2. fix	_____
3. book	_____
4. set	_____
5. do	_____
6. marsh	_____
7. pipe	_____
8. project	_____
9. dentist	_____
10. coast	_____
11. university	_____
12. alloy	_____
13. ally	_____
14. fall	_____
15. rock	_____

16. petrify   _____

17. inculcate   _____

18. adversary   _____

19. penetrate   _____

20. intensify   _____

Exercise 4

Correcting Word Endings

Correct any misspelled words in the following paragraph.

Several horses stamped nervously in the dirt near the water trough. Inside the saloon Luke Sutton was dealling a hand of blackjack. Three men looked on from the bar. Another man stood near the swinging doorrs, carveing an apple with a short knife. Sunlight from the windows brightenned the room almost beyond endurance. A fly, buzing in the dusty air, was the last sound anyone rememberred hearing. Sudden gunshotts tore the room in half.

SOUND-ALIKE WORDS

Spelling difficulties come from several sources. Sometimes one word sounds so much like another word that we confuse the two spellings. These sound-alike words are called **homonyms**.

Possessives and Contractions

There are many sound-alike words in English. Among the most confusing are the following possessive adjectives and contractions.

Its/It's
Its is a possessive adjective meaning "belonging to it." *It's* is a contraction of *it is* or *it has*.

The dog raised **its** head.

It's a beautiful day.

(**It is** a beautiful day.)

It's been good to see you.

(**It has** been good to see you.)

Your/You're

Your is a possessive adjective meaning "belonging to you." *You're* is a contraction of *you are*.

Did you bring **your** books?

You're the best storyteller in the class.

(**You are** the best storyteller in the class.)

Whose/Who's

Whose is a possessive adjective used in questions and adjective clauses. *Who's* is a contraction for *who is* or *who has*.

Whose car is this?

I know the woman **whose** car this is.

Who's willing to ask the obvious question?

(**Who is** willing to ask the obvious question?)

Their/They're/There

Their is a possessive adjective meaning "belonging to them." *They're* is a contraction of *they are*. *There* is an adverb that usually indicates a place.

Their holiday plans sound interesting.

They're working in the garden.

(**They are** working in the garden.)

We will plant the garden **there.**

In each of these groups, the word with the **apostrophe (')** can be expanded into a two-word subject/verb phrase.

When in doubt about which word to use in one of your sentences, try the expanded version. If the sentence still makes sense, the word you want is spelled with an apostrophe. If the sentence doesn't make sense, you probably need the possessive adjective or *there*.

Exercise 5

Possessives and Contractions

Correct any misused word in the following sentences. If a sentence is already correct, write **OK** in the margin.

She left the phone off ~~its~~ *its* hook.

1. Their trying to correct the problem now.

2. Whose explanation do you believe?

3. There sits an honest man.

4. The personal computer has left it's mark on Western culture.

5. They're working on the problem and will have a solution some time this week.

6. I read the text of you're speech in the campus newspaper.

7. They're is a young man waiting in the outer office for you.

8. Every dog recognizes its owner.

9. I'm looking for one juror whose on my side.

10. Michael and Inez left there books in the car.

11. Who's standing by the door?

12. Its time to start working on the anthropology project.

13. Their vacation has been delayed.

14. I was told that they're sending a person to repair the broken boiler.

15. Your the best man for the position.

16. The eggs are all packed in their containers.

17. I know it's a long trip to be taking on such short notice.

18. Who'se car are we taking to the lodge?

19. The horse stamped its feet nervously.

20. Your tests are graded and in my office.

Other Sound-Alike Words

There are other groups of common words that sound alike or similar to each other and are often confused with each other. A few common ones are these.

Accept/Except

Accept is a verb meaning "to receive" or "to acknowledge." *Except* is a preposition that shows that something or someone is excluded.

> She will not **accept** the truth about Aunt Marge.

> He scored better than everyone **except** Bennett.

Affect/Effect

Affect is a verb meaning "to change." *Effect* is a noun that shows the results of a change.

> The election will **affect** our schools in several ways.

> Some of the **effects** will be good.

Alone/Along

Alone is an adverb meaning "by oneself." *Along* is an adverb or preposition meaning "with someone else."

> I went to the film **alone**.

> I went **along** with Jim to the film.

An/And

An is an adjective. It is used instead of *a* when the next word starts with a vowel sound. *And* is a conjunction.

> **An** old tree has fallen behind the garage.

> Brad **and** Antony are going to Fort Lauderdale together.

By/Buy/Bye

By is a preposition meaning "next to" or "through the action of." *Buy* is a verb meaning "to purchase." *Bye* is a form of *goodbye*, meaning "farewell."

> The essay was written **by** Brad over the weekend.

> We **buy** a season ticket every year.

> Mickey stood on his toes and whispered, "**Bye**, Grandma."

Doing/During

Doing is the *-ing* form of the verb **to do**. *During* is a preposition that introduces a span of time.

> Are you **doing** well in Astral Geology?

> The cat sleeps **during** the day.

Find/Fine

Find is a verb meaning "to discover." *Fine*, as an adjective or adverb, refers to the quality of something; as a noun, it means "a penalty," such as a judge might give a traffic offender.

> Can Felicia **find** the restaurant?
>
> This is a **fine** day.
>
> Judge Watson levied a fifty-dollar **fine**.

Hole/Whole

Hole is a noun referring to a cavity carved out of something. *Whole* is a noun or adjective meaning "everything" or "entire."

> The back yard has a gopher **hole** in it.
>
> The **whole** story is being rewritten.

Idea/Ideal

An *idea* is a thought. An *ideal* is a standard of perfection. *Idea* is a noun. *Ideal* can be a noun or an adjective.

> Governor Black has a good **idea** for reforming the state income tax.
>
> Fairness is one of the governor's **ideals**.
>
> In an **ideal** class, students are free to ask questions.

Loose/Lose

Loose (Pronounced LOOS) is an adjective meaning "not tight," referring to how something fits. *Lose* (pronounced LOOZE) is a verb meaning "to mislay something" or "not to win."

> These shoes are too **loose** for my feet.
>
> I'm afraid the child will **lose** his way.

Loss/Lost

Loss and *lost* are both related to the verb "to lose." *Loss* is a noun made from this verb. *Lost* is a past participle used in verb phrases or as an adjective.

> **Noun**
>
> Mr. Allen's passing was a great **loss** to Mary.

> **Past participle**
>
> The money was **lost** at the roulette table.

Adjective

The **lost** child was discovered at the candy counter.

Mind/Mine

Mind is a noun that refers to a person's thinking tools. *Mine* is a pronoun related to *I* and *me*.

The coffee is **mine**.

He does all his adding in his **mind**.

No/Know

No is an adjective or adverb meaning "not any." It is also a negative response to a question. *Know* is a verb meaning "to be aware of" or "to understand."

I have **no** clean socks.

Did you **know** that Bill got married?

Pass/Passed/Past

This group is similar to *lose/lost/loss*. *Pass* (like *lose*) is a verb that has several meanings. *Passed* (like *lost*) is the past participle form of this verb, used mainly in verb phrases.

Past (like *loss*) is a noun, referring to time gone by. *Past* can also be an adjective, adverb, or preposition. *Past* is never used in verb phrases.

Verb

He cannot **pass** the final exam without more work.

Past participle

Antony has **passed** Biology at last.

Noun

Memories are shadows of the **past**.

Preposition

Silena drove **past** the old courthouse.

Sit/Set

These two verbs are often confused. *Sitting* is something you do to yourself. *Setting* is something you do to something else. If something rests undisturbed, it *sits*.

Please **sit** next to Marion.

The typewriter usually **sits** next to the file cabinet.

Set the shovel down and come inside.

Then/Than

Then is an adverb that tells "when." *Than* is a preposition used in comparisons.

Then Mrs. Marini rose to speak.

The Sears Tower is taller **than** the Empire State Building.

To/Too/Two

These are commonly confused words. *To* is a preposition and is also used to form infinitives. *Too* is an adverb. When it describes a verb, it means "also." When it describes an adjective, it indicates an excessive amount of something. *Two* is a number.

Study these words carefully. They occur frequently in writing.

Frank drives **to** the office at nine.

He started **to** sleep at ten.

Alicia wanted to go **too**.

This coffee is **too** hot.

She will return in **two** hours.

Were/Where

Were is a verb, the past tense form of *to be*. *Where* is an adverb or conjunction that indicates a place.

James and Doree **were** both raised in France.

Where is my brown jacket?

Whether/Weather

Whether is a conjunction (tip-off word) that usually introduces a dependent clause or phrase. *Weather* is a noun referring to the climate or atmospheric condition.

She wondered **whether** Randolph would visit soon.

The **weather** will be cool and dry.

Exercise 6

Other Sound-Alike Words

Correct any misused or misspelled word in the following sentences. If a sentence is correct, write **OK** in the margin. (All of the errors involve words discussed in this chapter.)

1. Bruno never did fine his loss books.

2. We past the store an several gas stations on the way to Walter's.

3. The find was levied against both of the defendants.

4. We searched every room except the storage chamber.

5. The credit sign said, "Bye now, pay later."

6. Brad changed his mine about lending us his notes.

7. My uncle doesn't like to loose on poker nights.

8. I have no idea weather you passed the restaurant or not.

9. Wendy rode alone with Felicia and her sister.

10. I spoke too soon.

11. How did you no the names of the authors?

12. These vendors do not except credit cards.

13. The test was shorter then I expected.

14. To many people wanted to use the pool at once, and it effected the water.

15. The Santini brothers are an idea circus act.

16. Miss Hays observed every holiday accept this one.

17. Herman never took a vacation in his hole life.

18. Please pass the cards too the dealer.

19. Would you mine if we borrowed these chairs?

20. He sets next to the minister and his wife.

COMMONLY MISSPELLED WORDS

Some words are commonly misspelled — everyone has trouble with some of them. Many of these words are listed below.

Use this list to help you learn to spell these words. They are also found in the dictionary.

Commonly Misspelled Words

accidentally
accommodate
acquainted
across
agreement
all right
already
analysis
appearance
argument
article
athletics
attendance
believe
benefit
Britain
business
changeable
choose
comparative
conceive
conscience
continuous
decision
definite
dependent
description
develop
dining room
disappearance
disappoint
dormitory
embarrass
environment
equipment
exaggerate
existence
extremely
familiar
fascinate
foreign
formerly
forty
grammar
height
hindrance
imaginary

immediately
incidentally
independent
intelligent
irresistible
judgment (*or* judgement)
knowledge
leisure
library
maintenance
manufacture
misspelled
monotonous
mysterious
necessary
neighborhood
noticeable
occasionally
occurred
occurrence
omitted
opportunity
particularly
pastime
perform
precede
prejudice
privilege
probably
procedure
pronunciation
proportion
psychology
quantity
receive
repetition
resemblance
schedule
secretary
seize
separate
similar
sophomore
succeed
sympathize
temperament
tendency

therefore   usually
tragedy   valuable
truly   weight
undoubtedly   writing
until

Exercise 7

Correcting Misspelled Words

Use the list above to correct any misspelled words in the following sentences. If a sentence contains no misspelled words, write **OK** in the margin.

1. We were embarrased by the noticable neglect of the environment.

2. Wes already took the baseball equippment back to the dormatory.

3. Incidentally, Michael took your books back to the psychology library.

4. Dr. Wescott is aquainted with fourty of the supervisors.

5. The applicant gave his heigth and weight.

6. Brad was a sophmore when the incedent occured.

7. I beleive Brittain will benifit from the bisiness.

8. The cabinet reached aggreement at four-thirty last night.

9. Page seven was omited from the catalog accidently.

10. It's hard to exadgerate the amount of prejidice in her earlier works.

11. I am dissappointed in his artical on the Atheletics Department.

12. The film wasn't divelopped until we returned to the city.

13. I wanted to see the maintainance agreement in writting.

14. Dr. Carnera offered an intelligent response to Benchley's analisis.

15. Desiree imediately walked to the dinning room.

16. The comparitive study was undoubtably valuble.

17. A fly droned monotinously.

18. The press chose to honor the court's dicision.

19. Packages are recieved in a seperate department.

20. An independant judgment would be welcome.

Chapter Review

In this chapter you learned that

1. *-ing* words are spelled as follows:

  a. Most *-ing* words are spelled by adding *-ing* to the present tense verb.
  b. Exception 1. Drop a final silent *e* before adding *-ing*.
  c. Exception 2. If the last syllable is accented (stressed), double a single consonant preceded by a single vowel before adding *-ing.*

2. *-ed* words are spelled as follows:

  a. Most regular past tense and past participles are spelled by adding *-ed* to the present tense verb.
  b. Exception 1. If the last letter is an *e*, simply add *-d.*
  c. Exception 2. Verbs that end in *-y* preceded by a consonant change the *-y* to *-i* before adding *-ed.*
  d. Exception 3. If the last syllable is accented (stressed), double a single consonant preceded by a single vowel before adding *-ed.*

3. *-s* words are spelled as follows:

  a. Most verbs and nouns spell the *s*-form by adding *-s* to the root word.
  b. Exception 1. Words that end in an *s, x, z, sh,* or *ch* add *-es* instead of *-s.*
  c. Exception 2. Words that end in *o* usually add *-es* instead of *-s.*
  d. Exception 3. Words that end in *-y* preceded by a consonant change the *-y* to *-i* and add *-es.*

4. Many words that sound alike (homonyms) are confused with each other. Among the most common are

  a. *Its* (possessive adjective)
      it's (contraction)
  b. *Whose* (possessive adjective)
      who's (contraction)
  c. *Your* (possessive adjective)
      you're (contraction)
  d. *Their* (possessive adjective)
      they're (contraction)
      there (adverb)

Review Exercise

Correct any misspelled words or apostrophe errors in the following paragraph. Then **recopy** the paragraph on the lines provided. (Note: Not all of the misspelled words are on the list provided earlier. Use a dictonary if you are unsure of a spelling.)

Much of the monney was never recoverred, even though it's owners searched countinuosly for nearly twelve years. Eventtually it was declarred lossed, and traces to its hidding place grew cold. Colonel Akroyd past the secret to his aunt in Georgia an quitely disapeared from the neiborhood. Twenty years later no one rememberred the military man who inhabitted the corner house. The aunt eventully placed his last letter in her safe deposit box and forgot it. The box and it's contents endded up on a closet shelf in Michigan.

_____

_____

_____

_____

_____

_____

_____

_____

_____

_____

_____

Writing paragraphs and essays

Though writing good sentences is necessary to all good writing, sentences usually do not stand alone. They are most often parts of paragraphs and longer units of writing, such as essays. The next two chapters discuss the basics of good paragraph writing.

c h a p t e r

19
The writing process

Chapter Preview

In this chapter you will learn about the **writing process** — a way of working that will help you write better paragraphs.

In addition, a RELATED SKILL section will show you several **prewriting methods** that will help you get started with writing assignments when you don't know where to begin.

NOTE: With the exception of some of the review exercises, which contain examples of errors studied earlier in the text, the chapters in this unit may be studied at any time.

THE WRITING PROCESS

Many people think good writing happens to some people automatically — that certain talented people just sit down and write well — and the rest of us don't have a prayer.

Nothing could be further from the truth. Anyone's writing can improve. And everyone's writing certainly will improve with practice — especially intelligent practice.

There are many ways to make your writing practice more intelligent and fruitful.

One way is to learn how good essays are constructed and to use that knowledge in constructing your own paragraphs. You have begun this task already in the chapter writing assignments. (In the next chapter you will study paragraph and essay structure in some detail.)

Another way is to practice a method of working called **the writing process**.

The writing process is, for most people, the most efficient way to do good writing. It divides writing into three stages.

1. Thinking about and planning your writing

2. Writing the rough draft

3. Improving and correcting the rough draft

Your work in other writing courses will probably focus, at least in part, on this same writing process. So our look at it here will be brief.

PLANNING YOUR WRITING

In previous writing assignments, you were asked to plan your writing in certain ways.

You had a subject to write about and something you wanted to say — some point you wanted to make about that subject. Then you made one or more lists, which you then edited. Eventually you produced a sort of summary or outline of the paragraph you wanted to write. From that summary you wrote a rough draft.

Why put so much emphasis on planning? To answer that, we need to take a look at what a good paragraph (or essay) is.

Unified Writing

Just like good speech, good writing is not just "about something." Good writing makes a point, then supports that point with evidence. If writing has both of these elements, it has **unity** and purpose. Just as speech with no purpose is almost "unlistenable," writing with no purpose is almost unreadable.

Writing has unity when it contains two important kinds of ideas — a **main idea** and **supporting ideas**, **details**, **or arguments**.

The **main idea** is a statement of the main point of your paragraph or essay. It includes

1. The **subject** of your paragraph.

2. The **opinion or point** you are going to make about that subject

The **supporting details** include all of the facts, arguments, reasons, stories, and examples you will use to prove that your opinion is correct.

Stating an Opinion

One of the most important parts of your paragraph is the opinion or point stated in the main idea.

Your "opinion" could take many forms. It is not always an "I like" or "I don't like" kind of statement.

You could try to prove, for example, that your subject has certain qualities. In your opinion, a certain person might be generous (opinion = "generous"), a certain film might be entertaining (opinion = "entertaining"), a certain teacher might be amusing (opinion = "amusing").

Other kinds of opinions are possible. You might show that your subject is different from another subject (opinion = "different"). That kind of writing makes a *comparison*.

You could show that your subject can be divided into certain groups (*classification*), that it can be defined in a certain way (*definition*), that a certain process will create it (*process*), that certain conditions caused it (*cause and effect*), and so on. Many of the Chapter Writing Assignments contain opinions like these.

No matter what your paragraph tries to prove, though, it must prove something. You cannot write simply "about" a subject and expect readers to be interested. If you are not making a point, you are not creating a unified piece of writing, and few readers will continue past the first few sentences.

The Need for Planning

How does a piece of writing become unified?

If all of our ideas were unified and well-thought-out the first time we expressed them, unity would just "happen" every time we wrote. But we know from experience that unified writing does not occur that simply.

It isn't just that our words could be better chosen. Our ideas are not always fully formed until we have expressed them several times. Sometimes we need to see the pieces of our thoughts before we can decide what conclusion those pieces add up to. And almost always, we cannot give the best evidence for our opinions immediately.

So if we sit down to write an idea without first planning out what to say, we are unlikely to be completely successful. It's almost impossible to write a good rough draft without knowing in good detail

1. The point you wish to make and

2. How to support that point.

It doesn't matter how you get this information, as long as you get it. Some writers make notes that lead to a summary page or outline, or they use other methods to help them collect their thoughts. Others write rough draft after rough draft, searching for what to say and the best way to say it.

If you are determined to do your best, almost any method will bring good results. Some methods get those results more quickly, however. The "rough draft after rough draft" method is absolutely one of the slowest, and the "summary page" method is one of the fastest.

Let's look at the summary page method more closely.

The Summary Page Method

The summary page method is used by writers of everything from novels to billboard notices. It is a "quick and dirty" approach to getting the job done. As a result, it is a very popular method. It also works.

In the **summary page method**, the writer makes written notes or lists of ideas she or he is considering for use in a paragraph or essay. These lists are then *edited* (added to and subtracted from), *organized*, and *recopied*. From these lists, an informal summary or outline is produced.

That final summary contains the two kinds of ideas your paragraph or essay must have.

1. A simple statement of your **main idea** — the subject of your writing and the point you are going to make about that subject

2. A list, in order, of your best **supporting ideas, evidence, or arguments**

By the time you have produced the summary you want to write from, much of your writing is already in your head. With your brain now full of ideas and your summary page to guide you in setting them down, the rough draft that follows often "writes itself."

It sounds simple, and it is. The key to the summary page method, though, is time. It takes time to make the lists complete and careful thought to edit and organize them. And the enemy of time is impatience.

To a beginning writer, the amount of time spent planning may seem excessive. Don't be fooled. A practiced writer knows that it's easier to rearrange disorganized notes than to recopy disorganized paragraphs — and far better to toss a bad summary than a bad essay.

Creating a Summary Page

How you create a summary page depends on how far along your idea is.

If you do not know the subject or main idea, do the following:

1. List all of the subjects you can think of that will fulfill the assignment.

If possible, take a few days to develop this list. Keep it with you and add ideas as they occur to you. Carry those ideas in the back of your mind and let them breed other ideas.

This list is important. You are creating your paragraph right now, in your mind. Don't settle for the first thing that comes to you. Instead, settle only for your best, the product of your careful thought. Let the list grow until you think you can add no more to it. Then go on to the next step.

2. Edit this list.

Sit down, and for one last time add to your list. Then cross things off, until only one item is left.

That item should be the one subject you would most like to discuss for this assignment. It should be the subject you think will produce the most successful piece of writing.

If you succeed here, you are well on your way. Believe it or not, your paragraph is almost half written — after all of that thinking, most of the pieces are now somewhere in your mind.

3. Decide what you want to prove about this subject.

This will be the "opinion" part of the main idea. You may know already what point you want to make. Keep in mind that without something to prove, you have nothing to say. Make notes, if you like, and do your thinking on paper. (The next chapter has more information about the "opinion" part of the main idea.)

4. On a clean sheet of paper, write the main idea.

A simple, one-sentence version will do. You should get, in writing, a clear statement of

   a. Your subject, and
   b. What you will prove about that subject (your "opinion")

This statement will control your paragraph and give it unity and purpose.

If you are writing a simple description, for example, your main idea might be

Description main idea

Mr. Romberg is usually well dressed.

(What you will prove = *well dressed*)

If you are writing a comparison (perhaps for your history class), your main idea might be

Comparison main idea

The invasion of Grenada required less skill than the war in the Falklands.

(What you will prove = *required less skill*)

Whatever your main idea is, don't let it sit vaguely in your mind. *Write it down* before you go further. You need to be very clear about what you are going to prove. Then follow the steps listed below.

If (or after) you know the main idea of your paragraph or essay:

1. Make a list of all of the things you could say to support your idea.

This list can include

Descriptions

Stories

Examples

Definitions

Statistics

Logical arguments

You probably know already what kind of support you need. You may, for example, be looking for stories. Your list will then be a list of stories you could tell. If you are trying to prove that something is created by a certain process, your list will include the steps in that process.

In any case, make this list as complete as possible. The more support you can choose from, the better (and more convincing) your paragraph will be.

2. Edit this list.

Add to and subtract from the list until you have included everything (stories, examples, steps in the process, etc.) that needs to be said to support your main idea.

Keep the needs of your audience in mind. Every audience is different. What will *your* readers need to see in order to be convinced? What kind of evidence, and how much of it, will you need to make your paragraph as effective as possible to the readers you are addressing?

3. Put this list in order.

Think about how you want the reader to encounter this information. What's the best order for your evidence?

Should the strongest evidence come first or last? What items on your list lead logically to the other items? Is there a natural place to start? What's the best place to end?

4. Now make the summary page.

On a clean sheet of paper, copy

  a. Your main idea
  b. Your supporting details (stories, etc.) in the order you want to present them.

You have just outlined your paragraph, and most of the details are fresh in your mind. With your summary page to guide you, the rough draft should go very quickly.

This part of the process is extremely important, even for short paragraphs. Taking extra minutes here could save hours later.

Exercise 1

Planning Your Writing

Use the steps listed above to produce a **summary page** for a long paragraph on *each* of the following subjects. When you are finished, **turn in all note pages**.

HINT: Don't forget to include an opinion (something to prove) in your main idea.

1. College football teams
2. How to study
3. The major causes of low grades
4. The condition of my room
5. The reason I am successful in school

RELATED SKILL   OTHER PREWRITING METHODS

Writing in college is unlike writing in the outside world in one important respect. In the world of your job or profession you will usually decide for yourself what needs to be written. You will rarely struggle for a main idea.

As a plant superintendent, for example, you know your next memo will argue for worker safety. As a nurse, you know your report will suggest a new lab technique. As a teacher, you know your essay will prove Dr. Fishbinder wrong. You may not yet know *how* to prove these things, but *what* to prove is not in question.

In college, on the other hand, students usually write because of a decision someone else makes. As a result, they often start without a clear main idea, perhaps not even a clear subject.

An English teacher, for example, might ask you to write a "cause and effect" essay — and the rest you will figure out for yourself. Or a history teacher might ask you to "discuss the reign of Louis XVI." To help students in this situation, writing textbooks offer a variety of methods (called **prewriting methods**) for creating ideas and outlines for essays.

The **summary page method** is one prewriting method. Others are listed below. Many of these other methods are helpful when you don't know where to begin.

Keep the summary page method in mind, though, and use it whenever you can. It is most like the method experienced writers use, and it's often the fastest. The sooner you can master it, the easier your future writing tasks will become.

Here are some other prewriting techniques:

Freewriting. The freewriting method attempts to stimulate your thinking through free association. It's a simple method — you just sit down with pen and paper and you write. Your only restriction is time — you must write for ten, fifteen, or twenty minutes, with no pausing or stopping.

You can write about anything, and change subjects whenever you like. If you run out of ideas, you write "I have run out of ideas," or words to that effect. When you are finished, re-read your work. Often there's the start of a paragraph or essay in there somewhere.

Focused freewriting. Focused freewriting is freewriting that stays with one subject. It lacks some of the freedom of free association, but when it works, the result is closer to a finished paragraph.

Looped writing. This technique, also called "looping," starts with either one of the freewriting techniques. This is the first "loop."

When you are finished with the first loop, re-read your work and choose one sentence that seems the strongest, most interesting, or most promising. Then on a clean sheet of paper, copy that sentence and do a focused freewriting that continues that idea. This is the second loop.

Continue the process through three or four loops. Find another strong sentence in the previous loop to start writing from, and write a new loop based on it. Stop when you have produced a paragraph that seems strong and interesting to you.

Branching. This technique is also called "clustering." Write a source word (like "sports") in the middle of a piece of paper and draw a circle around it.

Next, write as many related words and ideas as you can think of around the source word. Connect each word in the second group to its source word with lines.

Now, treat each word in the second group as a new source word — around each word in the second group of words, write a third group of related words. Draw lines to connect each word in the third group to its source word in the second group. Write small, and do this until the page is full.

When you are finished, the first word is like the trunk of a tree, with limbs and branches growing out from it. There should be a number of ideas for essays in the various branches. Pick the branch that seems most interesting or promising and build a main idea around it.

Cubing. Look at a subject from six sides, and see if one of them will start an essay. Those six sides can be

> What are the subject's qualities? (description)
>
> What are the subject's causes? (cause and effect)
>
> What is like the subject? (comparison)
>
> What is unlike the subject? (contrast)
>
> How is the subject produced?
>
> What are examples of the subject? (examples)

Other similar questions could be asked. Answer all six of your questions at some length on paper. At least one of your answers should be the start of an essay.

| Skill Exercise | Other Prewriting Methods |

Practice other prewriting methods by doing the following:

1. At three separate times, do three fifteen-minute **freewriting** exercises on any subject.

2. Do a **focused freewriting** on each of the following subjects.
   a. Parents
   b. Restaurants

3. Do three loops of a **looped writing** exercise on each of the following subjects.
   a. Careers
   b. Honesty

4. Do a **branching** (or "clustering") exercise for each of the following source words.
   a. War
   b. Government

5. Do a **cubing** exercise for each of the following ideas.
   a. Drinking
   b. Successful relationships

For methods 4 and 5 (branching and cubing), **produce a summary page** from the material you have generated.

WRITING THE ROUGH DRAFT

Writing the rough draft is the simplest part of the writing process. If your planning went well, the rough draft will almost write itself. That's the test, in fact, of good planning. A rough draft that becomes a struggle is probably not well planned.

Two general rules apply to rough-draft writing.

1. Write the rough draft in one sitting and without interruption. (This applies to all but the longest writing assignments.)

2. Do not edit your rough draft sentences, as long as they contain some version of the idea you need in that position.

Apply these rules to the rough drafts you will write in the following exercise.

Exercise 2

Writing the Rough Draft

Choose the two most successful summaries from Exercise 1 on page 494 and, using the lines below, turn them into rough drafts.

From summary number _____

_____

_____

_____

_____

_____

_____

_____

_____

_____

_____

_____

_____

From summary number _____

_____

_____

_____

_____

_____

_____

_____

_____

_____

_____

_____

_____

_____

_____

_____

IMPROVING AND CORRECTING THE ROUGH DRAFT

Changing the rough draft is the final stage in writing. It includes several processes.

1. Revising to improve the logical structure and the content of your work

2. Editing to improve the clarity and correctness of your sentences

3. Creating a clean, attractive, readable final copy

Each of these processes will be discussed below. Since the focus of this book is on sentences, however, we will devote most of this section to the editing process.

Revising the Structure

Revising for structure means rereading your rough draft to make sure that all parts of your paragraph or essay fit together smoothly and logically.
In particular, it means answering the following questions.

1. What is the main idea?

2. What is the subject stated in the main idea?

3. What is the opinion stated in the main idea?

4. Are your supporting details presented in the best order?

5. Do ALL supporting details help prove that idea?

If you find problems with the answer to any of these questions, fix the paragraph before going on — add sentences, move sentences, or take sentences out until your paragraph or essay says everything you think it needs to say to be convincing.

Some writing, of course, will need little or no revising for structure. But most rough drafts need at least some restructuring. It is a serious mistake, therefore, to ignore this step. Many otherwise good student essays are often marred by structural flaws.

| Exercise 3 | Revising for Structure |

Using the lines provided, **answer the following questions** for each of the rough drafts you produced in Exercise 2.

Then **rewrite** each rough draft as necessary to correct any errors in construction.

Rough draft 1:

1. What is the main idea?

   _____

   _____

2. What is the subject stated in the main idea?

   _____

   _____

3. What is the opinion stated in the main idea?

   _____

   _____

4. Why are your supporting details presented in the order you chose? Would another order be better? (If yes, explain what changes you would make.)

   _____

   _____

   _____

   _____

   _____

   _____

_____

_____

5. How does EACH supporting detail help prove the main idea?

_____

_____

_____

_____

_____

_____

_____

Rough draft 2:

1. What is the main idea?

_____

_____

2. What is the subject stated in the main idea?

_____

_____

3. What is the opinion stated in the main idea?

_____

_____

4. Why are your supporting details presented in the order you chose? Would another order be better? (If yes, explain what changes you would make.)

_____

_____

_____

_____

_____

_____

5. How does EACH supporting detail help prove the main idea?

_____

_____

_____

_____

_____

_____

_____

Improving the Sentence

If the structure of your writing is sound, you can begin to work on the sentences. This process is called **sentence editing**.

All rough drafts need sentence editing. In fact, writing the rough draft properly means that you have saved sentence editing for later. "Later" is now.

Editing sentences means altering the wording of sentences so that

1. Sentences flow smoothly from one to the other. This refers both to the flow of ideas and the flow of rhythm and sound. It involves the connectedness of ideas and the use of transition words and sentences to make that connectedness obvious.

2. Individual sentences are as

Clear

Concise

Correct

Graceful and pleasing to read

as you can make them.

Not all of these goals are met easily. Some writers, including the writer of this book, take years to improve their editing skills. Nevertheless, improving your editing is one of the most satisfying ways you can grow as a writer.

In this text, you will begin to edit for the following:

Clear writing

Concise writing

Correct writing

Other texts will deal more completely with sentence editing, including editing for a graceful style.

Clarity

Clear writing is writing that is easily understood. Unclear writing comes from two main sources — misused words and awkward sentence construction.

The following sentence, for example, contains errors of clarity that come mainly from misused words.

Misused words

Reality could be believed from watching that film.

Here, both *reality* and *believed* are misused. How does one believe reality from watching a film?

The author is really trying to comment, not on reality in general, but on the *realism* of the film, or how *realistic* it was. It is the realism of the film that is being believed. This sentence could be corrected as follows.

Corrected

I believe the film was realistic.

The following example is unclear because of its awkward construction.

Awkward construction

If you would read this script, I would appreciate it and add your comments for me.

Corrected

If you would read this script and add your comments, I would appreciate it.

In the first version, the writer (*I*) will add the comments. (Notice that *I* is the subject of both verbs in the main clause, *I would appreciate* and *add*. Obviously the second version is what the writer really means.

Exercise 4

Editing for Clarity

Each of the following sentences is unclear. If any word is misused, **circle** it. Then **rewrite** each sentence so that the meaning is clear.

example

Antonio will follow (to) us very soon.

Antonio will follow us very soon.

_____

1. He let himself in and made himself at home petting the cat and to read the newspaper.

_____

_____

2. Yelling started up again, but ended in friendly laughing as they all sat around looking at each in a very caring for each other.

_____

_____

3. About twelve o'clock on the sliding door we heard a knock.

_____

_____

4. Last Friday on the way to school I nearly fell asleep on the road.

_____

_____

5. I was starting to get afraid, so I called with great anticipation of any news.

_____

_____

6. Later I saw her talking to Sam, which put a biased opinion in my heart.

_____

_____

7. At eight o'clock she picked me up, being only fifteen minutes late.

_____

_____

8. She is generous to give, love, hope, and care very much.

_____

_____

9. I have an employee that sounds as though she is frustrated.

_____

_____

10. Everything that is obvious about her supports the image of the cosmopolitan girl on the go.

_____

_____

Conciseness

Concise writing states an idea with a minimum of unnecessary words. This does not mean that every sentence should be short, just that every sentence should, within reason, be as short as possible.

Not concise

It's really easy and not hard at all to see that the writer's goal in writing this short story is to deal with his relationship with his father when he was a child and growing up at home.

This wordy monster can be edited as follows.

Edited for conciseness

~~It's really easy and not hard at all to see that the writer's~~ ~~goal in writing~~ T|his short story ~~is to~~ deals with ~~his~~ *the writer's early*

relationship with his father, ~~when he was a child and~~ ~~growing up at home.~~

Result

This short story deals with the writer's early relationship with his father.

Notice how the important words are rearranged and the "deadwood" (unnecessary words) eliminated.

Sentence combining (and "uncombining") can be used to achieve conciseness. Notice how the following groups of sentences can be combined.

Uncombined

The children walked across a field. It was covered with snow.

Combined

snow-covered

The children walked across a field. ~~It was covered with~~ ~~snow.~~
∧

Notice that the second sentence in the uncombined example (*It was covered with snow.*) is built around a weak subject and verb (*It was*). Verbs should be strong and, wherever possible, active rather than passive. (See Chapter 2, pages 44–46, for more about active and passive verbs.)

Often the best editing comes from recognizing weak or passive verbs. You can then change them, often by finding another word in the sentence that has "verb possibilities."

The following sentence, for example, is weakened by a weak verb.

Weak verb

The bells made a ringing sound in the wind.

Made is a weak verb in this sentence. (It might be strong in another sentence, but it is weak here.)

The sentence, however, could easily be rewritten around another word with verb possibilities — *ringing*. Notice both the strength of the new sentence and its brevity.

Stronger

The bells rang in the wind.

Watch for opportunities to combine sentences as you edit, and wherever possible, eliminate weak and passive verbs. Your writing will improve noticeably if you do.

Correcting Errors

After you edit your sentences for conciseness, you should correct all grammar and punctuation errors.

Is it really that important that writing be completely correct? People are often judged on the correctness of their writing. In fact, in the business world, writing should contain no errors at all.

There is little "partial credit," for example, for mostly correct writing in a job application or an important report, just as there is little "partial credit" for mostly good grooming on an important occasion or business interview. On these and other occasions, either your writing is correct or it isn't.

Is it possible to correct writing completely? The answer is absolutely yes — anyone who wishes to learn can do it, including you.

Your work in this course is preparing you to correct most common sentence errors. Apply carefully what you learn. If it helps you, mark sentences as you have done in previous chapters to see how they are constructed. Do whatever you need to do to correct the errors your rough draft contains. (All rough drafts contain errors, including those of all professional writers.)

Hint: DON'T correct errors until you have done most of your other editing; there's no point in correcting sentences that will soon be crossed out. But DO search for errors after editing, and repeat your search one last time before you type the final copy. Then be sure to proofread the typed version!

Exercise 5

Editing Sentences

The sentences in this exercise are divided into two groups. The main problem in the first group is deadwood and in the second group, weak or passive verbs. Do the following.

1. **Edit** these sentences to make them more concise and error-free.

2. **Show your corrections** in the original printed sentence (as shown in the examples on page 506).

3. Then **recopy** the result.

Do NOT rewrite these sentences in your head and then copy the result. You will probably end up with new rough-draft sentences that then need editing of their own. Instead, improve the sentences that are here.

example

(Contains both deadwood and weak or passive verbs)

~~The logs were placed in a pretty careful way~~ My brother and I carefully stacked the logs in a corner of the garage. ~~against the wall by my brother and I.~~

My brother and I carefully stacked the logs in a corner of the garage.

A. Deadwood

1. We were no more than twenty yards away when I began to think to myself that these faces were not the faces of friendly people.

   _____

   _____

   _____

2. Halfway down the slope I got beside him and was telling him to do the thing we call "snowplowing" and to not lean back.

   _____

   _____

   _____

3. Toward the end of the concert the band stopped and then started picking people out of the concert audience to come on stage and help with the next part of the concert.

   _____

4. The story began in the ice cold north in January of 1967 somewhere in the Rocky Mountains of Colorado.

_____

_____

_____

5. It has been a long time since I heard the reasons she says were the reasons she did it.

_____

_____

_____

B. Weak or passive verbs

1. The beds had just been made, and they were fine to look at.

_____

_____

_____

2. Most of everything on the bike ride went well until my sister and I came up to a bump in the road and our bikes hit it hard.

_____

_____

_____

3. Joe Sporos was placed under arrest by narcotics agents.

_____

4. Since it was coming to an end, I felt better about getting back home from my vacation.

_____

_____

_____

5. She looked at the branches rustling in the high wind.

_____

_____

_____

Preparing the Final Copy

This easy step is often overlooked. Yet the impression made by the final copy will often determine how successful your writing will be.

Most people are swayed heavily by impressions. A messy, unreadable, unprofessional final copy of a well-written masterpiece will fail as often as a poorly written essay.

When working on the final copy, consider the following suggestions.

1. Use correct margins and line spacing.

For typed and handwritten college essays, a one-inch margin on all four sides is most common. All typed essays should be double-spaced.

Handwritten essays can be double- or single-spaced unless your teacher specifies otherwise. Difficult handwriting, however, should be double-spaced.

2. Make sure all typing and hand-copying is free of incidental errors (typos, etc.).

Errors in recopying or typing are easy to make, but they should not be left uncorrected. This kind of carelessness is distracting and makes a horrible impression.

When correcting errors on the final copy, be sure to correct them neatly.

3. Write a brief, interesting title and center it (without quotation marks or underlining) a few lines above the first paragraph.

Five words or less is a good length for an essay title unless the subject is either intentionally humorous or scientific. "My Description Essay" is an unimaginative and vague title.

4. Use only one side of a sheet of paper.

This makes the writing much easier to read.

5. Do whatever else enhances the readability of your final copy.

For example, if your typewriter ribbon is producing very light copy, change it so that the writing is darker. If the paper you are using is yellow with age, buy new paper. Number your pages (except for page 1). Don't justify word-processed writing.

You don't want your reader to struggle just to read your work. Impatient readers become nonreaders almost instantly.

6. Make your final copy as attractive to look at (and touch) as possible.

We are all swayed by beauty. Pretty things are more favorably received than those that aren't as attractive.

Use this prejudice to your advantage. Write or print well. Find a typewriter with an attractive, clean typeface. Use good paper, not pages torn from a notebook. Don't let your paper become wrinkled and dog-eared. Notice even the feel of your paper. Some chemically treated "erasable" papers are very uncomfortable to touch and easily smudge.

The final copy of your writing is really a sales tool. Much of your writing intends to make people respond favorably toward you. Your final copy is the only part of your work the reader will see. Don't let something you can control get in the way of your success.

Exercise 6

Final Copy

Edit and prepare a final copy of one of the rough drafts you revised for Exercise 3.

To help your teacher evaluate your use of the writing process, **turn in all of your work** including your notes, along with the final copy.

Chapter Review

In this chapter, you learned that

1. Every **unified paragraph** or essay has

    a. A **main idea** that states the subject being written about and the point the writer wants to make about that subject.

    b. Supporting details, ideas, examples, or evidence.

2. The **writing process** includes these stages.
   a. Thinking, planning, and note-making, which lead to a **summary page** or outline
   b. Writing the **rough draft**
   c. **Changing** the rough draft, including
      1. Revising the overall structure and order of ideas
      2. Improving (editing) the sentences
      3. Preparing a clean, readable final copy

In the RELATED SKILL section, you learned about the following **pre-writing methods**.

1. Freewriting
2. Focused freewriting
3. Looped writing
4. Branching
5. Cubing

Review Exercise

Edit the following paragraphs from student essays. Make sure the sentences are clear and concise.

In addition, watch for all the kinds of sentence errors you have studied in this book.

Then **make a final copy** of each paragraph.

A. This paragraph is the beginning of a longer essay about a camping trip.

Scared Stiff

Camping was meant to be fun but there was one trip in particular where I got a good scare. After the last day of school two of my friends and I decided to go camping. We got off to a late start so we didn't pull into Malibu Lake until about eight thirty. The sun had set in the west and the temperature was going down. Once the camper was set up our hands and feet became frigid. And at that moment we decided to search for some firewood as we slowly made our way through the dark misty air around the lake we spotted another campsite. We pushed on through the brush and trees and I noticed they had a nice little fire. My only thought at that time was to cuddle up with the flames. We drew closer. . . .

B. This is the introduction from a longer piece about a close escape the author had while walking his uncle's dog in a strange neighborhood.

A Close Escape

Through out my life I have had many close escapes from being punished in a violent way, namely a good beating. The escape in this story was one of the closest I ever encountered. Five years ago I flew back to Pennsylvania for the summer to visit some relatives. My uncle Ed has a pug, these dogs are born with bad breathing problems. At the time of this incident the weather was hot and humid making life for the pug very hard. Unfortunately there was a story about a similar dog who had died the day before from heat exhaustion, making Uncle Ed cautions about his own pet. Uncle Ed told us if the dog was taken out not to let him run around. Because Uncle Ed has such a bad temper, so you would think that my cousin Ted and I would obey his commands, but we wouldn't be stereotype kids. Anyway the story goes like this. . . .

20

The structure of paragraphs and essays

Chapter Preview

In this chapter you will learn about

1. The **structure of paragraphs and essays**

2. The basic and suspended **paragraph patterns**

Good writing always includes good sentences. As you learned in the last chapter, sentences should be clear, concise, and correct. Otherwise, readers may not understand them.

But there is more to good writing than just good sentence writing. Good writing has an overall structure that presents ideas in an orderly way.

In this chapter, we will discuss how good writing is organized. Before we do, however, let's define what we mean by two important terms — the **paragraph** and the **essay**.

PARAGRAPHS AND ESSAYS

An **essay** is a group of sentences that expresses the whole thought of the writer.

An essay has a beginning, middle, and end and contains the main idea and supporting ideas that you studied in the last chapter. When the essay is completed, the writer has said everything he or she wishes to say to convince the reader that his or her point is correct.

Though some essays are very short, many are long. Long essays are usually broken into groups of sentences, called "paragraphs." Short essays are sometimes only one paragraph long. Your chapter writing assignments, for example, have been one-paragraph essays.

So far in this book we have talked about paragraphs as though every paragraph were an essay. We will continue to do so now. For the purposes of this discussion, the term **paragraph** means "one-paragraph essay."

Keep in mind, though, that writers divide long essays into paragraphs in a variety of ways. For this reason, not every printed paragraph has the same structure as the one-paragraph essay.

PARAGRAPH STRUCTURE

Just as a random collection of words is not a sentence, a random collection of sentences is not a paragraph. A paragraph is a group of sentences that combine to make a point.

Every paragraph that is complete in itself must contain at least three main parts:

A main idea

Support for the main idea

A closing that feels like an ending

Let's look at these parts one at a time.

515 The structure of paragraphs and essays

The Main Idea

As you saw in the last chapter, the **main idea** is a statement of the main point of your paragraph. It includes

1. The **subject** of your paragraph

2. The **opinion or point** you are going to make about that subject

The following are valid main ideas for paragraphs.

Main ideas

Each of my high school science teachers influenced my career choice.

Barry's behavior is an example of good sportsmanship.

The poster was well designed.

The unrest in South Africa is caused by both political and economic injustice.

Each of these main ideas has a subject and an opinion. In addition, it is not difficult to imagine someone wanting to discuss or learn about them.

subject
Each of my high school science teachers
opinion
influenced my career choice.

subject
Barry's behavior
opinion
is an example of good sportsmanship.

subject
The poster
opinion
was well designed.

subject
The unrest in South Africa
opinion
is caused by both political and economic injustice.

Some sentences name subjects for paragraphs but do not make a point about these subjects. Sentences like these cannot be main ideas for paragraphs.

The following sentences are not main ideas for this reason — they name subjects but lack an opinion.

NOT main ideas

My brother is six feet tall.   (NO OPINION)

Arizona became a state in 1912.   (NO OPINION)

The Union of South Africa was founded by Dutch colonists.   (NO OPINION)

Notice that some statements contain opinions that are too obvious to need much proving. These would also not make good main ideas for paragraphs.

NOT a good main idea

If you cut all of your classes, you will probably get bad grades.   (OPINION DOESN'T NEED PROVING)

Every main idea contains a subject and an opinion worth discussing. A main idea without these elements is a poor foundation for a paragraph.

Personal and Impersonal Writing

Some paragraphs are about people and events in our own lives. They are derived from the writer's personal experiences. The writer is prominently featured in this kind of writing. Family, school, work, recreation, romance — all of these provide material for **personal** paragraphs.

Two of the sample main ideas, for example, introduce personal paragraphs.

Personal main ideas

Each of my high school science teachers influenced my career choice.

Barry's behavior is an example of good sportsmanship.

Other main ideas are not about the writer and his or her life directly. They are about people, things, and ideas that the writer is thinking about, but there are few references to the writer as a person in the paragraph.

The following main ideas could introduce **impersonal** paragraphs — paragraphs that are not about the writer and his or her personal preferences.

Impersonal main ideas

The poster was well designed.

The unrest in South Africa is caused by both political and economic injustice.

The first main idea deals with the design of the poster, not the fact that it is hanging in the writer's dining room. The second main idea analyzes the causes of unrest in South Africa, not the writer's emotional reaction to that unrest.

Most of the paragraph assignments in this book required personal writing. Personal writing is a good training ground for impersonal writing — it requires almost no research and is interesting both to write and read.

As you progress in college and move into your profession, however, you will find that impersonal writing is more and more important. Do not be concerned if you receive an assignment to write an impersonal paragraph. Just apply what you are learning in this Unit. The rules of good paragraph structure are true for both kinds of writing.

| Exercise 1 | Subject and Opinion of Main Ideas |

Each of the following sentences is a good main idea for a paragraph. Indicate which portion of the sentence states the **subject** and which states the **opinion** by underlining each sentence part and labeling it as in the following example.

| example | SUBJECT   OPINION
Student elections should be delayed until after the trial. |

1. Early marriage can create many problems.

2. Many former members of this fraternity hold highly respected professional positions.

3. The incumbent mayor will probably win re-election in June.

4. The money from the cable television company influenced his vote.

5. The prices for these apartments are too high.

6. Although Mr. Jonas and Ms. Henderson are different in many ways, they have similar teaching styles.

7. Although Mr. Jonas and Ms. Henderson have similar teaching styles, they are different in many ways.

8. Twenty million dollars will be raised in the latest effort.

9. Other opinions should have been sought before surgery was performed.

10. My skiing trips have all been unique and memorable experiences.

Exercise 2

Identifying Main Ideas

Some of the following sentences could be main ideas for paragraphs, and some could not. For each sentence, do the following.

1. Indicate the **subject and opinion** for each sentence that has them.

2. Write YES next to those that could be main ideas, and NO next to those that could not.

3. Give your **reason** for each sentence you marked NO — either **no opinion** or **opinion doesn't need proving**.

examples

    _____YES_____
SUBJECT   OPINION
Good writing skills are worth whatever work it

takes to acquire them.

_____

    _____NO_____
I received straight A's in high school.

        NO OPINION

    _____NO_____
SUBJECT   OPINION
My good grades helped me to get into a good

school.

OPINION DOESN'T NEED PROVING

    _____   **1.** The recent weather has broken several records.

    _____   **2.** The temperature on September 12 was 107 degrees.

    _____   **3.** This car can be purchased at a very reasonable price.

    _____   **4.** I will need a car during the spring semester.

    _____   **5.** Mr. Abbott spent most of his life behind bars.

_____ **6.** Your best investment advice will probably not come

from your banker.

_____

_____ **7.** Franklin Roosevelt did not create the "Democratic

coalition" by himself.

_____

_____ **8.** The Café Paris has been awarded two stars by the

Collegiate Diners' Association of nearby West

Penwicker.

_____

_____ **9.** The play received an "eight" from critic John

Bolliver.

_____

_____ **10.** Life had been especially kind to Mrs. Walstonberg.

_____

Exercise 3

Writing Main Ideas

On separate paper, work out **five good main ideas** for paragraphs. When you are satisfied with the results, **copy** your sentences here. Then mark the **subject** and **opinion** of each sentence.

1. _____

2. _____

3. _____

4. _____

5. _____

Supporting the Main Idea

The main idea is the foundation on which a paragraph is built. It states what the writer believes to be true. Now the writer must attempt to prove that the main idea is correct.

This is done with **supporting ideas**. Supporting ideas are the writer's evidence that the main idea is correct. Without supporting ideas, there is no paragraph, just a naked statement of the writer's opinion.

Supporting evidence can be of many types, including any or all of the following.

Descriptions

Stories

Examples

Process analysis

Comparisons

Definitions

Cause or effect analysis

Classification — division of a large group into smaller ones

Statistical evidence

Quotations from authorities

Logical and reasonable arguments

Some main ideas require certain kinds of support, while others can be supported in many ways. The following main idea, for example, requires physical description for its support.

Descriptive main idea

Mr. Romberg is usually well dressed.

The next main idea, on the other hand, could be supported in several ways.

An American in Paris is a history-making film.

It could be supported with *stories* about how the movie affected particular filmmakers, with *quotations* from authorities, with a *cause-and-effect analysis* of its influence on the history of movie-making, or with any combination of these.

You have practiced most of these kinds of writing in the chapter writing assignments.

Kind of Writing	Chapter
Description	1 and 2
Narration (stories)	3
Examples	4 and 5
Process analysis	6, 7, and 8
Comparison	9 and 10
Definition	11 and 12
Cause and effect analysis	13, 14, and 15
Classifications	16

For particular information about organizing and writing a paragraph of these types, refer to the Hints given in the appropriate chapter writing assignment.

The following sample paragraphs show the relationship between main ideas and supporting ideas.

In the first example, the supporting ideas are descriptions of Annette Dula's state of mind. This description helps convince us that her first main idea is true — that try as she might, she cannot escape her emotional ties to America.

The main idea of each paragraph is printed in *italics*.

Main idea

Supporting ideas

I am not patriotic, but I am a product of America. I believe in freedom of speech, even if it is only token. I take education for granted though we may not receive it equally. I believe in the working of democracy even though it never seems to work. I am forced to accept that I am an American and that here in America lie my cultural roots — whether I like it or not.[1]

In the next example, George Orwell uses both storytelling and description to convince us that his main idea is true — that as he walked with a man about to be hanged, he saw for the first time that life is important for its own sake.

Main idea

Supporting ideas

It is curious, but till that moment I had never realized what it means to destroy a healthy, conscious man. When I saw the prisoner step aside to avoid the puddle, I saw the mystery, the unspeakable wrongness, of cutting a life short when it is in full tide. This man was not dying, he was alive just as we were alive. All the organs of his body were working — bowels digesting food, skin renewing itself, nails growing, tissues forming — all toiling away in solemn foolery. His nails would still be growing when he stood on the drop, when he was falling through the air with a tenth of a second to live. His eyes saw the yellow gravel and the grey walls, and his brain still remembered, foresaw, reasoned — reasoned even about puddles. He and we were a party of men walking together, seeing, hearing, feeling, understanding the same world; and in two minutes, with a sudden snap, one of us would be gone — one mind less, one world less.[2]

[1]Annette Dula, "No Home in Africa," *New York Times*, 27 July 1975.
[2]George Orwell, "A Hanging," in *Shooting an Elephant and Other Essays* (New York: Harcourt Brace Jovanovich, 1956).

Writing Supporting Ideas

Write a few connected sentences of support for the following main ideas as though they were your own. Then tell what kind of support you are providing. (Use the list on page 521 to guide you.)

1. The view from the bridge is peaceful.

_____

_____

_____

_____

_____

_____

_____

_____

_____

_____

2. Many employees find themselves in situations that test their honesty.

_____

_____

_____

_____

_____

_____

_____

3. Most of the films released today fall into two groups.

4. It's not as difficult to learn to dance well as you might think.

_____

_____

_____

_____

_____

5. My boss is often too picky.

_____

_____

_____

_____

_____

_____

_____

_____

_____

_____

The Closing

Every paragraph that is complete in itself has an effective closing, something that makes the reader feel that the writer is finished.

The key word here is *feel*. When the New Ohio Spaceman, galactic hero, has phasered the last alien into a smoldering blue lump, the story will still feel incomplete without a quiet moment of good-bye, however brief. Anything that gives the reader a feeling of completion is fair game, so long as it works.

Effective closings for paragraphs include any of the following.

1. A summary or restatement of the main idea

2. A conclusion that can be drawn, now that the main idea has been proved

3. The repetition of a key phrase from the beginning of the work

4. A particularly effective supporting detail that feels like an ending

The most common closing for paragraphs is actually number four — the supporting detail that feels like an ending.

Let's look at the closings of the two paragraphs quoted earlier in this chapter. The closing of the first one is a restatement of the main idea.

For these examples, both the main idea and the closing are printed in *italics*.

Main idea
Supporting ideas
Closing restates main idea

I am not patriotic, but I am a product of America. I believe in freedom of speech, even if it is only token. I take education for granted though we may not receive it equally. I believe in the working of democracy even though it never seems to work. *I am forced to accept that I am an American and that here in America lie my cultural roots — whether I like it or not.*

George Orwell's closing is based on the main idea, but it gains its power by referring to a final — and very effective — detail from the story of a prisoner and his guards on the way to the gallows.

Main idea

Supporting ideas

Closing reflects main idea (effective final detail)

It is curious, but till that moment I had never realized what it means to destroy a healthy, conscious man. When I saw the prisoner step aside to avoid the puddle, I saw the mystery, the unspeakable wrongness, of cutting a life short when it is in full tide. This man was not dying, he was alive just as we were alive. All the organs of his body were working — bowels digesting food, skin renewing itself, nails growing, tissues forming — all toiling away in solemn foolery. His nails would still be growing when he stood on the drop, when he was falling through the air with a tenth of a second to live. His eyes saw the yellow gravel and the grey walls, and his brain still remembered, foresaw, reasoned — reasoned even about puddles. *He and we were a party of men walking together, seeing, hearing, feeling, understanding the same world; and in two minutes, with a sudden snap, one of us would be gone — one mind less, one world less.*

THE PARAGRAPH PATTERNS

You have seen that every paragraph needs

A main idea

Supporting details

An effective closing

These main parts of a paragraph can only be arranged in a certain number of ways. These arrangements are called **paragraph patterns**.

The most common are the **basic paragraph pattern** and the **suspended paragraph pattern**. Each starts in the same way — with a statement of the subject of the paragraph. Each places its body of support in the middle of the paragraph. These patterns differ only in the placement of the main idea.

The Basic Paragraph Pattern

The basic pattern places the main idea where most people would expect to find it — in the introduction of the paragraph, right before the supporting ideas.

The Basic Paragraph Pattern

Introduction	Subject introduced
	MAIN IDEA — subject + opinion
Body	SUPPORTING IDEAS
Closing	CLOSING

The basic pattern is illustrated in the paragraph below. (The main parts of the paragraph — introduction, body, closing, and main idea — have been marked for you.)

Introduction

Main idea

Body (descriptive details)

Closing (final descriptive detail)

A popular item for tourist shoppers in New York City is a poster originally designed as a cover for The New Yorker *magazine by the artist Saul Steinberg. It depicts the world, or at least the West, as seen from the blinkered perspective of a Manhattanite.* Most of the foreground is taken up by Ninth and Tenth Avenues, bordered by the Hudson River. New Jersey gets a good deal of space; but beyond that, the Middle West is vaguely defined, with obscure places such as Nebraska given uncertain location. The hump of California is depicted with more confidence, *bounded on the other side by the Pacific Ocean, dotted with some nameless islands against a distant backdrop of China and Japan.*[3]

[3]Andrew Cockburn, *The Threat: Inside the Soviet Military Machine* (New York: Random House, 1983), p. 3.

The Suspended Paragraph Pattern

The suspended pattern places the main idea at the end of the paragraph. There it serves as a conclusion as well, since it seems to sum up the ideas that came before.

The Suspended Paragraph Pattern

Introduction

> Subject introduced

Body

> SUPPORTING IDEAS

Closing

> MAIN IDEA — subject + opinion
>
> *Closing detail*

The following paragraph uses the suspended pattern and places the main idea at the end. (Once again, the main parts of the paragraph — introduction, body, closing, and main idea — have been marked for you.)

Introduction (subject stated)

For half a lifetime, Cyrus Vance had access to the innermost secrets of the American intelligence-gathering machine, which for $15 billion a year, has concluded that Soviet military power presented a clear and growing threat to the United States. In 1982 Vance took a $3 cab ride across midtown Manhattan. His driver was a recent Soviet émigré. Like most Soviet males, he had served a two-year draft period

Body (supports M.I. with a story)

in the armed forces. They talked about the driver's experiences in a tank unit during that time. It was Vance's first opportunity to hear the description of the Soviet threat from the inside, and it was very different from what the secret intelligence briefings had been telling him all along. Vance was surprised to hear that the living conditions of the men were deplorable and that the training for the crews was bad at

Closing (states main idea)

best. *It sounded like a very different Soviet army from the one depicted by the intelligence briefers over the years.*[4]

Use your knowledge of these writing patterns to organize the paragraphs you write.

[4]Ibid., pp. 21–22.

Chapter Review

In this chapter, you learned that

1. Every one-paragraph essay has **three main parts**.
   a. Main idea
   b. Supporting details
   c. Closing

2. The **main idea** contains
   a. The subject of the paragraph
   b. The writer's opinion about that subject

3. In the **basic paragraph pattern**
   a. The main idea is stated in the introduction
   b. The body supports the main idea

4. In the **suspended paragraph pattern**
   a. The subject is stated in the introduction
   b. The body leads to and supports the main idea
   c. The main idea is stated in the closing

Review Exercise 1

Identifying paragraph patterns

Mark the parts of each of the following paragraphs: **introduction, main idea, supporting ideas, closing**. Then write on the line the **pattern** of each paragraph.

A. Pattern: _____

    The rough draft is your first attempt to assemble all the elements on which you have been working, to bring order out of chaos. Now your characters must move into action; now they must speak through your dialog. Open the floodgates of your imagination. Write this draft without revisions or polishing and don't plague yourself about its literary quality. If something does not seem quite right, despite your painstaking planning, leave it and plow right along. Bring your work to the climax you have chosen for it.[5]

[5]Constance Nash and Virginia Oakey, *The Television Writer's Handbook* (New York: Barnes & Noble Books, 1978), p. 59.

B. Pattern: _____

Houses are like sentinels in the plain — old keepers of the weather watch.
There, in a very little while, wood takes on the appearance of great age. All
colors wear soon away in the wind and rain, and then the wood is burned
gray and the grain appears and the nails turn red with rust. The window-
panes are black and opaque; you imagine there is nothing within, and indeed
there are many ghosts, bones given up to the land. They stand here and
there against the sky, and you approach them for a longer time than you
expect. They belong in the distance; it is their domain.[6]

C. Pattern: _____

The view from the windshield is this: There's that three-to-six-story-high
screen, on which titanic monsters or car crashes of megaton explosiveness
suddenly appear. Hundreds of vehicles are lined up like pigs before a trough,
grunting their approval — horns honking, tape decks blaring, an odd rocket
arching toward the screen. If you look past the speaker hung from your
window, you gaze on the Texas moon riding high above this most remarkable celebration; you note hibachi campfires, smoke rising from barbequed
ribs, lawn chairs planted in the beds of pickup trucks, hammocks strung
between speaker poles, patrons splayed out on blankets atop cars, and a
Western Rocky Horror punk fest of sixteen-year-olds crowded around the
concession stand. You smell pot sweeping through the night, sweet as sagebrush. And all around you Texans are mating. That's summertime at the
drive-in movies in, say, Dallas.[7]

[6]N. Scott Momaday, *The Way to Rainy Mountain* (Albuquerque: University of New Mexico
Press, 1969), p. 10.
[7]Toby Thompson, "The Twilight of the Drive-In," *American Film,* July/August 1983.
Reprinted by permission of the author. Copyright © 1983 by Toby Thompson.

Chapter 20 Writing Assignment

1. Using the writing process as discussed in Chapter 19, create a **summary page** for a paragraph describing your special "hideaway" — the place where you go when you need to do your most important thinking.

2. Now write the **rough draft** of this paragraph. Use the **basic paragraph pattern** to organize your writing.

3. **Revise** your paragraph for structure and **edit** its sentences as discussed in Chapter 19.

4. Make a **final copy** of your basic pattern paragraph. Keep this final copy clean — it will be graded.

5. Now, using a photocopy of your basic pattern paragraph, **restructure** it using the **suspended paragraph pattern**.

6. **Revise, edit, and make a final copy** of this paragraph as well.

7. On separate paper, write a sentence that tells **which paragraph you prefer**. Then write a few sentences explaining your decision.

8. Finally, **turn in** all of your work.

Chapter 20
Exercise 1

1. Early marriage can create many problems.
   - SUBJ.: Early marriage
   - OPINION: can create many problems

3. The incumbent mayor will probably win re-election in June.
   - SUBJ.: incumbent mayor
   - OPINION: will probably win re-election

5. The prices for these apartments are too high.
   - SUBJ.: prices for these apartments
   - OPINION: are too high

7. Although Mr. Jonas and Ms. Henderson have similar teaching styles, they are different in many ways.
   - SUBJ.: Mr. Jonas and Ms. Henderson
   - OPINION: are different in many ways

9. Other opinions should have been sought before surgery was performed.
   - OPINION: Other opinions should have been sought
   - SUBJ.: surgery

Chapter 20
Exercise 2

__YES__ 1. The recent weather has broken several records.
   - SUBJ.: recent weather
   - OPINION: broken several records

__NO__ 3. This car can be purchased at a very reasonable price.
   - OPINION DOESN'T NEED PROVING

__NO__ 5. Mr. Abbott spent most of his life behind bars.
   - NO OPINION

__YES__ 7. Franklin Roosevelt did not create the "Democratic coalition" by himself.
   - SUBJ.: Franklin Roosevelt
   - OPINION: did not create the "Democratic coalition"

__NO__ 9. The play received an "eight" from critic John Bolliver.
   - NO OPINION

Chapter 20
Exercise 3

Each student will have an individual response.

Chapter 20
Review Exercise 1

Identifying paragraph patterns

A. Pattern: __BASIC PATTERN__

INTRO (MAIN IDEA) — The rough draft is your first attempt to assemble all the elements on which you have been working, to bring order out of chaos. SUPPORTING IDEAS — Now your characters must move into action; now they must speak through your dialog. Open the floodgates of your imagination. Write this draft without revisions or polishing and don't plague yourself about its literary quality. If something does not seem quite right, despite your painstaking planning, leave it and plow right along. Bring your work to the climax you have chosen for it. CLOSING

C. Pattern: __SUSPENDED PATTERN__

INTRO — The view from the windshield is this: There's that three-to-six-story-high screen, on which titanic monsters or car crashes of megaton explosiveness suddenly appear. Hundreds of vehicles are lined up like pigs before a trough, grunting their approval — horns honking, tape decks blaring, an odd rocket arching toward the screen. SUPPORTING IDEAS — If you look past the speaker hung from your window, you gaze on the Texas moon riding high above this most remarkable celebration; you note hibachi campfires, smoke rising from barbequed ribs, lawn chairs planted in the beds of pickup trucks, hammocks strung between speaker poles, patrons splayed out on blankets atop cars, and a Western Rocky Horror punk fest of sixteen-year-olds crowded around the concession stand. You smell pot sweeping through the night, sweet as sagebrush. And all around you Texans are mating. That's summertime at the drive-in movies in, say, Dallas. CLOSING (MAIN IDEA)

INDEX